ANIMATING THE LETTER

Xρι generatio

# ANIMATING THE LETTER

*The Figurative Embodiment of Writing*

*from Late Antiquity*

*to the Renaissance*

## LAURA KENDRICK

OHIO STATE UNIVERSITY PRESS

COLUMBUS

FRONTISPIECE: Chi-rho page. Book of Kells.
Dublin, Trinity College, MS 58, fol. 34r.
Photo courtesy of the Board of Trinity College Dublin.

Library of Congress Cataloging-in-Publication Data
Kendrick, Laura.
Animating the letter : the figurative embodiment of writing
from late antiquity to the Renaissance / Laura Kendrick.
p.   cm.
Includes bibliographical references and index.
ISBN 0-8142-0822-3 (cloth : alk. paper)
1. Initials.    2. Illumination of books
and manuscripts, Medieval.    I. Title.
NK3610.K46    1999
302.2′244′0902—dc21    99-19159
CIP

Type set in Granjon. Text and jacket design
by Wilsted & Taylor Publishing Services.
Printed by Sheridan Books.

9  8  7  6  5  4  3  2  1

*This book is dedicated to my parents,*

*James P. and Janet Kendrick*

# CONTENTS

# ACKNOWLEDGMENTS

I would like to express my deep gratitude to all those who have helped to make this a better book over the course of the last decade. Among those whom I am still able to remember by name are several fellowship-granting institutions that supported my research (the National Endowment for the Humanities, the John and Eliza Gardner Howard Foundation, the University of California Humanities Research Institute, and the Rutgers University Faculty Study-Leave Program); three conscientious and constructive press readers (Pamela Sheingorn, Laurence de Looze, and Derek Pearsall); two especially generous librarians, Stuart O Seanóir of Trinity College Library, Dublin, and Father Leonard E. Boyle, Prefect of the Vatican Library; several friends in need (Antonia Tripolitis for checking most of my Latin translations, Wai-Chee Dimock for last-minute photocopies, Gilles Delavaud for help with Greek and patience with the entire enterprise); and the Ohio State University Press team that acquired, improved, and produced the book (Barbara Hanrahan, Ellen Satrom, Ruth Melville, and Mira Nenonen).

# INTRODUCTION

# THE BEING OF THE LETTER/
# *L'ÊTRE DE LA LETTRE*

It is a paradox, but surely no coincidence, that this book about the fetishization and empowerment of the book, or of alphabetic writing in codex form, came into being electronically as a text fleetingly "written" in pixel letters on a video screen and entitled, in its embryonic version, "Founding the Order of Absence." The dematerialization of writing that has been made possible by the computer revolution initially aroused feelings of alienation or disconnection from the text I was producing—and still raises certain irrational fears in me. Why, for example, should my gut response to the possibility of publishing this text electronically be so negative? Had I written it a decade from now, when much more academic publishing will be done on-line, far greater numbers of people would have potential access to my ideas than through the increasingly small pressruns of academic publishers today. Readers could view my text on their video screens, "capture" portions of it as they pleased, and print them out in formats of their choice. Knowing there are now more efficient methods of communicating and stocking ideas than through the paper codex, why should I feel threatened by its imminent abandonment as the physical support for academic publishing? What am I afraid of losing? Authority? If so, how is it that writing in the form of the codex has come to be endowed with such authority? Why do I find it unsatisfying that the text expressing my ideas should become virtually intangible, invisible, weightless, and infinitely small, a speck on a hard disk that no longer takes up "real" space in the world? Why should I want my text to have a "body"?

Instead of repressing these fears and desires, I have tried to interrogate them and to investigate their historical and cultural foundations, even though the danger of allowing feeling to taint the scientific enterprise, much less to motivate it, was impressed upon me from an early age, as upon so many other scholars. If I can now safely acknowledge the genesis of this book in feeling and in the need to think about and understand emotional reactions, this is because contemporary scholars are more ready to admit that an absolute dichotomy between thinking and feeling, or between perception and emotion, is, essentially, wishful (emotional) thinking and, furthermore, that the attempt to maintain such a false dichotomy has sometimes resulted in falsified and censored narratives and reluctance to deal with emotionally charged subjects.

The discomforts of switching to electronic or "virtual" writing, to a new level of physical abstraction, made me more aware of and called into question the nature of my emotional and imaginative attachments to print, manuscript, and oral cultures, none of which any of us has entirely surpassed or abandoned. If electronic publishing threatens academics with a loss of authority, is this because, as some would claim, the very idea of "originality, or authorial substance and authority" depends on late eighteenth- and nineteenth-century copyright laws and is print based?[1] I believe my own sense of imminent loss derives from an even older layer of codex culture. Originality and authority were buttressed by copyright laws regulating the publication of printed texts, but even before these laws there were medieval ways, some of which carried over into print culture, of authorizing or giving authorial substance to writing in codices, ways that we might characterize as fetishizing.

As a response to the alienation created by a new technology, my interest in what I perceive as the figurative embodiment and empowerment of writing in certain kinds of medieval manuscripts might be labeled by some as regressive, a step backward from print as I am drawn forward into the electronic age. Yet, if we identify progress with increasing abstraction and disembodiment (a highly dubious notion), we would also have to judge as regressive attempts of software inventors to "warm up" electronic writing with pictures or graphics, colors, movement, morphing, and other state-of-the-art ways of enlivening electronic writing and creating illusions of presence. Indeed, taken literally, the title of this book, *Animating the Letter,* might as well describe current trends in software for electronic writing as it describes the efforts of medieval scribes.

The late twentieth century seems to share with the seventh through ninth centuries a desire to animate the letter by giving it the appearance of liveliness or of being, a desire provoked by the introduction of a more abstract, disembodied, "cold" way of communicating and saving knowledge. In the early Middle Ages, handwriting in codices was introduced into oral cultures whose sacred "texts" had always been conserved in people's memories and communicated in live performances; in the late twentieth century, the support of writing, the codex itself, is being replaced by the video screen and the magnetic disk for the display and storage of an intangible, invisible trace. It is not difficult to think of analogies between the imaging techniques being integrated into modern electronic writing and those used by early medieval scribes—for example, variable scaling or "zoom" effects and the greatly enlarged initial letters of the chi-rho page of the Book of Kells (color plate 1). However, to elaborate the list of such analogies would be beyond my level of sophistication as an electronic writer and would, I suspect, result in little more than an exercise in ingenuity. Given the enormous differences between pen, ink, and parchment, on the one hand, and a computer, on the other, the methods used by medieval scribes and modern electronic writers to animate their respective texts are inevitably far more different than alike.[2] This in no way diminishes the importance of the basic similarity: the desire to animate alphabetic writing.[3]

I am, of course, not the first person to fall under the spell of early medieval animated letters, although few scholars have talked about them in precisely these terms—at least not in print—for a variety of reasons that can only be touched on here. These reasons range from the way the subject matter of medieval studies has been divided up by professionals, to the iconoclastic bias of a print culture that would sharply distinguish between alphabetic writing and drawing, to the widespread reluctance to recognize in the Western Christian tradition—and especially in ourselves—"irrational" cognitive patterns such as animism, the projective perception of life and being in inanimate figures.

Until the rise in the last decade of a holistic, interdisciplinary "new codicology," professional medievalists had followed the generally accepted Western dogma that writing and depiction are two very different activities accomplished by different people; medievalists have defined their specialized fields so that the study of writing (paleography, textual editing, and literary analysis) has been divorced from the study of drawing and painting (art history). In consequence, designed or "decorated" letters have not been central to the interests of any discipline, although art historians specializing in manuscript illumination have made the greatest contributions to understanding them.

Some of the earliest art historical attention to designed letters in medieval manuscripts is dismissed today as amateurish, impressionistic "appreciation." For example, Emile Van Moé, who published in 1949 a beautiful volume of engraved, colored reproductions of designed letters from eighth-through twelfth-century manuscripts, entitled *La lettre ornée,* was content to present this "admirable flowering of letters," which he organized alphabetically, for their sheer aesthetic value. Van Moé did not hesitate, for example, to marvel over the liveliness of these letters: "what joy, what life the frankly beautiful colors of the initials give the page."[4]

Such forthright subjective response has been eliminated from studies with scientific ambition, such as Carl Nordenfalk's fundamental work, to which I am much indebted, on late antique "decorated" letters, *Die spätantiken Zierbuchstaben* (1970), which classifies and traces the origin and history of the earliest figurative motifs used to "ornament" alphabetic writing.[5] J. J. G. Alexander's *The Decorated Letter* (1978) provides, for a wider public, what he calls an anthology of forty high-quality color plates of decorated initials ranging from the fourth to the fifteenth century, as well as a good but brief introductory overview of their development, accompanied by reproductions in black and white.[6]

Now that much of the fundamental work of classification and dating has been done on these figures, we can consider more seriously why—to what effects—figurative representation has been combined with alphabetic writing at all. We need to consider the role of figuration in creating "images" of early Christian writing that served to empower and authorize it in various ways. This requires a reintegration of subjective response, present as well as past, into our science and a broader, more theoretical view of what "decoration" or "ornament" may do—if we want to retain such terms, for they have too often been used anachronistically (in accordance with a modernist, decoration-denigrating aesthetic)[7] to divorce, and even to dismiss, figuration from writing, as if it were merely a superficial and superfluous complement to the letter and had no transformative power.[8]

Scholars who study medieval writing have been chiefly interested in reading "through" the letters to the sense of the words they represent; when the visual shapes or figures of the letters have been scrutinized, it has usually been to interpret these as utilitarian signs or markers. Paleographers, for example, have traditionally paid less attention to the more elaborately designed initials (which they leave to art historians) than to the quirks in the shaping of ordinary letters, which may identify a particular scribe at work or help to date and locate the provenance of a manuscript.[9] Textual editors, on the other hand, pay attention to the special shapes of initial letters as markers of the main divisions and subdivisions of the text; they are interested mainly in the way designed letters "clarify" the logical relationship of a text's parts, and hence its sense. For example, this is Hélène Toubert's explanation of the function of designed letters:

> A medieval ornamented initial is a letter that has received a format, a coloring, and a particular decoration destined to distinguish it from other letters so that it can function for the reader as a signal. . . . [T]o the ornamental role of decorated letters was added that of guiding the reading of the text by emphasizing its principal articulations through the particular appearance given to the initial of each significant section. . . . This led to a hierarchization of initials that were ornamented and colored according to a format and decoration more or less rich depending on whether they indicated the beginning of a chapter or a secondary paragraph.[10]

The modern editor of a medieval text pays attention to specially designed letters in order to replace them with the significant "nothing" of the blank spaces or indentations that conventionally articulate a modern printed text. By eliminating whatever would call attention to the body of the medieval letter per se, modern printed editions have made it much easier for literary analysts to read "through" medieval texts, that is, to concentrate solely on the sense of the words.

Although it has been possible for over a century now to supplement printed editions of medieval writing with photographic or lithographic re-productions, it has not been customary to do so—in part because of the prevailing emphasis on, or ethic of, "reading through," but also because the cost of such reproductions, often prohibitively high even in black and white, has reinforced the iconoclasm of print. For example, an early model of scientific editing, Gaston Paris's 1872 critical edition of *La vie de Saint Alexis,* offers not one single image of the writing of this text in the base manuscript, the Saint Albans Psalter, a marvel of early twelfth-century il-lumination wherein the designs of the letter (in the Alexis section, as in the Psalter proper) suggest the richness of figurative meaning twelfth-century monks had discovered in these texts.[11] Although the cost of reproducing photographs is more of a problem than ever, this is being done with in-creasing frequency in editions and critical essays, owing to the exertions of a generation of interdisciplinary medievalists interested in more holistic representation of medieval texts.[12]

Literary scholars are no longer satisfied with just "reading through" modern editions of medieval texts. They insist on seeing them in manu-script and in seeing *everything* on the manuscript page—not only framed miniatures illustrating the literal or figurative senses of the words of the text, but also those aspects of illumination that have so long been disre-garded. For example, in *The Book of Memory* Mary Carruthers has sug-gested a more complex—mnemonic—function for medieval designed let-ters. Such a function requires editors and literary analysts to really *see* the figures of these letters, to examine them closely and study them, not just to note them as strictly utilitarian signs of textual divisions and subdivisions or to dismiss them as "merely" decorative, that is, irrelevant to the sense of the text's words:

> The idea that manuscript decoration had a practical use has begun to be broadly adopted by codicologists and art historians; as De Hamel says [*A History of Illumi-nated Manuscripts* (1986), p. 101], "Decoration is a device to help a reader use a manu-script." But ... if we take a wholly utilitarian approach to decoration, especially if

we identify it with some preconceived notion of "literate" as opposed to "oral" culture, we will misunderstand its full function as much as we did when we thought of it as "only" decoration, or as a help for those who couldn't read. Like reading, of which it is a part, decoration is "practical" in the medieval understanding of that word, having a basic role to play in every reader's moral life and character because of its role in the requirement of memory.[13]

For a designed letter to function mnemonically, we would have to decipher its figures and contemplate its shapes in order to discover (or invent for ourselves) relationships between these designs and the sense of the words of the text, which would not necessarily be illustrated straightforwardly by the designs. For example, Carruthers suggests that attentive consideration of the intricately designed letters of the chi-rho page of the Book of Kells (color plate 1)[14] may "help . . . to initiate the divisional and compositional process that is required to read [and inscribe in memory the book of] Matthew."[15]

Indeed, designed letters—especially those, as in the Book of Kells, designed to look alive—accomplish their mnemonic function in several ways: not only by proposing an abstract, intellectual technique of recollection based on the arts of memory taught in classical and medieval schools, but also, and perhaps even more effectively, by arousing emotions in the reader/viewer. Carruthers suggests that the "emotion of surprise" at discovering two cats too lazy to catch the mice that surround them at the bottom of the chi-rho page of the Book of Kells "makes the page effective in memory, whatever the meanings we may later give to its many forms."[16] But surprise is surely not the only emotion the designs of this page provoke. How would the untutored eye (or the tutored one, on first impression) react to greatly magnified letters with human heads and "bodies" filled with a seemingly infinite tangle of living and geometrical forms too complex ever fully to decipher or understand? Would these figurative shapes of the letters not serve to fetishize the writing of this text, and to impress upon the reader/viewer, emotionally even more than intellectually, the awful mystery, the divine power and authority, of the writing? How *dare* we forget a text apparently inhabited by such a powerful presence?

In Western cultures today, belonging to the ranks of the sane and rational requires that we treat images as mere representations; no person in his right mind, much less a scholar with scientific ambitions, would publicly admit to entertaining the impression that images are alive. Nevertheless, as David Freedberg has provocatively argued in *The Power of Images,* all human beings, whether they are willing to admit it or are conscious of it or not, project life upon figures that resemble living forms; there is no fundamental difference between "them" ("primitives," pagans, the insane) and "us" in this respect:

> *We* may be quite happy to believe that images in primitive cultures are felt to partake of the life of what they represent, or even of the life of things other than what they represent. But we do not like to think this of ourselves, or of our own society. We refuse—or have refused for many decades—to acknowledge the traces of animism in our own perception of and response to images: not necessarily "animism" in the nineteenth-century ethnographic sense of the transference of spirits to inanimate objects, but rather in the sense of the degree of life or liveliness believed to inhere in an image.[17]

This impression that there is living presence in figurative representations is just what Western viewers have been taught to deny.

The proper Christian attitude to images was a subject of controversy in the seventh through ninth centuries in the Western church as well as in the Eastern; the official doctrine that eventually emerged was that, whereas pagans might erroneously worship images as god(s), Christians were supposed to regard images as nothing more than representations. As Pope Gregory put this as early as 599, images were to be "read" rather than adored: "For a picture is displayed in churches on this account, in order that those who do not know letters may at least read by seeing on the walls what they are unable to read in books."[18] The comparison Gregory makes here between images and writing seems intended to purify our response to images by having us imagine them as a kind of writing, that is, as mere representations, conventional signs. Modern iconographers tend to read "through" images in precisely this way.

Monotheistic religions of the book—Hebrew, Muslim, as well as Christian—have traditionally contrasted writing to depiction and upheld writing as superior because of its greater abstraction or "spirituality"; in other words, writing is judged superior because disembodied representation does not lend itself easily to idolatrous responses. And yet—supreme paradox underlying this generally accepted *doxa*—these same religions of the book have created images of writing that encourage idolatrous, projective responses to the "body" of writing in the corpus of a codex. The covert agenda of religions of the book has been a transfer of affect from "graven images" to letters—and the creation of a new idol.[19]

Recently, Seth Lerer has argued that early Christian writers in England insisted on a difference between Christian alphabetic writing and pagan runic writing and, in so doing, deliberately mystified the latter. The superiority of Christian writing was its abstraction; it was supposed to function purely symbolically, whereas its diabolical Other, pagan runic writing, was supposed to function magically:

> Christian literates effectively "invent" the idea of a runic mysticism . . . an alternative literacy to that of the Roman alphabet. [Runes] stand not just for a different technology of writing but for a different conceptual understanding of the written sign itself. Unlike the letters of a Christian world, those of a pagan past derive their power from their own inscription. Runes, to put it bluntly, are not "symbols" of anything, but may instead be thought of as a power of their own . . . what Cassirer called the "word-magic" envisioned by early societies . . . where "word and name do not merely have a function of describing or portraying but contain within them the object and its real powers. Word and name do not designate and signify, they are and act."[20]

The will to purify Christian writing by distinguishing it from and contrasting it to a pagan writing contaminated by animism is contradicted by the visual evidence provided by contemporary Christian manuscripts of the Gospels, whose scribes and illuminators seem to have been trying to incorporate and redirect (rather than simply reject) the "magical" powers they attributed to earlier pagan alphabets such as the runic and the Greek, as well as of earlier pictographic scripts—and even of knots. As we shall see, initial letters and lines of Insular[21] scripts often begin by imitating and assimilating the shapes and figures of earlier (and in that sense "initial") kinds of writing.[22] Furthermore, these initial letters incorporate figural designs in the shapes of humans, animals, and plants.[23] Because we tend to perceive the shapes of living figures before deciphering the shapes of letters and words,[24] such depiction solicits animistic responses that then influence our attitude to the writing, serving to activate and empower it. As literate people trained to read "through," we may not even be consciously aware of this transformative influence of the figure upon the letter.

One of the most important challenges to a medievalist today, and one I have tried to take up in the series of essays that follow, is to hold learned responses at bay long enough to take "first impressions," emotional responses, and "naive" questions seriously. My forays exploring developments in the image of writing in the Middle Ages and the different ways in which images empower writing from approximately the sixth through the sixteenth centuries—but with much more concentration on the early period and on manuscripts of sacred texts than of secular ones—are more in the nature of intermittent ventures into promising regions than attempts to circumscribe and "cover" thoroughly. The territory is vast and will support many explorers. The particular examples I have chosen to discuss might easily have been replaced by others equally revealing. Nor have I made any special efforts to reproduce images of writing that have seldom or never been reproduced for modern audiences. On the contrary, I have sometimes deliberately dwelt on those manuscripts and images of writing, such as the chi-rho page of the Book of Kells, that are most familiar today. The value of the following essays does not lie in the number of never-before-reproduced pictures they present but in the novelty of their project instead: to take account of the image of writing in medieval books, not to treat it as transparent. It is not that we have never been here before, but that we have so often passed through looking for something else.

# 1

# WRITING AS RELIC

*The Mythologizing of Alphabetic Writing*

*as Bodily Trace*

I once walked up to a man at a cocktail party where I knew no one and asked bluntly, "Who are you?" The man immediately disappeared into the hostess's library and returned with a novel containing the word *immortal* in its title, held it up, pointed to the picture of the author on the back, and said, "This is me." Then he disappeared once more, leaving me with the book. This self-definition was clearly a sort of self-effacement, a substitution of an alternate—presumably more lasting, not mortal, therefore immortal—corpus for the writer's living body. In the context of a cocktail party, when I wanted a living body to speak with rather than to be left standing holding the book, the disappearing writer's "This is me" struck me as ludicrous. And yet he had dramatized part of what writing is supposed to do: replace the human body. This replacement, however, is only partial, for writing cannot convey (and thus may be considered to censor) many of the messages the body conveys through voice and gesture about the speaker's gender, age, social class, regional origin, and so on. The photograph of the author on the book jacket of contemporary fiction or academic writing is an attempt to supply this lack. Even more poignant is the testament of the contemporary American poet who wanted his own skin tanned after his death and used to bind his poetic works.[1]

Although we prefer to think of writing as a means of self-expression or self-presentation, it is in many respects a means of self-effacement. By writing, the writer plays, and thus imaginatively masters and controls, his own physical disappearance, his own death. As many writers have remarked, to write requires absenting oneself, not being present for others. Writing envisaged in terms of self-effacement would be a symbolic suicide were it not for compensating illusions of continuing presence: metaphors that animate and personify the "dead" letter (or page or book) by attributing to it voice or gesture or body, enabling a writer to say "This is me." Even as writers accomplish their own physical disappearance, they believe they are leaving permanent traces of themselves. Although writing is a way of controlling one's own physical disappearance, it also denies that disappearance by substituting for the body the continuity of the line in space, the line imagined as the trace of the body, the body's presence implicit in the linear trace. I help to sustain the illusion of the writer's continuing presence every time I follow the common practice of summarizing or citing the text of a long-dead author in the present tense, as if he or she were currently speaking or inscribing it as I myself, for example, write "Shakespeare *writes* 'lines that grow to time.'"

The high value we place on the autograph manuscripts of the works of famous authors or their correspondence stems in part from this belief that something of the person is preserved in the trace of his or her handwriting.[2] We feel closer to the writer in reading an autograph manuscript than in reading the same text in a modern printed edition. One of the pleasures of handling and reading medieval manuscripts (scripts written "by hand")— as compared, for example, to modern paperbacks—is the relatively greater sense of living presence they give us. To be sure, some of the "presence" of the medieval manuscript comes from the material support of writing: skin. We can feel with our fingertips the difference between flesh side and hair side of the leather page; we can see and touch the pores and sometimes old scars; we can even smell the parchment. Designs drawn or painted on skin (even that of a dead animal, smoothed and whitened) evoke that ancient form of writing on human flesh, the tattoo.[3] Getting to know a particular manuscript is like getting to know a particular person. No two are ever alike; even when, so rarely, they contain the "same" text(s), the placement of words and figures on the page is different, and the manuscripts are (or were, for many original coverings have been lost) "dressed" differently to further individualize them. Much as we might describe a missing person by his clothing as well as by the distinctive marks of his flesh (facial features, scars, birthmarks, and the like), medieval inventories distinguish one manuscript from another by describing the style and placement of marks of inscription as well as their coverings and ornamentation, sometimes right down to the missing jewel.[4]

Yet medievalists do not tend to discuss the peculiarly "personal"—even intimate—nature of reading and studying medieval manuscripts. Indeed, editing a medieval handwritten and hand-illuminated text for a modern printed edition has traditionally required the editor to be the suppressor of all that is personal or different about the medieval version(s). In the nineteenth and earlier part of the twentieth centuries, as Carlo Ginzburg has pointed out, the philologist's project tended to be reductive:

> At first, all the elements tied to orality and gesture and later even those tied to the physical characteristics of writing were thought to be irrelevant to the text. This twofold process resulted in a progressive dematerialization of the text, which was gradually purified at every point of reference related to the senses. . . . The abstract notion of text explains why textual criticism, even while retaining to a large extent its divinatory qualities, had the potential to develop in a rigorously scientific direction, as in fact occurred in the course of the nineteenth century. The radical conception of considering only the portions of a text which could be reproduced (first manually and later, after Gutenberg, mechanically) meant that, even while dealing with individual cases, one avoided the principal pitfall of the humane sciences: quality.[5]

A medievalist who alleged the seductive odor of old manuscripts as his reason for stealing them is perhaps the most striking exception I can think of in the past decade or so to this rule of silence concerning our sensual relationships to texts in manuscript and the personality we attribute to them.[6]

On the contrary, medievalists tend to treat openly the "problem" of the anonymity of writing in medieval manuscripts, which are often the work of unknown scribes and sometimes of anonymous authors. Yet our inability to name the scribe or the author of a text in a medieval manuscript does not impersonalize our experience of reading it; we still feel a human presence. When we cannot name the scribe or the illuminator, we can describe him (as a detective would) by the natural traces of his motor habits, his characteristic choices or errors, all the details that distinguish his "hand" and make up a personal "signature." The increasing interest in manuscripts today, among both scholars and visitors to museum exhibits, stems in part from nostalgia for the more permanent, more sensual, more "natural" trace of handwritten texts, nostalgia provoked by the recent changes in writing's (and reading's) material support, which is now increasingly the video screen, the fleeting, distanced, untouchable electronic image.

Writing (just as much as speech, although in different ways) has been mythologized in Western cultures as a natural, presence-bearing trace, a signifier that partakes of the very essence of the signifying subject: a Signifier. This mythology of writing as an extension of presence (rather than an absence of it) is what Jacques Derrida had to ignore in *Of Grammatology* in order to construct the Western metaphysics he has criticized: a metaphysics that consistently debases writing (as opposed to speech) as empty of presence or being, merely the sign of a sign.[7] Derrida states that the trace is the effacement of a presence: "The trace is the effacement of oneself, of one's own presence; it is constituted by the menace or the anguish of one's inevitable disappearance, by the disappearance of one's disappearance. A trace that is unerasable is not a trace; it is a full presence, an immobile and incorruptible substance, a Son of God."[8] This view is only partly right, for the presence may also be perceived as lingering in the trace. Derrida wants to see the glass as half empty, not half full. He imagines the trace in the process of disappearing completely, like the sound of a voice. Yet the trace may be and has often been imagined and imaged as a much more lasting—indeed, living—sign.

The opening lines of a recent book on the symbolism of handwriting amply attest to the vitality of the myth of a permanent presence in the trace of writing: "Your signature is, in effect, the imprint of yourself and contains, in a fashion just as unique as a fingerprint, what characterizes you and belongs to you alone in your innermost being. . . . More faithful than your shadow, it will accompany you all your life, preserving at every instant the essential traits of your character. . . . Each being is unique, likewise, his signature. . . . His signature will remain the affirmation of his passage on earth and the resumé of the very essence of his human nature."[9] Some graphologists even claim that a person's handwriting (not merely his signature) is much more expressive of his personality than is his voice, "because the writer does not know what he is doing by writing," that is, because the design of his handwriting is an unconscious projection of his inner nature: "Conscious writing is an unconscious design, sign and portrait of oneself."[10]

Just as we would like to think of the sounds of our voices as extensions of ourselves, so also we would like to think of alphabetic writing as a "natural" trace, a sign of our presence that is not arbitrary but inevitable because it literally conserves something of us. This impossible desire has been captured by a contemporary cartoonist as a series of fingerprints: first, in the voice balloon of a toga-clad orator; second, on the notebook of a woman writing with a pen; third, on the video screen of a man typing at a computer.[11] When an animal leaves a trace in the snow—of blood, paw prints, or even scent—this natural trace of the animal's body may be "read" by the hunter to track down the animal. These remnants of the animal or configurations of marks or imprints made by its moving body the hunter reads as signs, a "natural," inevitable, "writing." (A modern detective tracking a criminal will look for the same kind of "natural writing.") Alphabetic writing is very far indeed from actually being a natural trace (in which something of the body that made the trace still inheres). Even when we write with our own hands on parchment or paper, we do not usually write with our own molecules (but rather with a substitute marking substance), nor do the letters of the alphabet resemble the natural imprints of our bodies in any way. The hypotheses we have devised to explain how writing came to be invented—for instance, by an imaginative hunter who imitated the tracks of animals to convey a message about them—may well be manifestations of our lingering desire that alphabetic writing should be a natural trace, a desire we rationalize by trying to ground it historically, imagining that alphabetic writing had its *origin* in the perception of natural traces as natural "writing" and the consequent step of artificially imitating this natural writing.[12]

As we shall see, early medieval Christian scribes were some of the most

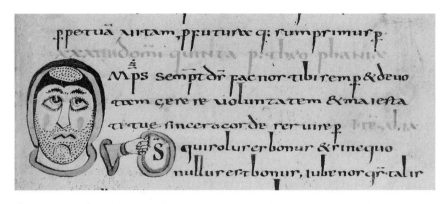

FIG. 1. Initial uncial *d* as the face and hand of a monk holding a loop. Sacramentary of Gellone. Paris, B.N.F., MS lat. 12048, fol. 18r. Photo Bibliothèque nationale de France.

ingenious mythologizers of writing as natural trace, for they departed from the conventional shapes of letters in different script styles to depict certain letters, especially initials, *as* bodies: whole bodies taking the place of all or parts of letters; contorted, stylized bodies turning into linear traces; vestiges of bodies still visible in the forms of letters. Late eighth- and ninth-century letters, for example, may have the hands or heads of their divine or human writers, as in the Sacramentary of Gellone (fig. 1) or the chi-rho page of the Book of Kells (color plate 1) and another Irish-influenced Gospel book (fig. 2). Instead of a hand emanating from the end of a letter in the early eighth-century Echternach Gospels, we see initial letters ending in spiral designs (called "mazes" by some art historians) that look like imitations of human fingerprints (fig. 3).[13] Pictorial amalgamations of bodily and literal forms from early medieval manuscripts are both incredibly various and virtually numberless; in the following chapters many more examples will be shown of letters figured as bodies.

Certain manuscripts of the Gospels, the Psalter, and other religious texts were thought to be both relics or earthly traces of God and also of the saintly men or women whose hands and heads were touched and inspired by God to inscribe them. Any object a saint had touched—but especially a text he or she had written—was believed to contain remnants of the saint's powerful presence; thus the seventh-century Irish Psalter known as the Cathach ("Battler") of Saint Columba, reputedly written by the saint under

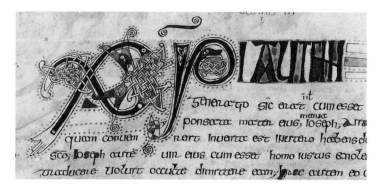

FIG. 2. Hand of the initial letter chi. Paris, B.N.F., MS nouv. acq. lat. 1587, fol. 2v. Photo Bibliothèque nationale de France.

the inspiration of the Holy Spirit, was borne to sites of combat to insure victory. Alphabetic writing was imagined in such cases as a trace conserving a powerful living presence. Today a similar mythology is at work in our reverence for autographs and autograph manuscripts as "relics" of the famous. The inscribed "relics" of the nonfamous are more likely to be perceived as worthless graffiti, but even these cryptic signatures are imagined, if only by those who write them, as natural traces enabling the writers to take possession of objects and their surrounding spaces by inscribing or "spraying" their own presence-bearing signatures upon them.

In all these cases, medieval and modern, the alphabetic writing that is to conserve the trace of the writer's presence is "designed," treated not solely as a representation of vocal sounds but also—and often more important— as a distinctive drawing. The Cathach of Saint Columba, for example, has initial letters designed to resemble living forms, such as the *Q* that terminates in a spiroid creature bearing a cross (fig. 4). My writing, punching keys, has nothing to do with drawing, whereas a medieval scribe's had everything to do with it. It is his (or as he might claim, God's) drawing, the pictorial aspects of his writing, his "signature," that I must censor if I want to transcribe his text, ever so partially, into a modern printed edition.[14] Yet it was precisely through the drawing or designing of writing that medieval scribes attempted to enliven alphabetic inscription, to mythologize it as a natural, presence-bearing trace. To design writing is, in effect, to de-sign it in the sense of de-conventionalizing and personaliz-

FIG. 3. Magnified detail of fingerprint patterns terminating the initial letter *N*. Echternach Gospels. Paris, B.N.F., MS lat. 9389, fol. 177r. Photo Bibliothèque nationale de France.

ing it, rendering it less abstract, more easily perceived as an extension of the person of the writer.

A modern example may help: How many graffitists would continue to leave their marks if their only recourse were to stencil their names in the exact same script and color used by every other graffitist? Indeed, contemporary graffiti, especially of the more elaborate, artful, and "monumental" sort on the exteriors of whole subway cars or walls, is worth considering for a moment here for how it gives the lie to the *doxa* that Western culture always has treated and will treat writing as the empty sign of a sign. Many regard such writing as sheer vandalism, "barbarian" destructiveness of higher culture that ought to be punished and suppressed, a sign of the failure of society to properly socialize (to inculcate an inner discipline in) its perpetrators. Yet the deliberately contestatory aims expressed through such writing are very hard to avoid seeing, very hard to dismiss as signs of the writers' "failure" to interiorize norms. That writing—the forms, colors, positions, and grounds of letters—should be a means of expressing difference, a field of contest, should not be surprising; Western culture has, for centuries, relied on the forming of characters to form character, on the teaching of writing to interiorize a much more far-reaching self-discipline and subservience to social standards. Proper printing (which is where the teaching of writing starts, and what we learn to read) is the order against which graffitists of the late twentieth century have deliberately transgressed to declare their difference.[15] And not only graffitists. Their practice is by no means marginal in contemporary Western culture. Professional

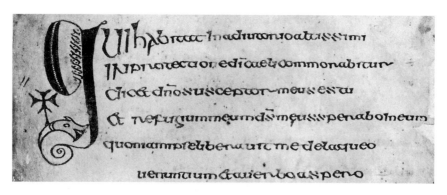

FIG. 4. Initial *Q* terminating in a spiroid, cross-bearing creature. Cathach of Saint Columba. Dublin, Royal Irish Academy, unnumbered MS, fol. 48r. Photo courtesy of the Officers of the Royal Irish Academy.

graphic designers, for example, are paid to make alphabetic writing seem to be more than the empty sign of a sign, to give it presence, to create more lively, powerful corporate logos, corporate identities.[16]

The letters of graffiti art (or graphically designed letters) are impossible to "read through." They call attention to themselves as form to such an extent that we may be unable to decipher what letters are being represented and how to combine these into words. Graffitists often magnify the shapes of printed letters and fill their hollowed-out "bodies" with bright colors. They twist and elaborate conventional letterforms and make letters overlap and jostle one another; such letters seem to have far too much energy to respect regular shapes, distances, or alignments. Magnified letters, often foreshortened for a three-dimensional effect, give the impression of moving toward the viewer, coming at us off their ground. They are intended to "impress," to imprint themselves on our memories. As one graffitist, who uses the signature "SEEN," put it, "the more you fill up the space, the more impression your piece makes. In the 'Blockbusters' [a lettering style] . . . I use a silver filling with a block or a red outline. That's why the letters sometimes look bigger than the train. When they drive into the station, you feel inclined to jump back."[17] The graffitist's ground of preference for his writing is one that will move—a train; his letters also refuse the conventional immobility of writing by appearing to move out at us.

The design or drawing of such writing (everything that is in excess with respect to conventionally printed letters) is supposed to make it seem alive. Often comic-strip characters replace and take the forms of the letter as character. A graffitist who works under the signature "QUIK" (and seems to play on an opposition to "dead") deliberately replaces the letter *I* with a childlike figure he identifies as himself. This same graffitist explains what he intended in a piece dedicated to his seriously ill father (who worked for a major institution of conventional graphic order, IBM, as did the graffitist himself for a short time): "It is a piece that says 'Ed,' which is his name, and it has a character, a portrait of myself, holding on to the 'D.' I'm holding on to my dad."[18]

As identifications such as this one suggest, graffitists treat the letters of names as if they were people. The graffitist Futura explains how his own logo works: "Futura is the name of a typeface. I discovered it in school, when I learned typesetting. The name and the tag [the stylized signature 'Futura'] were one; that's what you make public. That's what graffiti means: it's about identification, about a personal icon. It's a way of presenting yourself to the world, something like 'here I am.' "[19] The norms Futura learned in typesetting are those against which he develops his own difference, his "enlivened" letters that "are" himself. Some graffitists even claim a precedent for their own lettering styles in medieval art and envision themselves fighting an institutionalized "iconoclasm." Rammelzee, for example, proclaims, "If you look in the dictionary you'll see that the bishops stopped the monks because their power was becoming too strong with the letter."[20] Individualistically designed writing is intended to be an incarnation of the writer's presence and power—just the opposite of the empty sign of a sign. Although created by professional graphic artists in the service of a corporate image, the transgressively designed writing of many corporate logos is intended to have the same effect.

Not surprisingly, it was the drawing aspect of alphabetic writing that Lévi-Strauss's famously illiterate Nambikwara Indians apparently understood as they "wrote" by making "wavy horizontal lines," just as it is the drawing aspect of alphabetic writing that is repressed by our print culture (so that Lévi-Strauss distinguishes between writing and drawing in his description of the natives' gestures). Derrida quotes this passage from Lévi-Strauss's *Tristes Tropiques* in *Of Grammatology:*

That the Nambikwara could not write goes without saying. But they were also unable to draw, except for a few dots and zigzags on their calabashes. I distributed pencils and paper among them, none the less, as I had done with the Caduveo. At first they made no use of them. Then, one day, I saw that they were all busy drawing wavy horizontal lines on the paper. What were they trying to do? I could only conclude that they were writing—or, more exactly, they were trying to do as I did with my pencils. As I had never tried to amuse them with drawings, they could not conceive of any other use for this implement. With most of them, that was as far as they got.

Immediately after this passage, Derrida criticizes Lévi-Strauss for judging that the Nambikwara did not understand the meaning or purpose of writing because their word for writing was "drawing lines": "As if 'to write' in its metaphoric kernel, meant something else."[21] Why "metaphoric," we might ask? For the early medieval scribe (or the contemporary graphologist or graffitist or graphic artist), alphabetic writing *is* drawing.[22] Both the anthropologist and his critic have exhibited the bias of their accommodation to print culture in insisting that there be a divorce between drawing and alphabetic writing, a divorce that serves Derrida's thesis (that Western culture has always denigrated writing as the empty sign of a sign) by repressing the possibility—and the history—of imagining and imaging writing as presence.

The history Derrida blanks out is that of the so-called Dark Ages and Middle Ages, from the end of the Roman Empire to the fifteenth century. Early medieval scribes and illuminators (often the same person) were, as I will demonstrate more fully in later chapters, the most creative inventors of the myth of living presence in alphabetic writing, a myth to which at least some of us still cling in our print culture (as my anecdote about the contemporary author's "This is me" suggests, or the claims of modern graphologists and graffitists and graphic designers, or the humanized alphabets of artists such as Erté).[23] Everything that diverges from the regularity of type—all the deliberately designed differences, incongruities, and intricacies that give the impression of life and constitute an individualizing "signature"—must be suppressed to transpose medieval writing into print.[24]

The difficulty of accepting this reductive process, because of the sense of loss it provoked, was demonstrated in 1529 by a Paris bookseller and printer, Geoffroy Tory, in his *Champ fleury,* which we may understand as a kind of apology for—or attempt to remedy by altering our perception of—the apparently lifeless abstraction of the regular classical characters of humanist print. Tory argues that "Attic letters were so well fashioned by the Ancients that they have the proportions of the human body."[25] Not only does Tory heap up verbal analogies between the shapes of classical letters and those of the human body, but he also illustrates these by drawing different Attic letters on human bodies or faces that are themselves drawn on grids serving to demonstrate their regular proportions. For example, he superimposes the letter *I* on the figure of a man standing against the background of a grid to show that, "because a man erect on his feet must have them a little apart, otherwise he could not stand firm . . . so, for a like reason, our *I* must be broader at the base than at the top" (fig. 5).[26] As we read this treatise and gaze at its illustrations, it is as if human bodies were being regimented and sublimated into the regular shapes of the letters of a classical printed text. Tory seems to be trying, against all odds, to continue the medieval scribal tradition of animating the letter; he seems to be trying to convince us that there *is* a human body within the classical letter and that the regularity of the letter's shape should not prevent us from seeing this, for regularity, as Tory tries to prove, is human.[27] But no two humans are exactly alike in their regularity, as is every printed Attic *I.* Tory's imaginative attempt to humanize classical characters succeeds as long as we have his drawings of humanized letters before us, but once we return to reading regular print, we no longer imagine a standing man in each *I.*

Except in expensive facsimile editions, on microfilm, and in manuscript rooms and museum exhibits, the medieval contribution to the myth of presence in writing is not visible today, and even many medievalists are relatively unaware of it. Most of the time it is in modern print that we medievalists encounter medieval texts, and when we have occasion to edit them, our very function is to separate drawing from writing and thus to suppress all traces of the myth. The designed aspects of alphabetic writing in medieval manuscripts are usually dismissed by editors as mere ornament, superficial, added later, having nothing to do with the "content" of the text. Specialists also tend not to see, to take for granted, anything that is too obvious, as is the "life" of the letter in medieval manuscripts—in the "bodies" of

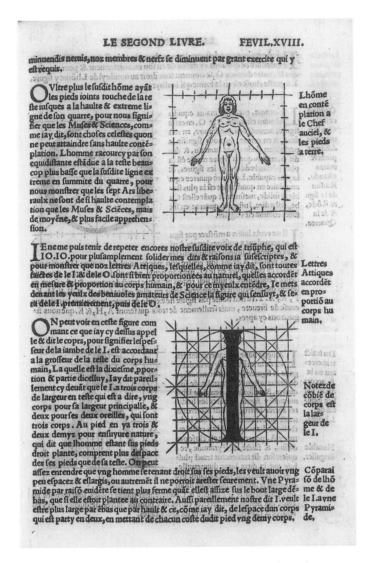

FIG. 5. Initial *I* as a standing man, from Geoffroy Tory, *Champ fleury* (Paris, 1529), p. 18r.

letters designed as birds, fish, plants, and humans; in letters that reveal such animate forms within their loops; in letters that grow into and harbor living forms in the page's margins.

By depicting letters in the act of moving, growing, or struggling, the medieval designers of sacred texts presented alphabetic writing as a living force, mythologized it as a natural trace or manifestation, not primarily of themselves, but of God. The animated writing these medieval draftsmen designed was supposed to be God's "signature," signed by divinely directed human hands. Like the distinctive and often illegible design of the letters composing the modern signature of a person's name, God's writing, Holy Scripture, was distinctively and often illegibly designed to manifest the presence of its writer. The mythology that empowers the modern Western signature—"the line become a trace, tasked with manifesting the presence of a single and unique body, inscribed on the page"—is not a postmedieval invention, as Béatrice Fraenkel has suggested,[28] but rather it is an early medieval one, elaborated for the purpose of empowering God's writing (i.e., man's). Before entering into a more detailed analysis of the medieval history of developments of the myth of writing as living presence, we should consider why such a myth needed to be elaborated at all.

Testimonies from quite various sources suggest that neither illiterate nor literate people automatically respected writing. What alphabetic writing enables—the physical absence of the signifying subject (through his replacement by lifeless marks)—made writing seem empty of presence and hence of authority. Lévi-Strauss's illiterate chieftain was not awed by the magical powers inherent in alphabetic writing, or else he would not have been so quick to make a few marks himself, reinforcing his own authority over his subordinates by pretending to be able to read them. Like the illiterate chieftain, Irish druids and prophets, whose power lay in the spoken word, and who were in some respects the opponents of Christian monks, regarded alphabetic writing mainly as a technique for duping people.[29] Although unfamiliar with alphabetic writing, illiterate peoples were not unfamiliar with the interpretation of traces and imprints, with "reading" as tracking or prediction.

What people in these earlier cultures revered was not the marks or the writing per se but rather the interpretive power of the reader, the living person capable of making meaning out of a pattern of marks in a delimited space. Power and authority were unimaginable without a living, enforcing presence. It was for this reason that, as Plutarch recounts, the Pythagorians did not use writing; they did not believe in confiding religious secrets to the keeping of "inert, undiscerning, soul-less things such as letters" (lifeless and therefore powerless to enforce, propagate, or protect).[30] Likewise, Plutarch writes that the early Roman priest-king Numa ordered his sacred books buried with him because he did not want "religious secrets guarded in lifeless letters." As long as he was alive, Numa used writing as a memory aid to teach other priests orally; death meant loss of control over the meaning of the written text, for power and authority were located in the living interpreter, not in the lifeless and defenseless text. Better to bury such lifeless letters with the dead body that had used them; better not to separate the signifier from the signifying subject.[31]

The most famous testimony to the emptiness of writing, and the historical example that founds Derrida's thesis in *Of Grammatology,* is the passage near the end of Plato's *Phaedrus* where Socrates denigrates alphabetic writing as a mere memory aid. Socrates argues that writing is not capable of retaining memories (thus replacing a person), but only of renewing memories the reader has already acquired (serving as a reminder). Citing the Egyptian king Thamus's warning that writing would make readers presume themselves wise when they were in fact empty of knowledge, Socrates denies writing the capacity to impress and leave traces in men, to *create* memories in them. In his view, only living men speaking have the power to impress.

The unbroken line of letters of a classical script is an arbitrary representation, as abstract in its principles as a digital sound recording. The letter *a,* for example, is by no means the trace of the sound it represents: there is no physical resemblance between the shape of the mark and the sound; the sound is not the origin of the mark; the mark is not the direct imprint of the sound. Although the continuous classical Greek script might have provided a satisfying image of linear (suggesting temporal) continuity and was economical of surface space, it was felt by men like Socrates to be a very poor substitute for a person speaking. In order to mean, the series of letters had to be translated back into sound by a living body hearing himself speak and analyzing (articulating) into meaningful units the sequence of sounds produced by his voice. To do this correctly, in Socrates' view, the reader had to be the original writer (or dictator) of the inscription or to know already what the inscription meant because he had been orally instructed.

Although Socrates was surely aware how ephemeral spoken words can be, he chose to deny this with metaphors that depict oral teaching as an act of generation or propagation. He argued against trying to disseminate ideas through writing, because it "drifts all over the place, getting into the hands not only of those who understand it, but equally of those who have no business with it; [it] doesn't know how to address the right people, and not address the wrong. And when it is ill-treated and unfairly abused . . . [it] always needs its parent to come to its help, being unable to defend or help itself."[32] The only way to impose one's ideas reliably and permanently is, in Socrates' view, through the oral teaching of capable pupils, which leaves an indelible trace in them that they will, in turn, transmit to future generations of pupils: "The dialectician selects a soul of the right type, and in it he plants and sows his words founded on knowledge, words which can defend both themselves and him who planted them, words which instead of remaining barren contain a seed whence new words grow up in new characters, whereby the seed is vouchsafed immortality, and its possessor the fullest measure of blessedness that man can attain unto."[33]

Socrates likes to imagine that his oral teachings are a living writing—living because impressed upon the living "support" of his pupils' memories—with all the power and authority of a person (his person living through his pupils). He imagines oral teachings born of his own mind as "legitimate sons," and he carries the image of oral teaching as engendering further to imagine that his oral discourses (the "legitimate sons") inseminate the souls of his pupils to produce further progeny. The goal of this scheme is continuation of the same through perpetual renewal, without any mutation (and without any females); Socrates' dream is to clone himself, and for these clones to clone themselves.

Elsewhere he uses the image of pupils as plants that grow from the seed of his oral teachings (with himself, implicitly, the "parent" plant). Metaphors such as these, of oral teaching as engendering or propagation, tend to mythologize oral teaching in much the same way that early medieval scribes would later mythologize alphabetic writing. Although Socrates explicitly denigrates alphabetic writing as lifeless and powerless compared to oral teaching, his wishful images of teaching as a *living* writing also suggest how the continuous script of classical alphabetic writing (wherein the geometrically shaped, evenly spaced, and uniformly sized letters cover the writing surface with maximum efficiency and regularity) might be made to seem a more satisfactory replacement for the signifying subject: by designing the letters differently, so that they might seem to be alive.

According to Eric Havelock's theory, in his *Preface to Plato,* it was the very abstraction of alphabetic writing that broke the "spell" of the highly physical, participatory oral poetic tradition and thus prepared the way for analytic thinking in pre-Socratic Greece:

> [The Homeric and post-Homeric Greek] is required as a civilised being to become acquainted with the history, the social organisation, the technical competence and the moral imperatives of his group.... This over-all body of experience (we shall avoid the word "knowledge") is incorporated in a rhythmic narrative or set of narratives which he memorises and which is subject to recall in his memory. Such is poetic tradition, essentially something he accepts uncritically, or else it fails to survive in his living memory. Its acceptance and retention are made psychologically possible by a mechanism of self-surrender to the poetic performance, and of self-identification with the situations and the stories related in the performance. Only when the spell is fully effective can his mnemonic powers be fully mobilised. His receptivity to the tradition has thus, from the standpoint of inner psychology, a degree of automatism which however is counterbalanced by a direct and unfettered capacity for action, in accordance with the paradigms he has absorbed.... His mental condition, though not his character, is one of passivity, of surrender, a surrender accomplished through the lavish employment of the emotions and of the motor reflexes.[34]

Havelock suggests that the rhythms and images of performed oral poetry appealed to the body, to all the senses, so strongly that memory retained the whole experience in which the body had participated, including the words. In the oral tradition, the performing body left its traces or imprints on the audience. Socrates, analytic thinker though he was, participated in this oral tradition and wanted his oral teaching to be such a living writing, to leave such physical impressions or traces.[35]

The inscription via alphabetic writing of "encyclopedic" oral poetry tended to take it out of the corporeal realm of the trace and of lineage. For this very reason there were many who regarded the abstraction of alphabetic writing—its apparent censorship of the body—as a threat to the continuance of cultural values (which could only be effectively impressed orally) and wanted writing to be used solely as a memory aid. Writing was considered not only impotent to impress but dangerously open to interpretation; once dead, the writer had no power to correct inadvertent misunderstandings or deliberate twistings of the sense of his text. Indeed, the continuous script offered even greater possibilities for misinterpretation than does this page full of marks carefully articulated via spacing and punctuation into words and larger units of meaning. Because the earliest Greek and Roman inscriptions do use some marks of punctuation to articulate words,[36] it would appear that the rigorously continuous script was, in both Greece and Rome, a later invention; it is almost as if the lack of visual articulation were a deliberate way of assuring that writing could not so easily replace a body remembering.

For many centuries alphabetic writing served mainly as a mnemonic device to spark the traces of memories in those who already knew the poetic text by heart or nearly so and would thus have no great difficulty articulating the sounds represented by the inscription into meaningful words and phrases. Pierre Riché has reminded us that far into the Middle Ages reading was taught in monasteries largely to aid in the recollection of the Psalter, which each monk was supposed to memorize in its entirety. Monastic schools followed the example of rabbinical schools, whose goal was to teach the Torah to youngsters, chiefly through oral recitation, so that the words "passed into their blood and naturally flowed from their lips."[37] People in predominantly oral cultures have difficulty imagining the possibility of conserving human experience in media other than the human body. Even though their sacred texts were written down, the Hebrews took care to keep them alive through oral transmission, that is, through constant oral performance during religious celebration, teaching, memorization, and study. Christian monks did likewise by constantly performing the divine word liturgically and in more private devotions and thus embodying it in themselves. Knowing the Psalter was not having read it, having deciphered its written text, but knowing it "by heart," interiorizing it and "ruminating" over it ("chewing it over") regularly in private as well as voicing it in common song.[38]

Marcel Jousse argues in *La manducation de la parole* that "one takes the words of the teacher into one's mouth and eats them" in oral cultures;[39] as evidence, he cites the famous example of Ezekiel, whom God ordered to eat the scroll and, having thus incorporated the divine message, to go prophesy (Ezekiel 2:9–3:3): "And I looked, and behold, a hand was sent to me, wherein was a book rolled up: and he spread it before me, and it was written within and without: and there were written in it lamentations, and canticles, and woe. And he said to me: Son of man, eat all that thou shalt find: eat this book, and go speak to the children of Israel. And I opened my mouth, and he caused me to eat that book: And he said to me: Son of man, thy belly shall eat, and thy bowels shall be filled with this book, which I give thee. And I did eat it: and it was sweet as honey in my mouth." John in the Apocalypse (10:8–11) reports receiving a similar divine command to eat an inscribed scroll and prophesy.

Memorization in oral cultures is, according to Jousse, a verbo-motor activity involving the whole body, and it is greatly encouraged by rhythmic bodily movements, balancing back and forth in rhythm to the balanced oral formulaic style, as in the parallel phrases of a text such as the psalms (or Anglo-Saxon alliterative verse or French octosyllables divided by a caesura).[40] Like Havelock, Jousse emphasizes the highly physical nature of the identificatory participation involved in this kind of memorization, which brings into play all the senses, but especially the mouth (rather than the eyes) as a means of taking into the body what was exterior to it. Indeed, behind the "eating of words" one glimpses less abstract (cannibalistic) kinds of ingestion of embodied wisdom to assure its survival. The "orality" of oral cultures—and the continuation of oral mentalities in our own print culture—is perhaps most powerfully exemplified for us today in the Christian Eucharist, founded on Christ's injunction to his disciples to eat in remembrance of him his flesh and blood (or bread and wine that are supposed to become these). Eating is remembering in the sense that the body of the disciple, by ingesting the body of Christ, is marked and partly made up of Christ, bears the physical trace of Christ within himself or herself. In oral cultures, one remembered important poetic compositions and customary lore because, through identificatory participation in repeated live performances of these, they were believed to pass into one's body, one's blood, one's breathing, one's very being—so that one *became* the other.

Eventually, despite much resistance, alphabetic writing did come to replace bodies remembering as the most authoritative way of preserving a cultural heritage. In order for this to happen, however, writing had to be treated—mythologized—as a relic, that is, a repository of living presence and authority, a trace superior in its fixity to other, more ephemeral, natural traces of the human body such as the "imprint" of a voice or a touch. In oral cultures, it was the living body in action or the living body in the act of remembering (even with the written text as memory aid) that commanded respect, and not any black marks on papyrus or on a piece of dead sheep.

We are probably wrong to think, as we would like to do, that illiterate people, when they first saw alphabetic writing, would regard it as magical and awe-inspiring. This is, for example, the opinion Peter Meyer expressed in his introduction to the 1950 facsimile edition of the late eighth-century Irish Book of Kells: "writing *per se* long retained its numinous quality for the north, which was emerging but slowly from a prehistory in which writing was unknown. Accessible only to a few initiates, its ultimately magical character was powerfully felt. Writing enabled fleeting thoughts to be preserved in signs, and a stranger might later reawaken those signs to life without ever having seen or heard the writer. That in itself was magic to those who had only known communication by word of mouth."[41] If such power was perceived to lie in alphabetic writing per se, why did the designers of medieval manuscripts such as the Book of Kells go to such effort to animate their script by designing it in the shape of such an infinite-seeming variety of colorful living forms? Why did they not simply do the most economical thing and write the Gospels in a continuous script? It seems much more likely that the illiterate person would see unembellished writing for what it really was—nobody, therefore not worthy of respect—and that the designers of the Book of Kells sought ways to overcome such indifference.

Peter Meyer was surely right to remark the magical quality, indeed, the impression of living presence, one senses in viewing a page of the Book of Kells, but this impression is not due to alphabetic inscription's ability to fix the spoken word (or a mythology to this effect, for there are no "spoken" words fixed on any pages anywhere). Rather, the effect of living presence in the letters of the Book of Kells comes, as we shall see in more detail later, from their pictorial design, that is, their depiction of life turning into the trace of alphabetic writing—or the reverse, of the trace revealing itself as life.

In the Book of Kells, we see human and animal bodies turning into or

FIG. 6. Lesser initial *A* as a knotted man. Book of Kells. Dublin, Trinity College, MS 58, fol. 53v. Photo courtesy of the Board of Trinity College Dublin.

emerging from traces before our eyes as their limbs, tongues, and ears elongate and twist around their bodies and intertwine with other body traces. Human speaking and movement (or gesture) seem to turn into the trace of the letter *A,* for instance, in one of the lesser initials of the Book of Kells (fig. 6). On the same page, we might see the elongated spiral of a lionish creature's ear, which, along with other bodily members, forms the shape of an initial letter *T.* In what may at first seem to be little more than a stylized series of complex knots and abstract linear forms, the mere suggestion of the shape of a head or an eye is all it takes to evoke life. To perceive the animal's "presence" in the tangle of knots, one literally has to follow the trace to a head or other recognizable body part. Appreciating "ribbon-style ornament," as this is conventionally called in Anglo-Saxon metalwork, from which it was adapted for letter design, is a kind of tracking or hunting. The same may be said of the animated lesser initials of the Book of Kells, some of which betray their inner life with the mere hint of a claw or paw or tail emerging from a relatively conventional letter shape.

Rather than considering knotting, ribbon-style animals as ornament extraneous to the letter, we might think of them as a kind of pictorial writing incompletely abstracted into alphabetic writing. Pictographic writing is believed to be the earliest kind of writing and to have expressed not the sounds of words but an even more primary, embodied language: living things' actions—even the most fundamental of actions, "being there." One thesis that attempts to account for early cave paintings, as at Lascaux in southern France, posits that early people traced the outlines or shadows of animal presences that they believed existed within other forms, such as stone. From darkening and signaling the "natural" trace of a presence to render it more visible, these early peoples may have turned to copying the "natural" trace on other surfaces capable of receiving inscription, surfaces that were more permanent or more portable. To copy the natural trace onto another surface was to denature it. Yet as long as the copy was a fairly close pictorial imitation of the natural (or supposedly natural) trace, the presence that supposedly manifested itself in the original trace might still seem to inhere in and motivate the copy.[42]

Gradually, through the course of repeated copying, the artificial trace of early pictographic "writing" was simplified, stylized, and further denatured. The table showing the development of cuneiform symbols from pictographs into classical Assyrian, reproduced from David Diringer's *Writing* (fig. 7),[43] demonstrates this stylization of the trace, a stylization in this case strongly influenced by the qualities of the writing surface, a soft clay tablet. As Diringer's table suggests, the progressive stylization of the trace, in this as in other pictographic writing systems, was accompanied by its phonetization. As the trace came to resemble less and less the outline or imprint of a body in nature, it came more and more to represent the word for the thing (rather than prolonging and manifesting the presence of the thing itself). Without this association with a word, the increasingly stylized trace was difficult to identify. Thus the classical Assyrian signs in the right-hand column are logograms, pictures for words. Some of these same signs also came to represent vowel sounds or the sounds of two- or three-letter syllables.[44]

Alphabetic writing completely denatures the trace, which is no longer the copy, however stylized, of the supposedly natural trace of a living thing or presence, but rather is the arbitrary representation of the sounds of the word for the thing. This difference in the way the graphism means can be unsatisfying in its abstraction. In the "writing" of the natural trace, what is signified *is* the signifying subject. The rabbit leaves a track of itself in the snow. Even Christ was thought to engage in this sort of writing as bodily trace, although the natural corporeal imprints he left were miraculous—supernatural—in their extraordinary imprinting capacity. On the cloth of

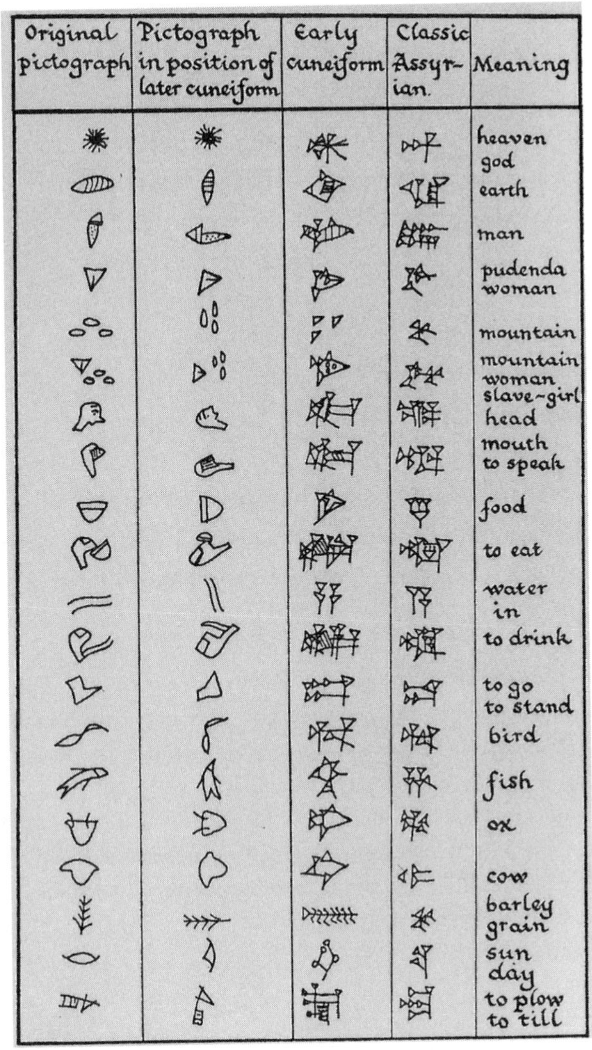

| Original pictograph | Pictograph in position of later cuneiform | Early cuneiform | Classic Assyrian. | Meaning |
|---|---|---|---|---|
| | | | | heaven god |
| | | | | earth |
| | | | | man |
| | | | | pudenda woman |
| | | | | mountain |
| | | | | mountain woman slave-girl |
| | | | | head |
| | | | | mouth to speak |
| | | | | food |
| | | | | to eat |
| | | | | water in |
| | | | | to drink |
| | | | | to go to stand |
| | | | | bird |
| | | | | fish |
| | | | | ox |
| | | | | cow |
| | | | | barley grain |
| | | | | sun day |
| | | | | to plow to till |

FIG. 7. Table of the "evolution" of cuneiform symbols from pictographs to classical Assyrian. Reproduced from David Diringer, *Writing,* p. 38.

the Veronica with which his face was wiped on the road to Calvary, and on the stone column to which he was tied when he was flagellated, Christ was believed to have left traces of his face and his chest and hands, imagistic impressions of divinity in which divinity still inhered, *achiropiites* that had not been made by merely human hands, and thus were not representations but relics.[45]

Alphabetic writing, unless it is mythologized as a natural, presence-bearing trace, breaks the equation between signifying subject, signifier, and signified, for it substitutes a signifier and a signified that are different from the signifying subject as the objects of our tracking effort. Today, we may find it difficult even to imagine the possibility that the primitive artists of Lascaux were not trying to represent animals (signifieds) but acknowledging these animals as signifying subjects (by retracing and thereby emphasizing the original traces by which the animals manifested their presence).

Yet it was as a direct impression or imprint (what he calls an "erasure" and we would now call a "rubbing") of a divinely designed writing that the twelfth-century cleric Gerald of Wales first perceived the pages of the now lost Gospel Book of Kildare:

> Here you may see the face of Majesty, divinely drawn, there the mystic symbols of the Evangelists, each with wings, now six, now four, now two; here the eagle, there the calf, here the man, and there the lion, and other forms almost infinite. Look at them superficially, with the ordinary casual glance, and you would think it an erasure and not tracery. Fine craftsmanship is all about you, but you might not notice it. Look more keenly at it, and you will penetrate to the very shrine of art. You will make out intricacies so delicate and subtle, so exact and compact, so full of knots and links, with colours so fresh and vivid, that you might say that all this was the work of an angel, and not of a man.[46]

Gerald goes on to narrate the legend that accounted for the Gospel Book of Kildare as the perfectly accurate retracing of designs revealed to the scribe by an angel:

> On the night before the day on which the scribe was to begin the book, an angel stood beside him in his sleep and showed him a drawing made on a tablet which he carried in his hand and said to him, "Do you think that you can make this drawing on the first page of the book that you are about to begin?" [When the scribe said no,] the angel said to him, "Tomorrow, tell your lady [Saint Bridget] so that she may pour forth prayers for you to the Lord, that he may open both your bodily and mental eyes so as to see the more keenly and understand the more subtly, and may direct you

in the guiding of your hand." All this was done, and on the following night the angel came again and held before him the same and many other drawings. By the help of the divine grace, the scribe, taking particular notice of them all, and faithfully committing them to his memory, was able to reproduce them exactly in the suitable places of the book. And so with the angel indicating the designs, Bridgit praying, and the scribe imitating, the book was composed.[47]

Such supernaturally exact copying—for the scribe, aided by the angel and the saint, did no modifying—would deny mediation and representation and be a worldly "imprint" of the divine design itself, an imprint of the "face of Divine majesty" (as Gerald puts it), an *achiropiite,* a natural trace that reveals God's presence to acute reader-trackers.

Although Gerald of Wales does not make this explicit, the "drawings" of the lost Gospel Book of Kildare, drawings executed by its scribe, were almost certainly not separate from alphabetic writing, but rather were completely integrated into writing, as in the Book of Kells and earlier Insular Gospel books. What the depiction of a letter of the alphabet as a ribbon-style animal does in the Book of Kells is attempt to reunite the signifying subject with the signifier by depicting the latter as if it were the bodily trace of a living (indeed, divine) presence. The elaborate "decoration" or "ornamentation" of the letter in early medieval religious manuscripts was not motivated solely by aesthetic impulse or the desire to embellish God's Word, as we have tended to suppose, but also by an attempt to compensate for the dissatisfying lack of presence perceived in ordinary alphabetic writing by integrating (or reintegrating) pictorial design into alphabetic inscription. To draw a letter that terminates in a hand was to suggest that the letter was (and had the same power as) a person—a person whose hands enabled him to act and enact, to hand over or transmit. In Roman law, as Jean-Claude Schmitt has reminded us, this power was named *manus* (literally, "hand").[48]

The pictorial design of the medieval letter, far from being superfluous decoration, can be an attempt to de-sign it, to reintegrate into alphabetic writing the trace of physical presence—the body—that alphabetic writing has censored and repressed in its replacement both of earlier kinds of pictographic writing and of the speaking, gesturing human body.[49]

# 2

# WRITING VERSUS IMAGE
# IN CHRISTIAN THOUGHT
## *Writing as Image in Christian Practice*

Lf not one medieval manuscript had survived the centuries, we would have few clues that early medieval Christian scribes regularly combined writing, that is, the letters of the Latin alphabet, with figurative, pictorial designs—much less that they did so with enormous virtuosity and ingenuity, and at great cost to the monastic and ecclesiastical patrons that commanded these laborious endeavors. As we have just noted, even the twelfth-century secular writer Gerald of Wales did not explicitly mention that the shapes of letters were combined with "divine" designs, although this was almost certainly the case with the early Gospel book he described in Ireland. In short, the image of writing that the church fathers and later medieval observers have left us in their own written texts seems to exclude the possibility that medieval Christians could regard writing *as* image. Yet the evidence of surviving medieval Christian manuscripts amply belies this. How are we to account for the paradox of an iconoclastic Christian theory of writing and an iconodule practice of it in the inscription of the most sacred texts?

Part of the answer may lie in the classical tastes and values of highly influential early Christian fathers such as Jerome and Augustine. E. H. Gombrich has argued that classical aesthetics (which was also an ethics) had its origin in Greek rhetorical theories about the proper—or virtuous—use of words to express ideas. In short, words were to *serve* argument, to serve ideas, not to seduce the listener by calling attention to themselves and provoking admiration for stylistic ornaments and display of the forms or "body" of language. Praise of the Athenian, or Attic, style—defined as a plain, functionalist use of language to express persuasive ideas with as much *perspicuitas* or transparency as possible—was coupled with denigration of "Asiatic" style—defined as a highly ornate use of language for its own sake, appealing to the senses but irrational, intellectually opaque. Gombrich further points out how the classical aesthetic, in censuring ornament, aligned itself with reason, with the abstract and intellectual, as opposed to the corporeal: "[H]ostility to decoration could easily be defended on rational grounds. Decoration was not only a wasteful indulgence, it was an offence against reason. Moreover, and this proved a powerful argument, it was an unnecessary offence, because rationality by itself was productive of beauty. We tend to connect what is called functionalist aesthetics with the radical reform movement of the 20th century, but the case for the beauty of the efficient machine had also been made in antiquity and can be found in Cicero's writings on oratory."[1]

To Saint Jerome's Attic taste, the ideal inscription of Holy Scriptures would draw so little attention to itself as to be nearly transparent, like Quintilian's ideal rhetoric. All the glory should derive from the meaning of the inscribed words, none from their physical appearance. Jerome's famous late fourth-century criticism of religious texts written in silver on purple-dyed pages or with decorated and enlarged letters is one of the rare surviving instances of discussion of the actual image of early Christian writing. He advises in a letter to Laeta, for example, that correctness and accurate punctuation are to be preferred to "gilding and Babylonian parchment with elaborate decorations."[2] A few of these religious manuscripts on purple-dyed parchment in uncial scripts written in silver or gold have survived from the fifth and sixth centuries to give us an idea of what Jerome was censuring.[3] None of these manuscripts, or its parchment, is of "Babylonian" provenance. Jerome's description is not an identification to be taken literally, but a deliberate slur meant to stigmatize what he considered to be the decadence of these manuscripts. For Jerome, "Babylonian" was the pejorative equivalent of "Asiatic." To the extent that shiny golden letters on a purple ground elicit admiration of their material beauty and splendor, such deluxe manuscripts do call attention to the image of writing to the detriment—so Jerome would say—of the meaning of the inscription, its spiritual "content."

We can only imagine, had he lived a few centuries longer to see a page from the Book of Kells, Jerome's scandalized reaction to the contamination of writing, not just by colors more various than purple and gold but by the deliberate transformation of the shapes of the letters of the Gospel texts—almost beyond recognition—into the tangled bodies of animals and humans. According to the classical aesthetics (and ethics) of writing, alphabetic inscription was purely functional: letters were mere instruments for representing the sounds of words, which in turn represented thought. In order to function well as visual signs of aural signs, classical letters were made to be as rapidly and mechanically translatable into sounds as possible. The continuous classical script, with its absolutely regularly formed characters lined up like bricks in a wall, is the epitome of the utilitarian use of signs, which call no attention to themselves per se, so unremarkable as to seem nearly transparent. (A modern printed page is just as utilitarian, and it enables us to "read through" even faster because the basic component for translation is longer—not the letter, but the word set off by blank space.)

Ideally, every letter shape in a continuous classical script was always the same, each *a* like every other one. Roman schoolboys learned to form their letters (and discipline their own characters) by drawing their styli down the grooves of incised letters.[4] Any distinctive or eccentric design of the letter was considered excessive and distracting and was to be eliminated, for it had nothing to do with representing the sound (and thereby the sense) and even detracted attention from this, the proper goal of alphabetic writing.

Augustine's view of inscription is just as utilitarian as Jerome's; the purpose of the material signs of letters is to point beyond themselves, to the immaterial signs of spoken words, which, in turn, evoke immaterial ideas: "But because vibrations in the air soon pass away and remain no longer than they sound, signs of words have been constructed by means of letters. Thus words are shown to the eyes, not in themselves but through certain signs which stand for them."[5] Writing, as Augustine reminded Christians, was comprised of the signs of signs. Anything that complicated or impaired the function of the letter as sign of the sound of a spoken word—such as the deformation of the letter's shape through the incorporation of pictorial designs—would have seemed as inappropriate to Augustine as to Jerome.[6]

From the evidence of surviving manuscripts, it is apparent that Jerome did not entirely succeed in suppressing patrons' and their scribes' efforts to embellish and call attention to writing as image. From the mid-sixth through the seventh centuries, Christian scribes inventively incorporated pictorial designs into the shapes of letters of the alphabet, and no censor spoke out against their transformation of sacred writing into figurative image. Perhaps this was because a much more flagrant sort of image worship was then on the rise among Christians. Ernst Kitzinger has argued that, at this time, there was a "vastly increased desire to make the presence of the Deity and of the saints and the succour which they could be expected to give visually palpable."[7] Even in the early fifth century there were indications of Christian image worship, which Augustine located around tombs. A number of wall paintings from the Roman catacombs have survived, as have tomb inscriptions,[8] some of which offer, as I will suggest later, the first evidence of the combination of Christian hieroglyphic (pictorial) and alphabetic writing.

Although the rise of image worship—the imaginative projection of life and power upon an image—gradually and profoundly influenced the way in which the text of Scripture was presented, Christian theologians turned a blind eye to these changes in order to hold up the reading of Scripture as the ideal way of knowing God, precisely because reading was supposed to be an abstract process that deemphasized and turned away from the physical. Indeed, it was not until the later Middle Ages that theologians began to apologize for religious images by insisting that the Holy Scriptures are pictures or images too: "[H]e who would forbid images to the laity will next forbid Scripture to the clergy. For what is writing but a certain picture and an image of a word of the mind or voice?"[9] Even in such cases where the image of writing is foregrounded, there is no explicit reference to any combination of pictorial representation with writing, no acknowledgment of any figurative designs of the letter. In general, medieval theologians maintain silence on the pictorially designed letters of Scripture in those very texts where they compare writing and depiction, nearly always to the detriment of the latter.

In his highly influential epistle to Bishop Serenus of Marseilles in 599 chastising Serenus for destroying images worshiped in local churches, Pope Gregory I argued that pictures displayed in churches *ought* to serve as a kind of substitute for Scripture for those who were unable to read writing:

> Meanwhile I note that some time ago it reached us that your fraternity, seeing certain people adoring images, broke the images and threw them from the churches. And certainly we praise you for your zeal lest something manufactured be adored, but we judge that you should not have destroyed those images. For a picture is displayed in churches on this account, in order that those who do not know letters may at least read by seeing on the walls what they are unable to read in books. Therefore your fraternity should preserve those things and prohibit the people from adoring them, so that persons ignorant of letters may have something whereby they may gather knowledge of the story and the people may by no means sin through adoration of a picture.[10]

Although the solution Gregory proposed was different from that of Serenus, images were a problem for Gregory, just as they were for Serenus, and would be for iconoclasts over the next two centuries; all these early ecclesiastics recognized that people have an idolatrous tendency to imagine that images of God or Christ or saints are not mere signs or representations, but *are* God or Christ or saints.

Knowing whether Gregory actually believed it possible to "read" pictures (which are almost inevitably more ambiguous than writing)[11] is less important, for my purposes, than recognizing two things about his argument: first, in 599 Gregory seems to assume that writing is pure of images, and that the only way we can respond to writing is by deciphering the words it represents; second, he argues that the way to purify our response to pictures is by treating them as if they were more like writing, that is, by treating pictures as if they were signs of the words of a narrative, signs to be "read"—in short, what we might call illustrations (of texts written elsewhere, in Holy Scripture or saints' lives). As signs, what pictures represent are the words of an authoritative narrative.[12]

Nevertheless, as Gregory makes clear, those who can read Scripture should use this superior way of knowing God, which does not need any pictorial supplementation. Only the illiterate need have recourse to images, and then only as a substitute sort of "writing" for them to "read." One wonders whether Gregory could have been totally unaware, when he wrote to Serenus, that scribes were already working figures into the capital letters in religious manuscripts, and what he might have thought of this development.

Over a century after Gregory's apologetic attempt to sanitize images by insisting that our response to them be modeled on that of reading alphabetic writing, Bede cast a similar argument in favor of religious images in considerably more animistic terms in his commentary on the temple of Solomon (written about 730):

> [T]here are some who believe that God's law forbids us to sculpture or to paint, whether in a church or any other place, the figures of men or animals or the likeness of any other object, on the grounds that it is said in the Decalogue: "Thou shalt not make unto thyself a graven thing, nor the likeness of any of those things that are in heaven above, or on the earth below, or in the waters under the earth." . . . Now if it was permissible [for Moses] to lift up a brazen serpent on a piece of wood so that the Israelites who beheld it might live, why should it not be allowable to recall to the memory of the faithful, by a painting, that exaltation of our Lord Saviour on the cross through which he conquered death, and also his other miracles and healings through which he wonderfully triumphed over the same author of death, and especially since their sight is wont also to produce a feeling of great compunction in the beholder, and since they open up, as it were, a living reading of the Lord's story for those who cannot read [et eis quoque qui litteras ignorant quasi vivam . . . lectionem]? The Greek word for *pictura* is indeed . . . "living writing" [Nam et pictura Graece id est viva scriptura vocatur].[13]

Bede's insistence that images are, for those who cannot read, a *living* writing (and a *living* reading or interpretation) tends to project life upon images, which is precisely what the Tenth Commandment would prevent. Furthermore, Bede's animistic expression tends to undermine the conventional purpose of equating images with writing from Gregory on, which was to *disempower* images by insisting that they were mere representations, signs of signs. Although Bede alludes implicitly to Gregory when he argues for the use of images on those who are "ignorant of letters," the authority Bede explicitly cites here is more ancient: the etymological sense of the Greek word meaning "picture."

In writing this passage and using the term *living writing,* Bede was probably thinking of panel paintings depicting Old Testament events and their New Testament fulfillments (such as Moses holding up the brazen serpent juxtaposed to Christ on the cross), which hung on the walls of the monastic churches of Wearmouth and Jarrow (brought from Rome by Benedict Biscop).[14] Even so, when he associated images with writing, Bede could not have been unaware of Insular attempts to animate writing by combining images with the shapes of letters, especially in ceremonial Gospels that would be viewed by worshipers who were not fully literate. The fact that Bede and other exegetes likened pictures to writing, but never the reverse, is significant. There is a certain refusal in these theoretical texts—but not in scribal practice—to see writing as image, for to do so would be to contaminate alphabetic writing with materiality, to destroy its superior abstraction.[15]

We encounter the same reluctance to see Scripture as image in the *Libri carolini,* written by Theodulf of Orléans for presentation at the Council of Frankfurt of 794 in order to clarify the position of the Western church with respect to images. For Theodulf, Scripture, even though copied by human hands, belonged in the category of sacred objects, as opposed to unconsecrated artistic images. Celia Chazelle has summarized the difference between sacred objects and artistic images according to the *Libri carolini*: "[T]he Carolingians argued, the *res sacratae* differ radically from such art because their existence was ordained and blessed by God, a blessing that endowed them with invisible, spiritual qualities and powers. As opposed to the utter materiality of ordinary artistic productions, these objects are places in which it is possible to achieve, in a very immediate sense, contact with the holy."[16] Theodulf does not discuss contemporary copies of Scripture and their physical appearance, but he stresses the immaterial aspects of the writing of the Holy Scriptures, their predestination "before the ages by the highest, secret and prophetic judgment of God alone," and their revelation over time to inspired human authors, that is, saintly or venerable men—or Christ himself. That writing is material and visible is acknowledged by Theodulf, but he deemphasizes this as much as possible by insisting on alphabetic writing's abstract mode of functioning; he argues that, as opposed to artistic images that evoke material things through visual resemblance and thus can never get beyond materiality, writing enables "the reader, within his mind or soul, to [conceive] an idea of that which [is] totally immaterial and invisible."[17]

Furthermore, Theodulf points out that writing, not pictures, was the method these inspired human authors chose for recording knowledge of the divine, just as God chose to give Moses not a pictured law but one written in letters. For Theodulf pictures occupied the same position with respect to writing that for Socrates writing had occupied with respect to speech. Pictures could spur recollection of something one already knew, but they could not teach something new: "Images . . . transmit the memory of things past to the soul. . . . Wherefore, the use of images ought not and can not be equated with books of the holy law; for it is from books, not from images, we attain instruction of spiritual doctrine."[18] The implication of such statements is that Theodulf did not perceive, or turned a blind eye to, writing as image.

The makers of the early twelfth-century Saint Albans Psalter,[19] who were sensitive to the dangers of substituting pictures for writing, seem to have been oblivious to any danger in the combination of picture with letter and the (by then quite conventional) transformation of the shape of the letter into a figure in the historiated initials with which each new verse of this Psalter began. Their concern was to justify the relative novelty of a series of full-page illustrations of biblical history with which they prefaced the text of the Psalter proper, and they did this by diverting Gregory's famous apology for illustrative images on walls to those in books. Thus they placed the Latin quotation and French translation of Gregory's apology for religious wall paintings within the sequence of full-page, color illustrations of biblical history. (More precisely, Gregory's apology appears on the lower part of the final page of an illustrated vernacular saint's legend, *La chanson de Saint Alexis,* inserted into the series of full-page illustrations.)[20] The compilers of the Saint Albans Psalter quoted and translated Gregory for two reasons: to justify their massive prefatory recourse to images, in lieu of writing, by implying that this tactic was required by an imperfectly literate audience (because the manuscript was intended for presentation to a pious female recluse who had female followers); and to make sure that their own intentions in creating images would not be misunderstood or the images misused by their viewers.[21] By translating Gregory into the vernacular, they warned an audience not proficient in Latin that "it is one thing to worship a painting and another thing to learn from the story of the painting [*par le historie de la painture*] what should be adored; for that which Scripture teaches readers [*lizans*], painting teaches the illiterate [*ignoranz*], for the illiterate see in it what they should follow." The full-page illustrations in the Saint Albans Psalter manuscript are not presented for adoration but for "reading."

Had they been asked to justify the combination of pictorial figures with the shapes of the letters in the initials of the Psalter proper, it is likely that the makers of the Saint Albans Psalter would have used a similar argument: the images of the letter—even more obviously than those not imbricated in writing—were for "reading," for interpretation, not for adoration. Yet no one explicitly made this argument; no one seemed to see or consider it necessary to apologize for the way in which figures enlivened initial letters and, in so doing, "contaminated" writing's superior abstraction.

Even Saint Bernard seems to have turned a blind (or indulgent) eye to the figures of the letter. A surviving Bible with annotations in Bernard's hand, and reputedly "his," has colorful initials whose shapes are partly made up of the bodies of dragons and other monstrous creatures.[22] When sacred texts were regularly "ornamented" with equally fantastic and monstrous initials, we wonder why he unleashed such indignation against the monstrous fantasies of cloister carvings for diverting the monks' attention from their reading: "But apart from this, in the cloisters, before the eyes of the brothers while they read—what is that ridiculous monstrosity doing. . . . In short, everywhere so plentiful and astonishing a variety of contradictory forms is seen that one would rather read in the marble than in books, and spend the whole day gawking at every single one of them than in meditating on the law of God. Good God! If one is not ashamed of the absurdity, why is one not at least troubled at the expense?"[23] This famous tirade, ad-

dressed in 1125 to William of Saint-Thierry, helped to sustain an iconoclastic Christian theory of writing that is belied by the evidence of extant
manuscripts, which turn the very shapes of initial letters into pictures.

As we have seen, the dominant theory of Christian theologians contrasted alphabetic writing with depiction—and Scripture with pictures or
sculpture—in order to insist on the superiority of writing, owing to its relative immateriality and transparency (in the sense that alphabetic writing
does not call attention to itself but rather serves to lead us to the sounds
of words and thus to ideas beyond itself). The authority of this theory of
writing, reinforced by the iconoclasm of the Protestant Reformation, was
so strong that nineteenth-century art historians had difficulty imagining
that Christian scribes could have initiated the combination of pictorial
figures with letters in sacred texts; they preferred to argue, instead, that the
first Christian scribes who combined figures with letters were not the inventors but the imitators of lost oriental (i.e., "Asiatic") examples, even
though the earliest surviving oriental examples are dated centuries after
their Christian "imitations."[24]

However, if Christianity is a religion of the book and the written word,
it is also a religion of incarnation, a religion that animistically "enfleshes"
the Word by giving it the human body of Christ. As we shall see, early
Christian scribal exegetes suggested, by their combinations of figures with
letters and by their representations of Holy Writ, that Scripture itself, if
perceived spiritually, was also the body of Christ. They suggested that
Christ-the-Word was materially present in the form of Scripture before his
incarnation in human flesh and after his return to heaven. Robert Lafont
has put this suggestively:

> [T]he alphabet is posited not only as a universal, but as the foundation of a [Chris-
> tian] metaphysics that orients the sense of the universe from a Beginning to an End
> in a teleological perspective: "I am the Alpha and the Omega, the First and the Last,
> the Beginning and the End." Such are the words of the one who incarnates the
> Word, the *Logos,* in the Apocalypse of Saint John. An ontology positing Being as
> the divine principle governs the function of the Spirit, which inspires writing by in-
> carnating itself in a body, in matter, in the letter. Although defined as the Beginning
> in the form of the Alpha, the letter remains subordinate to an original speech, but
> especially to a Being existing prior to all creation, all matter, all letters.[25]

The lively and life-giving "verbum" that was "with God" and "was God" in the beginning, according to the opening words of John's Gospel (1–4), was conventionally understood to be Christ: "In principio erat Verbum et Verbum erat apud Deum et Deus erat Verbum; hoc erat in principio apud Deum; omnia per ipsum facta sunt et sine ipso factum est nihil quod factum est; in ipso vita erat et vita erat lux hominum." (In the beginning was the Word, and the Word was with God, and the Word was God. The same was in the beginning with God. All things were made by him; and without him was made nothing that was made. In him was life, and the life was the light of men.) Nor was this lively "verbum" understood exclusively as the spoken word, as we tend to assume.

As early as the sixth century, in a wall painting in the vault of the monastery of Saint Apollo at Bawit (now in the Coptic Museum in Cairo), Christ is depicted holding up an open codex with the edge of his mantle interposed between his fingers and the sacred pages (fig. 8). Enthroned and cross-nimbed in the upper register, encircled with a heavenly mandorla, Christ is flanked by two adoring angels, and the wheel-like shape of his mandorla floats on four eye-covered wings from which emerge the heads of the different animal symbols of evangelical inspiration (thus alluding to the visions of Ezekiel and John). This image tends to identify Christ-the-Word with an original *written* word, that is, with the words inscribed on the codex of Holy Scripture he displays. Immediately under this heavenly scene, in the lower or mundane register, is a depiction of Christ's incarnation in human form: as an infant enthroned on Mary-Ecclesia's lap, holding a scroll (representative of his oral teachings), and flanked by the apostles who spread these teachings (signified by their codices with ornate covers). Jean Wirth has remarked that the reduction of the size of the body of Christ, from mature adult in the upper register to child in the lower, indicates how much the spiritual power of the Word was diminished through the process of incarnation.[26] This hierarchical juxtaposition also seems to give priority to the written word: the Word that was "in the beginning" is not spoken but inscribed in a codex.

The two material forms of Christ-the-Word—as written codex and as speaking man—are depicted somewhat differently in the mid-ninth-century Moûtier-Grandval Bible in a full-page illumination preceding the

FIG. 8. Christ, with covered hand, holding open a codex. Vault painting from the monastery of Saint Apollo at Bawit. Coptic Museum, Cairo, Egypt.

Book of Revelation (fig. 9). In the upper register, a huge, closed codex stands upright on its side on a draped, altarlike throne before a closed curtain; this codex is flanked by a lion and a lamb and surrounded by the four animal symbols of evangelical inspiration reading open books. In the lower register, surrounded by evangelist symbols without books, a man sits on a throne and holds high above and slightly behind his head a long piece of cloth, which both divides the lower from the upper registers (earth from heaven) and suggests an unveiling or act of revelation of the man's head and face. Although the lower figure has been diversely understood, it seems most likely that we are meant to see depicted on this page two forms of Christ-the-Word: above, as Holy Scripture, the preexisting Word that inspired the four evangelists (and that they copied down on parchment—pages of flesh—to reveal to the world); and below, "in the flesh," as a human speaker. In both cases, the conventional configura-

FIG. 9. Christ-the-Word as codex
and as man. Moûtier-Grandval Bible.
London, British Library, MS Add.
10546, fol. 449r. Photo by permission
of the British Library.

tion of surrounding evangelist symbols identifies the central image—
codex or man—as Christ-the-Word.[27]

These depictions powerfully authorize the written text of Holy Scripture. Hardly the empty sign of a sign, Christ-the-Word *is* the Signifier. Although deluxe editions such as the Moûtier-Grandval Bible would have
been seen by few, this same mythology of the divine presence in Scripture
(always there but perceived only by those capable of spiritual vision) was
represented in much more widespread and public ways for ordinary people—for example, in innumerable sculpted and painted images on tympana, apses, or walls of churches showing a mandorla-encircled (visionary)
Christ-the-Word holding up a codex, revealing to the viewer his dual "incarnation" in human form and in Scripture. Christ's gesture of displaying
the codex means "This is me."[28]

An iconoclastic Christian theory of writing as superior in its abstraction
to depiction was countered by the need to empower and authorize writing
by mythologizing it as divine presence, attributing to it a body. The doc-

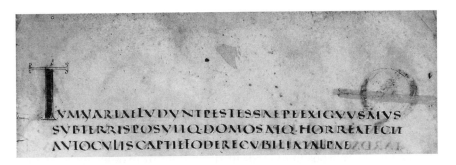

FIG. 10. Decorated letter *T.* (Decorated letter of the reverse side showing through the parchment at the end of the line.) Vergilius Augusteus Codex. Vatican, MS lat. 3256, fol. 2v. Photo courtesy of the Biblioteca Vaticana.

trine of the incarnation of the Word had, as we shall see, a profound effect on the ways in which Scripture, and writing associated with the divine, was presented visually. When, then, did Christian scribes first begin combining pictorial figures with letters, and to what purposes?

The late fourth-century Vergilius Augusteus manuscript, a fragment of Vergil's *Georgics,* is the earliest surviving example of designed letters: the first letter of each page is drawn larger, filled with simple geometrical designs, and colored with shades of red, green, and yellow (fig. 10).[29] These designed letters do not serve any utilitarian marking purpose with respect to the logical or syntactic structure of the text, for they appear at the beginning of each new page of the continuous classical script, regardless of whether the page begins in midsentence or midword.

That the first surviving designed letters appear in a text of Vergil does not mean, however, that designed letters were originally pagan or had anything to do with the classical tradition (except in an oppositional sense). On the contrary, as Nordenfalk has pointed out, book decoration, such as ornamental colophons, was kept separate from the letter in pagan antiquity, so that the enshrinement of the letter in decoration was not only anticlassical but typically medieval (and, he might have added, typically Christian): "Late-Antiquity considered the decoration to be an enrichment of the book itself, an idea which could be encouraged in so far as it did not encroach on the clarity of the text. The Middle Ages, on the other hand, regarded ornamentation as a medium for emphasizing the sacred text—clothing the word as it were in a precious garb in the same manner as a relic was encased in a casket of gold and precious stones."[30]

The likely owner and patron of the Vergilius Augusteus manuscript, with its decorated letters, was Pope Damasus, who was an admirer of Vergil's verse and an imitator who used Vergilian quotations to evoke Christian meanings, as did other contemporary Christian composers of *centones* ("patchwork" compositions made up of citations from other authors), such as the poetess Proba, who used quotations from Vergil to describe the events of the Old and New Testaments.[31] Two later Vergil manuscripts, the fifth-century Vergilius Vaticanus and the sixth-century Vergilius Romanus, illustrate the literal sense of the text in narrative images boldly framed off from the writing.[32] If such a tradition of narrative illustration was available to the scribes of the Vergilius Augusteus manuscript a century earlier,[33] they abjured it in favor of one enlarged and "ornamented" initial at the beginning of every page. The forms of these initials, especially the hooks or curls emanating from their ends, have been compared to those Filocalus carved in the Roman catacombs for the poems Pope Damasus had had composed in honor of the martyrs buried there.[34] The so-called *capitalis quadrata* ("square capital") script used for the blocks of text in the Vergilius Augusteus manuscript are also copied from epigraphy in a deliberate (and at this date relatively rare) attempt to monumentalize the text written in a codex. The result is that, compared with the way literary works by classical authors were usually inscribed, each page of the Vergilius Augusteus manuscript looks, in Nordenfalk's words, "as much 'designed' as 'written.' "[35]

Nordenfalk speculated that the dearth of surviving examples of decorated letters after the Vergilius Augusteus manuscript until the sixth century, from which time they appear in ever more elaborate forms, was probably due to Christian scribes' and book patrons' respect for Jerome's authority and their fear of being stigmatized as followers of pagan ("Babylonian") precedent. Because of the lack of surviving examples, Nordenfalk argued it was not until the sixth century that "book craftsmen appeared who saw in the ornamental letters so little of heathen outrage that they actually considered them a most worthy attire for the Holy Word."[36] Yet contemporaries—such as Pope Damasus, who apparently paid for the designed letters of the Vergilius Augusteus manuscript—may have perceived nothing "Babylonian," nothing heathen, in designed letters and have recognized Jerome's slur as a conventional Atticist one having little basis in reality. It would have been easier for Jerome's contemporaries and immediate successors to see what designed letters truly were than for us readers of print: they were anticlassical and, in that sense, antiheathen.

There is no evidence that the enlarged, designed initials of the Vergilius Augusteus manuscript owe anything besides their basic outlines—again, except in a deliberately oppositional sense—to pagan Greek or Roman traditions of inscription, which prized absolute regularity and clarity of letterforms so that these would not call attention to themselves to the detriment of their "content" (the spoken word and the thing or idea for which it stood); as we have seen, classical writing was supposed to be strictly utilitarian, meant for pronouncing rather than admiring. For precedents involving the enlargement and filling of letters, we might look, instead, to the earlier fourth-century Christian poems of Porfyrius.

By transgressing against the regularity of a continuous classical script, by giving the figure precedence over the letter of alphabetic writing, Porfyrius celebrated Constantine the Great's victory as the victory of Christianity over paganism—symbolized by the regular "background" of the continuous classical script, out of and against which he made his Christian figures seem to surge forward. In surviving ninth-century manuscripts of these poems (which imitate visually a much earlier exemplar, presumably based on the visual effects of the copy Porfyrius sent to the emperor Constantine), a double red outline creates larger letters or figural patterns, such as the chi-rho monogram, the palm branch, and the ship with a chi-rho for mast. At the same time, these red outlines also create a ground different from that of the square page upon which to perceive and reread the letters of the text. The act of drawing red outlines on either side of certain letters effectively "reinscribes" them, and this is stressed by the writing of these letters in gold or silver (for Constantine's copy) or in red ("*minio scripte,*" in the terms of the Latin prose explanation accompanying the verse).[37] Thus the smaller red (or shining gold or silver) letters within the red outlines of the larger letters or pictorial figures form new verses, new texts within the main

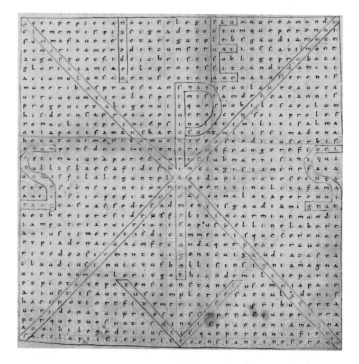

FIG. 11. Figural poem by Porfyrius. Paris, B.N.F., MS lat. 2421, fol. 49r. Photo Bibliothèque nationale de France.

textual block, ones that we read diagonally or in other unconventional directions, following the shape of the figure.

Let us take for example the literal patterns of Porfyrius's poem number 8 (according to the numbering of Polara's edition). The thirty-five Latin verses of this poem are inscribed in a continuous script to form a solid block. In manuscripts such as the ninth-century Paris, B.N.F., MS lat. 2421, this square is outlined in red to create the "page" ("*pagina*"), as is explained in the upper margin (fig. 11). Within this red-outlined textual block, the letters of Jesus' name are drawn in red, with each letter seven lines high and enclosing within its "body" certain letters, written in red, of the continuous script. The effect of such enlargement and bright coloration is to make letters treated this way appear to come forward at the reader, to turn the continuous classical script into a "ground" for the figures of larger, brighter letters.

On an even grander scale, the letters of the chi-rho monogram (standing for the first two Greek letters of Christ's name) are inscribed within red outlines across the entire length and width of the page, the rho being twenty-one lines tall and the chi thirty-five lines tall, each containing rubricated letters. By reading the red letters contained in the huge rho from top left to bottom right, and then from bottom left to top right (along diagonal reading trajectories), we discover the verses "Alme, salutari nunc haec tibi pagina signo. Scripta micat, resonans nominibus domini." Proceeding then to read, along various trajectories, the messages contained in the letters next largest in scale, those of the name "IESVS," we add two further verses, "Nate deo, solus salvator, sancte, bonorum. Tu deus es iusti, gratia tu fidei." Finally, returning to the center, we read down the leg of the rho and around its loop for the verse "Sit Victoria comes Aug. et natis eius." Thus the same letters that form the words of the verses of the continuous script also, when read in different directions, indicated by the figures of the large letters containing them, form the words of different verses written within the large letters. For example, the letter *a* at the very center of the crossing of the large chi-rho participates in four different words, "h*a*ec" and "reson*a*ns" in the two legs of the chi, "victori*a*" in the leg of the rho, and "pl*a*cida" in the underlying continuous script.

The most powerful way Porfyrius broke the rules of classical inscription to make alphabetic writing convey multiple meanings was by using letters as pictorial figures. Here the sheer size of the red-outlined letters of the chi-rho monogram works to turn these letters into an abstract image of Christ on the cross (the rho suspended in the center of the chi). (The illuminators of the Book of Kells would later make this symbolism even clearer on their own chi-rho page by terminating the loop of the rho with the head of Christ [color plate 1].) Porfyrius reinforced the figural import of the chi-rho monogram by surrounding it with the name of Jesus in enlarged letters. The fundamental meaning of Porfyrius's poem is revealed in the pictorial figure of the crucifixion; it is revealed to anyone who is willing to see the design in the text, the picture present in the letters.[38]

Before or approximately contemporary with the designed initials of the Vergilius Augusteus manuscript, the only letters that seem to call attention clearly to their own forms as pictures or images are Porfyrius's chi-rho

<small>FIG. 12. Roman funerary inscription from the catacomb of Callistus with the letter *I* juxtaposed to a cluster of grapes and a dove. Reproduced from G. B. de Rossi, *La Roma sotterranea,* vol. 1, table 26, no. 1.</small>

monogram as crucifixion, the enlargement of the letter *T* to suggest the crucifix in the Filocalus script and in some apparently earlier catacomb epigraphy,[39] and certain other letters of late third- and fourth-century funerary inscriptions in the Christian catacombs in Rome. "Writing" in the catacombs was meant to be seen and contemplated, not just pronounced. Furthermore, in these funerary inscriptions alphabetic writing was often juxtaposed to conventional Christian "hieroglyphic" or ideographic symbols—the dove (representing the soul flying away with a victory wreath), the fish (representing Christ, the Eucharist, the baptized Christian), the anchor of faith (alone or combined into a monogram with the crucifix and/or the fish), the palm branch of victory, and others.[40] Already in the second century, the Greek father Clement of Alexandria, in his *Paedagogum,* had listed the dove, fish, ship, lyre, and anchor as symbols appropriate for Christians to have engraved on their rings.[41]

The close juxtaposition of alphabetic writing with the pictorial writing of Christian hieroglyphs sometimes has the effect of changing the way the letter is perceived. For example, in the inscription of the name "PRIMI-TIVA" on the lower level of the fourth-century Roman catacomb of Callistus, a bunch of grapes, pecked at by a dove, appears to grow out of the bottom of a letter *I,* thus turning the *I* (in our perception) into a vine stock (fig. 12).[42] Such an effect seems intentional, for it revises the pagan imagery of

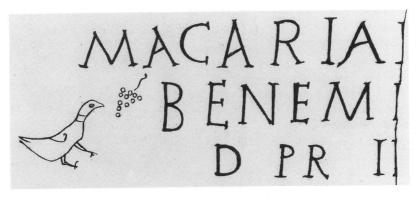

FIG. 13. Roman funerary inscription from the catacomb of Callistus with the letter *A* juxtaposed to a grape cluster and a dove. Reproduced from G. B. de Rossi, *La Roma sotterranea,* vol. 2, table 57, no. 32.

paradise, which was often symbolized by birds pecking at grapes. *I* is the first letter of Jesus' name, and his likening of himself to a vine in John 15:1, "I am the true vine," was a text much favored by the early fathers of the Christian church. The sense of the letters of Primitiva's name is enriched by pictures and thus shown to contain the first letter of the name of Jesus; the dove that nourishes itself on the grapes that hang from this letter may represent the spirit of the deceased. Primitiva's funerary inscription suggests that she has incorporated Jesus (and can therefore expect salvation in paradise). In two other epitaphs from the same cemetery, a similar idea is conveyed using the same pictures close to different letters: a dove pecks at grapes right under an *x* symbolic of the cross or of Christ,[43] and again under an *a* (fig. 13), which may recollect the alpha and Christ's saying, as repeated in Apocalypse 22:13, "I am the Alpha and Omega."[44]

On a child's grave bearing no other inscription in the catacomb of Callistus, a dove points an instrument that may be a paintbrush or a candle toward a chi-rho monogram (fig. 14).[45] No matter how we identify the instrument, a connection is being made here between the letters of the monogram and the picture of the dove. Is this the soul of the dead pointing to (lighting or inscribing) its faith in Christ? Or is this a dove of the Holy Spirit pointing to the true, Christological, sense of these letters? At the bottom of another epitaph, this time in the cemetery of Momitilla (fig. 15), fish

FIG. 14. Roman funerary inscription from the catacomb of Callistus with a dove pointing to a chi-rho monogram. Reproduced from G. Wilpert, *Römische Quartalschrift für christliche Altertumskunde* 6 (1892): 375.

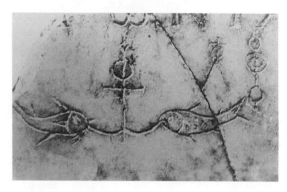

FIG. 15. Roman funerary inscription from the catacomb of Momitilla of two fishes hooked on an anchor-ansata cross. Reproduced from G. Wilpert, *Nuovo bulletino di archeologia cristiana* 8 (1902): table 6, no. 3.

are hooked on an anchor that has been given a crossbar and large ring that evoke the form of the ansata cross (⚷, a stylized and probably later combination, like the staurogram ⚷, of the letters chi and rho).[46] Anchors (symbolizing faith or hope) were often turned into crosses by the addition of a crossbar, which, along with an anchor ring, could evoke a staurogram or ansata cross and thus make the hieroglyphic statement "Hope in Christ." The two fish attached to the prongs of this anchor-monogram may make us see it as a fishhook as well, which would not be inconsistent with the image, elaborated by Paulinus of Nola, Ambrose, and Augustine, of the faithful Christian as a fish hooked and pulled up from the deep by the word of God (preached by the disciples, whom Christ would make "fishers of men").[47] This hieroglyphic monogram (fish coming to the bait of or caught on the hook of the ansata cross) would express the faith of the defunct baptized Christian in salvation through Christ's crucifixion.

By no means every juxtaposition of a Christian hieroglyph with alpha-

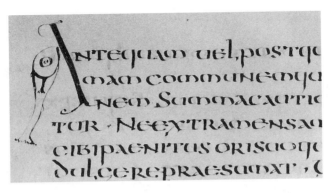

FIG. 16. Loop of an initial uncial *a* as a fish. Paris, B.N.F., MS lat. 12634, fol. 69r. Photo Bibliothèque nationale de France.

betic writing in the epitaphs of the Roman catacombs changes our perception of the letter by overlaying it with a figurative meaning. This happens often enough, however, to suggest that there was an attempt in the fourth century, at least in the inscriptions of the catacombs, to distinguish Christian writing from pagan, classical writing precisely by treating the letter as a pictorial design to enrich literal with figurative meaning (enlarging a *T* to evoke a cross, for example, or juxtaposing a bunch of grapes with an *I* to evoke a vine stock). However, with the exception of geometrical designs in enlarged initials (as in the Vergilius Augusteus codex), figural treatment of the letter does not show up in surviving manuscripts, of which there are very few, until the sixth century.

Perhaps the most striking and long-lived of these figured letters in manuscripts (one that is prepared for by the hieroglyphic configurations of epigraphy but does not appear in epitaphs) is the uncial *a* with its loop depicted as a fish, a hieroglyphic letter that would seem to mean "Christ is the alpha," or, more generally, "Christ inhabits the letter" or "This is Christian writing" (fig. 16). In the fourth century much was made of the discovery (given credence by such writers as Eusebius and, later, Augustine) that certain sibylline verses were an acrostic prophecy of Christ: the first letters of successive lines of these pagan verses made up the Greek words for "Jesus Christ, Son of God, Savior," and the initials of this epithet, in turn, made up the Greek word for "fish," ΙΧΘΥΣ, which earlier Christian exegetes such as Tertullian and Origen had explained as a figure of Christ.[48]

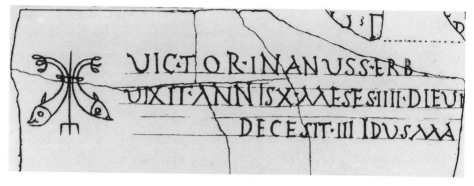

FIG. 17. Roman funerary inscription from the catacomb of Callistus of two fishes attached to a trident-cross. Reproduced from G. B. de Rossi, *La Roma sotterranea,* vol. 2, table 57, no. 25.

Not only was the Greek word for fish engraved in epitaphs as an abbreviation for Christ, but the picture of a fish (virtually any sort of fish) was also used as a hieroglyphic representation of Christ. Thus one or more fish were often shown flanking, superimposed upon, or hanging from the crossbar of a cruciform anchor (or even a trident as cross) to signify Christ on the cross or the baptized Christian's hope of salvation through the crucifixion, as in the epitaph of Victorianus in the catacomb of Callistus (fig. 17).

The idea of elaborating the loop of an uncial *a* into a fish seems to have been provoked by the similarity of two hieroglyphic configurations originating in epigraphy, a cruciform anchor flanked by fish and a cross or chi-rho monogram flanked by alpha and omega. Whereas a depiction of Christ with the letters alpha and omega on either side appears in fourth-century catacomb paintings in recollection of Apocalypse 22:13, the "portrait" is replaced in many epitaphs by a more easily engraved cross or a chi-rho monogram,[49] which produces the same hieroglyphic statement—"Christ is the alpha and the omega"—and with the same implications: not only that Christ is the beginning and the end (as symbolized by the first and last letters of the alphabet) but that he *is* the alphabet, that he is incarnated in the written word.[50] Likewise, a staurogram flanked by alpha and omega, which prefaces a late fifth- or early sixth-century miniature Gospel of John (enclosed in a reliquary in the eleventh century along with a relic of the Virgin's shirt), seems to admonish the reader that this alphabetically inscribed text *is* an incarnation of Christ (fig. 18).[51]

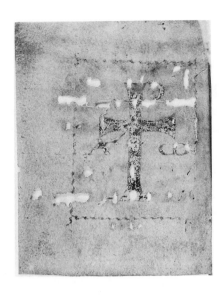

FIG. 18. Staurogram flanked by alpha and omega. Gospel of Saint John. Actual size. Paris, B.N.F., MS lat. 10439, fol. 1v. Photo Bibliothèque nationale de France.

To ensure that the reader perceives Christ in the letter, and thus to combat pagan with Christian writing, the scribe of a mid-sixth-century manuscript from Ravenna of Orosius's *Historia adversum paganos* combines the fish hieroglyph with the form of the uncial *a* in a series of variations that transform and make each letter "new"; the loop is designed as a fish and the upright decorated as a column slightly differently for each uncial *a* (fig. 19).[52] In the Gospels inscribed by Valerianus a few decades later, at the beginning of the seventh century, Valerianus experiments at combining Christian hieroglyphs with the letter in ever different, renovating ways: an uncial *a* is formed by a staurogram tilted to the left, with a fish forming the loop of the letter and a dove (of the Holy Spirit) perched atop (fig. 20); elsewhere, omegas hang from the broken crossbars of more angular alphas, while a dove with a cross perches on the letter, or a leaf sprouts from it (Christ as vine) (fig. 21). Such creative transformation of pagan letters, formed at least partially out of Christian hieroglyphs to signal the Christianity of the text, continued without interruption in manuscripts into the Merovingian period and beyond. The double-page spread opening the mid-eighth-century Gelasian Sacramentary, for example, presents, on the left, an arch framing a large cross from which hang the letters alpha and omega formed by fish and, on the right, in the last line of

FIG. 19. Loop of an initial uncial *a* as a fish. Orosius, *Historia adversum paganos*. Florence, Biblioteca Medicea Laurenziana, MS Plut. 65.1, fol. 120v. Photo courtesy of the Biblioteca Medicea Laurenziana.

the *incipit* page, an entire word, "NOVERIT," formed by the bodies of eleven fish and two doves (fig. 22).

Anyone who recognized Christian hieroglyphs might look at such figural letters or at the large monograms outlined in red and filled with colored letters in one of Porfyrius's poems and perceive, before reading the Latin letters, that this was "Christian writing." The enlarged initials beginning pages of the fourth-century Vergilius Augusteus manuscript declare their Christianity differently: through their curling edges (a beginning of liveliness) and their multiple colors and interior geometrical designs (which suggest a richer than ordinary sense). All such pictorial elements, which Nordenfalk labels "filling" or "substitution ornament" and other scholars have called "purely" ornamental (meaning completely irrelevant to the verbal content expressed), were highly transgressive of the conventions of classical inscription and thus served to distinguish Christian writing from pagan, or to Christianize pagan writings by enriching the letter and suggesting figurative interpretations that might transform pagan writings—for example, literature by Vergil, science or history—into prophetic or divine texts ("written" by God).

To signal that the book of nature is ultimately God's writing, and not its pagan author's (in short, to Christianize a pagan text through enriching interpretation), may be the intention behind the earliest dated initials involving fish and vines, in the index (and solely there) prefacing the Dioscurides of the Princess Juliana Anicia, written in Constantinople in 512 and

FIG. 20. Initial uncial *a* as a tilted staurogram with a fish as loop and a dove perched on top. Valerianus Codex. Munich, Bayerische Staatsbibliothek, MS lat. 6224, fol. 33r. Photo Bayerische Staatsbibliothek.

FIG. 21. Initial *A* with an omega dangling from its crossbar and sprouting a heart-shaped leaf. Valerianus Codex. Munich, Bayerische Staatsbibliothek, MS lat. 6224, fol. 29v. Photo Bayerische Staatsbibliothek.

given to the princess in thanks by the burghers of a town where she had endowed a church. The index to this medicinal herbarium contains, for example, an initial rho (P) with a tendril-like curl sprouting above and dots forming a bunch of grapes below (fol. 9v), as well as a squid and a dolphinlike creature apparently hooked to two different letters that extend below the line.[53] Instead of illustrating the literal sense of the words in a textual space separate from the inscription (as was conventionally done in classical scientific treatises, such as the text of Dioscurides's herbarium), Christian writers first juxtaposed pictorial elements to letters of the alphabet and then integrated them into letters. They did this initially with recognized Christian symbols or hieroglyphs (doves, fish, crosses, vines, palm

FIG. 22. Fishes forming the letters alpha and omega dangling from the cross (*left*); fishes and birds forming the word NOVERIT (*bottom right*). Frontispiece pages of the Gelasian Sacramentary. Vatican, MS reg. lat. 316, fols. 131v and 132r. Photo courtesy of the Biblioteca Vaticana.

branches) to suggest the greater power of signification of Christian writing—indeed, in some cases, to create the impression of a living writing in which divine presence still inhered and revealed itself.

We "classicize" medieval writing in our own minds (and try to render it as transparent as print) when we dismiss the figural aspects of the early medieval Christian letter as "pure decoration." When we take the view that such aspects are "only the outer shape of a letter of the alphabet," and that they do not "stand directly for the thing," as in hieroglyphic writing,[54] we try to censor all but the literal sense of the text; we censor the figures that may be intended to reveal the true import of or to authorize and empower the Christian letter. As we have seen earlier in this chapter, early Christian scribes deliberately transgressed the formal conventions of classical inscription to signal the difference—the transcendence—of Christian over pagan writing (just as Christian interpreters refused to be limited by the rules of Donatus, by "correct" Latin grammar, but sometimes preferred a transgressive "barbarism" to make a doctrinal point).[55] Those who were willing to break the rules of classical reading and, instead of reading straight through the letters, to contemplate also their figurative designs might find a supraliteral import revealed there. What is more, this supraliteral sense was available, through figures of the letter such as well-known Christian hieroglyphs, even to those who could read Latin very little or not at all. Illiterates may even have had a cognitive advantage over accomplished readers in "reading spiritually," for they might perceive the figures of the letter without the distraction of attempting to decipher the words and their literal sense.

# 3

# ANIMISTIC EXEGESES

*Christ's Incarnation in Holy Scripture*

*and the Figures of the Letter*

Although early Christian theologians in theory preferred the superior abstraction of writing to the dangerous materiality of images, the language in which some of these men described or explained Holy Scripture was full of figures of speech that served to animate writing through mental images. It was these same figures of speech that early medieval scribes, some of whom were themselves educated biblical interpreters, realized or "literalized" by depicting them as letters.

One of the most influential animators of Scripture was the apostle Paul. Like Socrates, Paul implicitly denigrated alphabetic writing (and Scripture, that is, the Old Testament) when he preferred "living writing," texts inscribed in the memories of living people; more precisely, Paul exalted the Christian story "written not with ink, but with the Spirit of the living God; not in tables of stone, but in the fleshly tables of the heart" (2 Corinthians 3:3). In his epistles, Paul used the letter, the inscribed mark, as a metaphor for the literal sense conveyed by the inscription (the "letter"), and this metaphoric equation enabled him to transfer Greek disparagement of writing to the literal sense it conveyed, thus devaluing the literal sense of the Hebrew Scriptures. Yet Paul was unwilling to deny the Old Testament any authority whatsoever. On the contrary, he argued that the texts of the law and the prophets were in fact a living writing in which was revealed—but only to Christians, whose hearts had already been inscribed by the Holy Spirit—"the glory of God, in the face of Christ Jesus" (2 Corinthians 4:6).

Such a formulation holds up the vision of a human face (God's) as the ultimate aim of reading, and not just the deciphering of alphabetically inscribed words. Only Christians might surpass the letter of the Old Testament to perceive Christ; for all others, the letter (the literal sense and also their concentration on deciphering alphabetical characters) acted as a veil that prevented recognition of the divine presence, and thus "condemned to death" the literalist reader: "For the letter killeth, but the spirit quickeneth" (2 Corinthians 3:6). Paul's figurative language addressed to the Greek churches mythologized and empowered Scripture as a living—divine—presence, while at the same time condemning anyone (especially the Jews, at this point) who valued chiefly the literal sense of Scripture: "And if our gospel be also hid, it is hid to them that are lost" (2 Corinthians 4:3).

Although Paul did not himself dwell on the presence of Christ in the Old Testament—on the way the signifying subject was present in the signifier, God in writing—later exegetes elaborated on this idea. Origen, in his Greek homilies on the Book of Leviticus, compared Christ's flesh to the letter of Scripture in that both veiled divinity (because only a few people were capable of recognizing God in Christ or Christ in the letter of the Old Testament): "[F]or the Word came into the world by Mary, clad in flesh; the seeing was not understanding; all saw the flesh; knowledge of the divinity was given to a chosen few. So when the Word was shown to men through the lawgiver and the prophets, it was not shown them without suitable vesture. There it is covered by the veil of flesh, here of the letter. The letter appears as flesh; but the spiritual sense within is known as divinity. This is what we find in studying Leviticus. . . . Blessed are the eyes which see divine spirit through the letter's veil."[1] The fifth-century monk Eucherius, later bishop of Lyon, wrote that "the body of Holy Scripture is in its letters."[2] Even Gregory the Great, who in his letters to Serenus tried to purify response to religious images by treating them as a kind of writing for the illiterate, elsewhere animated Scripture through his figurative comparisons; for example, in explaining 2 Corinthians 3:6 ("the letter killeth, but the spirit quickeneth") Gregory equated the letter of Scripture with the body, and the spirit with the soul enlivening the body.[3]

Maximus the Confessor, a Greek exegete, considered that the divine word or Logos became flesh both in "approaching men ... borrowing a language of objects familiar [to men], wrapping Himself in the medley of stories, enigmas, parables, and obscure words" and in the materialization of human language in the form of writing: "The Logos, in effect, by each word set down in writing, became flesh."[4] In his exegesis of the Gospel of John, influenced by his translations of Maximus the Confessor, the ninth-century Irishman known as John the Scot focused on the carnality of alphabetic inscription (rather than of the spoken word) by explaining that there had been, in effect, more than one incarnation of the divine: in the human form of Christ through a virginal birth and, long before that, in his "incarnation-like condensation into the visible forms of letters" (of the Old Testament texts of the law and the prophets).[5]

The equation of the body of Christ with the letter of Scripture became a venerable formula and was incorporated, citing Origen, into the *Glossa ordinaria*.[6] Jerome's version of this idea, in his explanation of Psalm 145, is that Christ, when he urged his disciples to eat his flesh and drink his blood, meant that they should ingest the discourse of Scripture, the divine doctrine: "vere corpus Christi et sanguis eius sermo scripturarum est, doctrina divina est."[7] For Jerome, then, Christ was incarnate in the "doctrine" of Scripture, not in the letters per se; however, to get at the "veins and the marrow" of that hidden doctrine, he testified that he spent his days and nights thinking about the single syllables and letters of Scripture.[8] Augustine, like Maximus, and even Origen himself at times, considered that the expression of divine knowledge through the inadequacies of human language constituted a kind of incarnation, so that the "body" of Scripture was human language. In his explanation of Psalm 103, for example, Augustine took this view: "[W]e should not be astonished if, because of our feebleness He stoops to the particles of our speech, considering that He also lowered himself even to the point of taking on the infirmities of our body."[9] Whereas modern readers may prefer these more sophisticated, abstract definitions of Christ's "incarnation" into the language or doctrine of Scripture, early medieval writers seem to have preferred to think, in more material and visual terms, of alphabetic inscription itself as an "embodiment" of the divine.[10] Indeed, the trope or figure of the letter as body founds a Christian art of illumination.

The design of early medieval initial letters is based on a fundamental equation between the recognizable (because conventional or regular)[11] shapes of the letters of the alphabet and the literal sense of the words of the text: the letter = the "letter." According to this logic, a text that should be understood solely on a literal level ought to be inscribed conventionally, and pagan texts inscribed in perfectly regular continuous scripts manifested thereby their lack of any figurative or spiritual sense. By the same logic, the richness of spiritual sense and the authority embodied in sacred religious texts could be demonstrated by their deviation from regularity to combine pictorial designs (at first well-known Christian hieroglyphs like the fish and the dove) with the shapes of letters of the alphabet. Such combinations added the specifically Christian sense of the hieroglyph to the literal sense, as well as, in many cases, transforming the letter itself into a figure. By transforming the ordinary shapes of the letters, Christian scribal exegetes indicated that there was more to the text than its "letter"; by creating ever new design variants and figures of the letter for successive initials, they showed the sacred text to be an inexhaustible source of figurative or spiritual (that is, nonliteral) meanings—and they could make this point not only to the literate but to whoever had occasion to look searchingly at the text, whether capable of deciphering written Latin or not.

The design of the early medieval letter—everything in excess with respect to a conventional letterform—was a kind of "signature" manifesting its divinity, and some of the most proficient scribal designers of such divine letters were thought to be inspired instruments whereby the mystical word of God was revealed. For example, in the passage quoted at the end of chapter 1, Gerald of Wales reported the story that the scribe of the Gospel Book of Kildare (whose illuminations Gerald found full of "intricacies so delicate and subtle, so exact and compact, so full of knots and links, with colours so fresh and vivid, that you might say that all this was the work of an angel, and not of a man") was in fact merely the human hand that executed divine designs revealed to him by an angel. The scribe of the Gospels of Kildare and his inspiring angel were not concerned with the correctness and accurate punctuation of the literal text of the Gospels (as Jerome might have preferred), but rather with the design of the writing, that is, with perfectly accurate reproduction of the seemingly infinite richness of patterns transfiguring the letters and thereby demonstrating a divine presence.

Four centuries before Gerald, Aethelwulf had recounted a similar story about the divine inspiration of the early eighth-century Irish scribe Ultan, who "made the shape of the letters beautiful one by one" when "the creator's spirit had taken control of his fingers, and had fired his dedicated mind (to journey) to the stars." Because it had been the instrument with which "the Lord's mystic words" (that is, the words of the New or Old Testament written with elaborately designed letters) had been written, Ultan's hand was thought to work miracles even after his death.[12]

By the way they transformed the ordinary shapes of letters, the most highly skilled and inventive medieval scribal exegetes could authorize their inscription as a work of divine inspiration, a miraculous writing given to them by the Spirit (God in one of his aspects). This was to empower the medieval copy of a sacred text more directly than by the claim that the words the scribe copied had originally been divinely inspired (at the time when the Holy Spirit directed the "incarnation" of the Logos into human language, that is, into the words written by the evangelists, Moses, or the Old Testament prophets). Indeed, as we shall see in chapter 5, "portraits" of the evangelists prefacing their Gospel texts in medieval manuscripts show the human writer as a copyist who receives the revelation of a text already inscribed in writing in the form of a codex or scroll held up in the heavens by a figure (man, lion, calf, eagle) representing the Holy Spirit in the act of inspiring the evangelist. Christ was considered to be incarnate not only in the written text of the Old Testament but also in that of the Gospels.

The evangelists, like Ultan or the scribe of the Gospel Book of Kildare, were imagined as perfect copyists of mystical words "written" by God. The design of such writing was what set it apart as God's writing—indeed, as a material embodiment of God—and was more important in authorizing the text than were more "petty" matters such as spelling, word forms, punctuation, and the like (matters of literal accuracy that would determine the authority of the text for a modern editor). Through the elaborate designs of their copies of the Old Testament or the New, through pictorial figures intended to suggest the "spirit" of the letter, medieval scribes presented their texts as reincarnations of divine presence (of God as Christ or the Spirit)—and themselves as inspired instruments of divine revelation in the tradition of the evangelists, Moses, and the Old Testament prophets. That the copying of wonderfully designed divine words conferred power and authority on the scribe is clearly suggested, especially in the Insular world, by the number of surviving manuscripts with elaborately designed letters that have been attributed, by colophons or other inscriptions or by monastic tradition, to scribes who were or became abbots, bishops, and saints.[13]

The pictorial designs of early medieval Christian letters are revelations of the Spirit "quickening" the letter. What to the modern eye may look like superfluous decoration (because it does not illustrate the literal sense of the text) was, to the eye of an exegetically inclined medieval reader, evidence of divine senses. The twelfth-century exegete Rupert of Deutz claimed that whoever had eyes to see would, in many passages of Scripture, perceive the "ornament of spiritual understanding covering the poverty of the letter."[14] "Ornament" or pictorial design could figure the Spirit in the medieval letter, a Spirit that visibly "gave life" to the conventionally abstract (or "dead") forms of alphabetic inscription by turning letters into the likenesses of living things, especially, in the sixth through eighth centuries, fish, doves, sprouting vines, and the leafy cross as Tree of Life.

A Christian scribe who designed a fish as part of an uncial *a* (Christ as alpha), or formed other letters with combinations of fish and doves (of the Holy Spirit), or turned the terminals of letters into sprouting vines (Christ as the vine) might be revealing the presence in the letter of Christ and the Holy Spirit—and demonstrating his own spiritual inspiration. Thus, for example, the scribe of a late seventh-century manuscript of Gregory of Tours's *Historia Francorum* animated an initial *P* by drawing eyes all over it, both on the loop (to turn it into a fish) and, more enigmatically, on the leaf-sprouting body of the upright (to give it the appearance of being formed out of triangular fish heads placed nose to nose) (fig. 23). The inventive scribes of the late seventh- or eighth-century Lectionary of Luxeuil combined versions of several Christian hieroglyphs into single letters, such

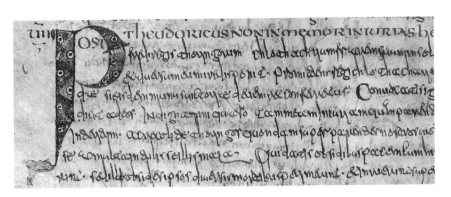

FIG. 23. Initial *P* with a fish as loop and an eye-covered shaft. Gregory of Tours, *History of the Franks*. Paris, B.N.F., MS lat. 17655, fol. 33v. Photo Bibliothèque nationale de France.

as the *T* whose upright is an abstract fish and whose crossbar is formed by two doves bearing in their beaks leafy sprigs that dangle, in the usual position of the letters alpha and omega, on the *T* as cross and turn it into a Tree of Life (fig. 24).

Not surprisingly, a number of the metaphors the early Christian fathers used to describe the spiritual sense of Scripture or the act of interpreting spiritually are realized in the designed letters of early medieval Christian texts. Their figures of speech are turned into the figural designs of letters. Drawing on the ancient equation of Christ with a fish (ιχθυς), one exegete wrote that the goal of "searching the depths of prophecy" was "to pull up from the profundity of Scripture, as with a fishhook, the fish of Christ the Lord."[15] Rupert of Deutz could well have been thinking of manuscripts with fish initials, as well as developing earlier patristic commentary, when he declared Christ to be present in Scripture "like a fish in water."[16] Yet it was not only in the Old Testament that exegetes might go fishing but also in the New. Ambrose had equated the text of the Gospels to a sea full of fish: "The Gospel is the sea in which the Apostles fish."[17]

A slightly different way of understanding fish initials is to say that their liveliness signals that they live in "living water," that is, waters that support or give life (with reference to John 4:10). The "living water" that Christ offered the Samaritan woman was understood to be his preaching, the Christian message, and by extension the texts of the Gospels. We might think that depicting the letters of the Gospel texts as "living water" would

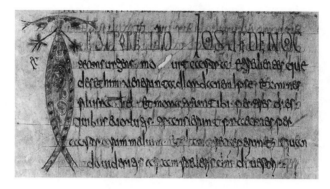

FIG. 24. Initial *T* formed by a fish and doves. Lectionary of Luxeuil. Paris, B.N.F., MS lat. 9427, fol. 120v. Photo Bibliothèque nationale de France.

be too difficult for early Christian scribes and that they would renounce even trying to realize this figure literally. Not so. Lois Drewer has pointed out, with specific reference to the iconography of mosaics in early Christian churches and baptisteries, that "the sea and related images of marine and river life are also commonly used as metaphors for 'living water' . . . which in varying contexts is understood as a symbol of God as the source of life, as a reference to the baptismal waters, or as an image of the Holy Spirit."[18] By depicting a text teeming with fish initials, scribal exegetes suggested both the immanence of Christ in the text and the life-supporting potential of the Christian text as "living water."[19]

The seemingly infinite variety of fish initials in Merovingian religious manuscripts may be understood not only as a demonstration of the life-giving power or spiritual fecundity of these Christian texts but also as a demonstration of the perpetual innovation, the "liberty" of interpretation, the freedom from the confining "narrowness" of the letter, that exegetes, following Paul, claimed to be characteristic of spiritual understanding. Paul (Romans 7:6) wrote that Christians must live in "newness of spirit, and not in the oldness of the letter," and Origen explained that both Testaments were, when understood spiritually, "ever new . . . not in chronological age, but in the novelty of [spiritual] understanding."[20]

Such incitation to innovative interpretation Christian scribes put into practice with elaborately designed initials that took great liberties with the

FIG. 25. Initial uncial *a* with its loop as a dove topped by a cross. Ecclesiastical canons. Oxford, Bodleian Library, MS e.Mus.101, fol. 27r. Photo Bodleian Library.

conventions of alphabetic inscription (ordinary letter shapes) to create ever different figures of the letter, all intended to reveal the same divine presence immanent in writing. Thus, on a single page and in a single text, no two fish-*a*s, for example, were designed or colored exactly alike; furthermore, within the same text scribes deliberately varied the Christian hieroglyphs they drew into their letters so that different kinds of fish, for example, might alternate or be combined in various ways with doves, vines, columns, and crosses, to name but a few possibilities. The deliberate variety and novelty of designed initials signaled the "liberty" of the spirit (and the inspired scribe) at work animating and transfiguring the letter and surpassing the literal sense. The mnemonic utility of such variety may well have been a secondary consideration for early medieval scribal exegetes.

To perceive a spiritual sense in the letter was to interpret "with the eyes of the dove," according to Richard of Saint Victor in an elaboration upon the centuries-old Christian symbol, common in catacomb epigraphy, of the dove of the Holy Spirit.[21] One way of figuring the spiritual sense of the letter in manuscripts from the sixth century on was by incorporating the head or the whole body of a dove into the letter, as for example in the uncial *a* terminating in a bird's head in the sixth-century Gospels of Split,[22] or the dove (with a cross on its head) that substitutes for a fish as the loop of an uncial *a* in a late sixth- or seventh-century Italian manuscript of ecclesiastical canons (fig. 25). At the risk perhaps of diminishing the force of the literal sense of church law, the scribe of this text of canons, followed by many

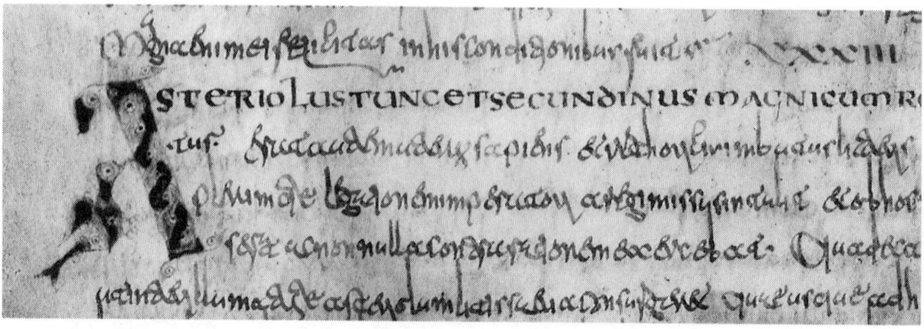

FIG. 26. Initial uncial *a* with a dove as loop. Gregory of Tours, *History of the Franks*. Paris, B.N.F., MS lat. 17655, fol. 42v. Photo Bibliothèque nationale de France.

others over the next centuries, incorporated pictorial figures such as the dove into initial letters to suggest that the letter of church law contained spiritual senses, was spiritually inspired, divinely authorized and empowered. The same spiritualizing, authorizing intention seems to motivate the dove (as well as fish) initials in the late seventh-century manuscript of Gregory of Tours's Christian *Historia Francorum* (figs. 23 and 26).

Whereas the fish symbol assumed a variety of particular forms from the very beginning, so that Christ might be depicted as a dolphin or a sturgeon or virtually any other fishy form, the dove symbol of the Holy Spirit was more gradually varied into undovelike shapes and assimilated to the Spirit-as-eagle (that inspired John) or to the peacock. For example, in the title of a late eighth-century manuscript of Ambrose's exegetical *Hexaemeron,* where we might expect to find letters depicted as doves and fish, the birds' hooked beaks suggest eagles (and their bright colors make them look, to the modern eye, far more like parrots) (color plate 2). In the late eighth-century Sacramentary of Gellone, the extender of an uncial *d* takes the shape of an undovelike bird—with crested but ducklike head and beak, partridge-plump body, and claws—engaged in pecking at the foliage of an abstract Tree of Life enclosed in the circle of the *d* (fig. 27). In the Lectionary of Luxeuil, the dove seems to have turned into a peacocklike creature with a long floral-patterned tail (fig. 28); and a different uncial *d* from the Sacramentary of Gellone more clearly assumes the form of a crested peacock preening or holding its tail with its beak (fig. 29). Like the dove, the eagle, and other birds, the peacock could figure the supraliteral

FIG. 27. Initial uncial *d* formed by a partridge-like dove pecking at a Tree of Life (*above*). Initial uncial *d* formed by a hand spearing a fish (*below*). Sacramentary of Gellone. Paris, B.N.F., MS lat. 12048, fol. 99v. Photo Bibliothèque nationale de France.

senses of the letter, but this was not so much because it might soar in flight as because of the many colors of its feathers. In the seventh century, Cassiodorus had compared the array of meanings in the Book of Psalms to the beautiful variety of colors in the eyes of a peacock's tail; two centuries later, John the Scot applied the same metaphor to Scripture in general.[23] By shaping letters out of colorful peacocks, scribal exegetes realized this metaphor.

Color in itself was an extremely important "figure" of the letter. Not only might color be used to give an appearance of liveliness to (and thus help to empower) Christian letters,[24] but, from Porfyrius on, color could be used to call attention to a figure, and the distinction of colors could create figures within figures. For example, at the center of the crossbar of an initial *T* in the late eleventh- or early twelfth-century Sacramentary of Figeac, blue-black, sky blue, and bright green grounds emphasize or reveal the various cross shapes of the interlace (color plate 3).[25]

Exegetes frequently used color as a metaphor for supraliteral, spiritual senses. The early Greek father Basil, for example, compared the richness of meanings in the Book of Psalms (and Scripture in general) to a royal bride's dress of cloth of gold reflecting a thousand colors.[26] We know, from Jerome's condemnation of them, that some of his contemporaries appreciated manuscripts written in gold letters on purple. To write letters in gold or silver enriched them both materially and figuratively; gold signified a "wealth" of meaning, and the mirroring shine of gold leaf might also, as Basil so finely observed, reflect the richness of surrounding colors. Only when the patron was affluent and willing could a scribe afford to use the reflective power of gold to multiply the colors with which he designed his

FIG. 28. Initial uncial *d* as a peacock. Lectionary of Luxeuil. Paris, B.N.F., MS lat. 9427, fol. 149v. Photo Bibliothèque nationale de France.

letters. More usually, without the aid of precious metals, the variety of colors alone (these, too, could be expensive) figuratively enriched the meanings of the letters.

The use of color as a figure for the spiritual sense of Scripture or its Christian "fulfillment" is especially striking among early Greek exegetes, as Herbert Kessler has cogently demonstrated. To explain Paul's Epistle to the Hebrews 10:1 ("For the Law contains but a shadow [*skia*], no true image [*eikon*], of the good things which were to come"), John Chrysostom compared the Old Testament to a preliminary drawing and the New Testament to the completed picture: "As in a painting, so long as one only draws the outlines, it is a sort of 'shadow'; but when one has added the bright paints and laid in the colors, then it becomes 'an image.' Something of this kind also was the Law."[27] Although never explicitly stated, this artistic analogy seems to underlie the integration of colored pictorial designs into the forms of letters in Christian texts, where the colored image represents the spiritual fulfillment of the shadowy, dark-inked outline of the letter. Kessler's interpretation of the theological discourse implicit in one ninth-century illumination, from a manuscript of the *Christian Topography* of Cosmas Indicopleustes, might serve to summarize the point implicit in the pictorially designed and colored letters of many a medieval Christian text: "Images, the miniature declares, . . . allow for a uniquely Christian appropriation of Hebrew Scripture. Jews persist in reading the Bible as law, as a closed and rigid written document; Christians understand it as art—to quote Cyril of Alexandria—'as a picture fertile with truth.' "[28]

In the arguments of eighth- and ninth-century iconophiles, color is asso-

FIG. 29. Initial uncial *d* as a peacock. Sacramentary of Gellone. Paris, B.N.F., MS lat. 12048, fol. 6v. Photo Bibliothèque nationale de France.

ciated with image, spiritual sense, and with the incarnate Christ. John of Damascus stressed color as the sign of spiritual fulfillment: "As the Law [is] a preliminary adumbration of the colored picture, so Grace and Truth are the colored picture."[29] Methodius, in the ninth century, deliberately contrasted writing with depiction to the detriment of the former: "Why might one not describe Jesus Christ our Lord with the brilliance of colors as legitimately as with ink? He was never presented to us as of ink, but was manifested as a true man, truly endowed with form and with color."[30] The conventional hierarchy of a religion of the book that grants supreme authority to written texts, especially the Gospels, is overturned by such a remark. Although Methodius seems to suppose a Christian writing devoid of depiction, his critique of it ought, at least in theory, to sanction the integration of colorful depiction into Christian writing to reveal Christ. According to the logic of such arguments, as Kessler put it, "art is not simply a pictorialization of texts [as Gregory the Great would have had it], but actual evidence of God's plan."[31] This, in turn, suggests that the only way for writing to compete with the authority of colorful depiction (understood as divine revelation) was to incorporate it. Christian scribes in the West accomplished this much earlier and in a much grander way than in the East.[32]

With rare exceptions, we must read Christian scribal exegetes' theory of color out of their practice. In the first half of the twelfth century, in his description of how to paint *The Mystical Ark of Noah* (the literal form of which is a cross inscribed in a square), Hugh of Saint Victor explained the symbolism of the colors to be used: green signified the historical or literal sense; saffron yellow signified the tropological or moral sense; and deep blue signified the allegorical or Christological sense.[33] Hugh's scheme might seem to offer a key to understanding the intentions of medieval scribal exegetes, especially in fine French religious manuscripts of the twelfth and thirteenth centuries (which make abundant use of the vivid hues, such as yellow, red, blue, and green, as well as gold leaf), but it is impossible to project such a hierarchy of colors back upon earlier scribal exegetes, who seem not to have had deep blue or bluish reds at their disposal. For example, an early glossed Psalter from the late eighth century (the Mondsee Psalter, Montpellier, Faculté de médicine, MS 409) opens with two full-page pictures of David and Christ (as figure and fulfillment, Christ being the "true" David) and exhibits various kinds of fish initials (to reveal Christ in the letter of the psalms) colored in green, orange, and yellow, with sparing use of gold and silver. In this Psalter, letters beginning verses of the psalms receive more elaborate variations of design and color than do the green-painted initials of the allegorizing gloss. In much brighter tones, the scribe of a later eighth-century manuscript of Augustine's *Questions on the Heptateuch* alternated green, orangey-red, and yellow as his main colors (color plate 4).[34]

Both the depiction of letters as themselves composed of several different colors and the outlining of letters against multicolored grounds, as in three lines of the title page to the *Questions on the Heptateuch* reproduced here (and in the Book of Kells and other Insular and continental religious texts), are ways of complicating our perception of the letter and preventing us from translating it directly into sound and literal sense. Through such incongruities of coloration, along with complexities of figural design, scribal exegetes encouraged consideration of the multiple spiritual senses of the letter. It is doubtful whether these scribes, in their own imaginations, made such clear and precise equations concerning a particular color and a particular kind of meaning as Hugh of Saint Victor later did. Yet it should be clear that visual pleasure was not the sole motive for such display—no matter how decorative and aesthetically satisfying the mosaic of color in the designed initial. From as early as the fifth century, color became one of the contestatory liberties Christian scribes took with the conventions of alphabetic inscription in order to distinguish Christian letters by making them seem to come alive with brilliant pigments suggestive of a wealth of meaning surpassing that of the conventionally colorless, "dead" letter.

In his sermons and writings Augustine repeatedly identified the cross as the "key" to unlocking the meaning of Scripture: "The key of the Old Testament is the cross."[35] Scribes evidently took this idea of the cross as universal key or, as Henri de Lubac put it, as "sign that changed the signs"[36] quite seriously and discovered (and invented) crosses everywhere to reveal the spiritual sense or the Christianity of the texts they were copying. Any *T* could be enlarged or emphasized by designs to reveal that it was a figure of the cross;[37] from the mid-eighth century on, this became a conventional scribal treatment of the *T* of the phrase "Te igitur" beginning the canon of the mass, as Jürgen Gutbrod demonstrated in a chapter of *Die Initiale* devoted solely to these *T*s as crosses.[38] In the Sacramentary of Figeac, for example, the great *T* beginning the "Te igitur" page forms a red knotwork cross that harbors many other crosses figured by knotwork crossings and colored grounds (color plate 3). Even in the remaining letters of the phrase "Te igitur" at the bottom of this page, the scribe has taken the opportunity to superpose a small *I* over the crossbar of a *G* to form a cross encircled by the curve of the *G*. Centuries before such sophisticated treatments, carvers of funerary inscriptions in the Roman catacombs deliberately enlarged *T*s and used crossbars to transform into crosses the uprights of certain letters, such as the *P* of the word "PAX" (thereby also turning the *P* into a chi-rho monogram, with the cross as the chi and the *P* as rho).[39] We find this same method of transfiguring letters by giving them crossbars used in the chi-rho page of the Book of Kells, where the upright of the rho is barred and the resultant step-patterned cross emphasized in bright yellow (color plate 1).

Every time a scribe wrote certain letters (such as *T* or *X* ) or designed two letters to overlap, he created a crossing whose potential spiritual significance he might emphasize pictorially in various ways to reveal Christ in the text. In the mid-sixth-century manuscript of Orosius's *Ten Books of History against the Pagans,* the same scribe who invented a variety of early fish-*a*s (fig. 19) also placed crosses within the circular loops of initial *d*s and *p*s,[40] or on top of one *p,* as well as forming monogrammatic combinations of initial

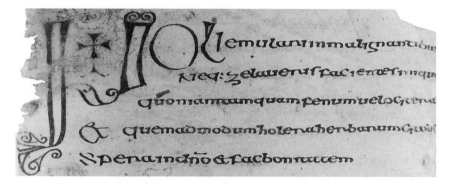

FIG. 30. Initial *N* with a fish as crossbar and a cross above this. Cathach of Saint Columba. Dublin, Royal Irish Academy, unnumbered MS, fol. 6r. Photo courtesy of the Officers of the Royal Irish Academy.

letters including *t* in such a way as to emphasize its cruciform shape.[41] We find such crosses inserted in initials also in the seventh-century Irish Cathach of Saint Columba (fig. 30). In the first part of the eighth century, Eadfrith of Lindisfarne considerably altered the ordinary shape of the letter to design as a cross the crossbar of a great letter *N* at the opening of the Gospel of Mark (fig. 31).[42] On the first page of the Sacramentary of Gellone, in addition to including a host of other animating Christological motifs such as vine leaves sprouting from letters and a *D* figured as part fish, a scribe enlarged the final *T* of the word *incipit* and surrounded it with red dots to suggest the cross (color plate 5).[43] In the lesser initials of this same manuscript, scribes sometimes seem to have been playing a game of hide-and-seek-the-cross with the reader. For example, directly under the previously discussed bird pecking at the Tree of Life (a version of the cross) (fig. 27), the oblique extender of another uncial *d* is drawn as a human hand spearing a fish (possibly a variant on an ancient hieroglyph of Christ crucified). In the round paunch of this same uncial *d* in the Sacramentary of Gellone, four-petaled, cross-shaped flowers alternate with crosses in an outer circle, and an inner circle is filled with a flower or a cross (or both) depending on which one perceives as figure or ground. Furthermore, in this instance the viewer may link the outer crosses with the inner, or the outer flowers with the inner petals, to form larger cruciform shapes.

The examples one could give of scribes transfiguring a letter or combina-

FIG. 31. Initial *N* with a cross as crossbar. Lindisfarne Gospels. London, British Library, MS Cotton Nero D.IV, fol. 95r. Photo by permission of the British Library.

tion of letters into a cross are legion (and would include figural poems such as those of Porfyrius and Rhabanus Maurus, discussed earlier [fig. 11], in which a sequence of letters forms the shape of a cross). To transcend the "narrow confines" of ordinary reading by perceiving the figure of the cross in the letter was, for the Christian scribe—and for readers attentive to the scribe's pictorial emphases—a sign of spiritual enlightenment and "liberation." In the Sacramentary of Gellone, an initial *d* depicted as a man digging with a pick and discovering the true cross (which art historians have cited as an early example of literal illustration of the adjacent text, a prayer commemorating the cross's discovery) also points up the purpose of reading: to "find the cross" in the letter (fig. 32).

Medieval scribal exegetes revealed Christ's presence in the letter in yet another manner: they realized pictorially as parts of letters those figures of

FIG. 32. Initial uncial *d* as the discovery of the true cross. Sacramentary of Gellone. Paris, B.N.F., MS lat. 12048, fol. 76v. Photo Bibliothèque nationale de France.

speech or metaphors that Christ used to describe himself in the Gospels, especially ones drawn from nature. To make letters shine with light (as in "I am the light of the world," John 8:12), scribes used the reflective power of thin layers of gold or silver and, in manuscripts such as the Book of Kells, the luminosity of bright yellow. There is an especially long tradition of enlivening the letter by picturing it as sprouting leaves, flowers, and fruit in recollection of Christ's "I am the true vine" (John 15:1).

One could provide endless examples of the metamorphosis of letters into plants, beginning with the tendril-like curls that add a semblance of liveliness to the Filocalus script of Christian catacomb epigraphy and eventually developing, voided of their original spiritual import, into the leafy borders, called vignettes, so common in later medieval manuscripts.[44] In a mid-eighth-century manuscript of Augustine's homilies, the leafy extender of an uncial *d,* whose loop is a rosette, stretches up and runs horizontally along the top of the page in a precocious instance of a semivignette (fig. 33). Such vegetal outgrowth and overgrowth of the letter may figure not only Christ's "I am the true vine" but also certain patristic metaphors for the spiritual senses of the text. Ambrose, in opening his fifth-century exegesis of the Book of Psalms, compared their moral (tropological) sense to the leaves and their mystical (allegorical or anagogical) sense to the fruit of a plant.[45] In his explanation of the Book of Job, Gregory modified the plant metaphor somewhat by considering that the historical sense was the root from which germinated the "spiritual fruits of allegory." A letter depicted

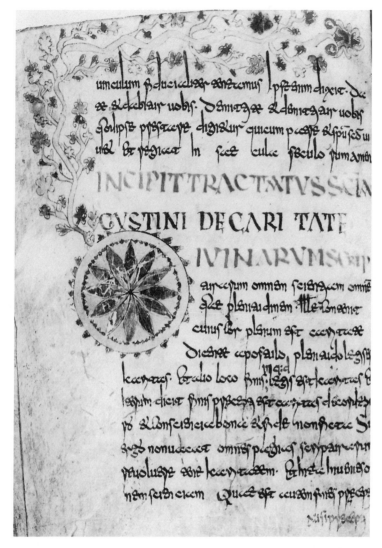

FIG. 33. Initial uncial *d* sprouting into a vine bordering the top of the page. Augustine, *Homilies.* Wolfenbüttel, Herzog August Bibliothek, Cod. Guelf. 99 Weissenberg, fol. 56v. Photo courtesy of the Herzog August Bibliothek.

as a flourishing vine would at least promise such allegorical fruits to the contemplative reader.[46]

In the ninth-century Drogo Sacramentary, for example, shiny golden, and in some cases flowering, vines enwrap the initials and seem to enliven

FIG. 34. Vine-wrapped initial *T* of the "Te igitur" page. Drogo Sacramentary. Paris, B.N.F., MS lat. 9428, fol. 15v. Photo Bibliothèque nationale de France.

the letters of a manuscript in which are inscribed the words of Christian rites ("sacraments" or mysteries) of transformation. Pictorial transfigurations of letters into flourishing vines were often meant to reveal Christ's presence in the letter (fig. 34). Such a transfiguration is particularly appropriate in the case of the *T* of the phrase "Te igitur," which opens the canon of the mass—whereby, according to Christian belief, bread and wine are transformed into the real presence of Christ. In effect, as Gutbrod has suggested, the pictorial designs of the letter *T* in the manuscript of the Drogo Sacramentary, which would lie open on the altar as the priest officiated, revealed that Christ was immanent in the letter of the text of the mass before the accomplishment of the miraculous transformation of bread and wine into the real presence of Christ. Just as the bread and wine retained their material forms despite this divine immanence, so did the transfigured, spiritualized letter.

But Christians who read with the "eyes of the heart" would pay much less attention to deciphering the conventional form of a letter *T* to read a word than they would to deciphering the meanings of the figures of the letter. The great red *T* of the "Te igitur" page not only is wrapped in gold vines that suggest Christ-the-vine clinging to the support of the cross (an image of the Tree of Life), but the ends and center of the letter also open to reveal, against light blue grounds, Old Testament figures of Christ's self-sacrifice: in the center, the priest Melchizedek; at the ends of the cross-bar, Abraham and Abel offering sheep; at the bottom, bulls as sacrificial beasts.

The spiritual significance of the fact that the letter *T* opened the celebration of the mass received explicit verbal (as well as pictorial) exegesis; in the twelfth century, Innocent III wrote that it was an act of "divine providence" that the canon began with the letter *T*, which had been understood by exegetes from Tertullian on as a figure of the cross.[47] To wrap in gold vines the initial letters of a Sacramentary, a collection of the verbal texts of Christian rites (which, as opposed to the writing in a Lectionary or a Psalter, were not, strictly speaking, Holy Scripture), was to try to authorize these words and this writing as divinely inspired, in effect, to turn them into Holy Scripture visibly animated by the same divine immanence as the Old and New Testaments.[48]

The early church had been remarkably hesitant to picture Christ's human person, using instead figures such as the fish, the vine, the lamb.[49] However, after the decisions of the Nicene Council in 787 and their confirmation in 843 helped allay fears that more realistic depiction was idolatry,[50] Western scribes began to use the option of evoking the spiritual sense of the letter by depicting Christ's human body within it. After all, they might consider themselves to be showing what Paul had said the enlightened Christian might perceive in Scripture: "the knowledge of the glory of God, in the face of Christ Jesus" (2 Corinthians 4:6).[51] Thus, for example, the scribe of the "Te igitur" page of the late eighth-century Sacramentary of Gellone audaciously formed the *T* by the crucified body of Christ

FIG. 35. Initial *C* encircling the head of Christ. Jerome, *Epistles*. Paris, B.N.F., MS lat. 1163, fol. 1r. Photo Bibliothèque nationale de France.

revealed against a deep blue, star-studded ground in the shape of a cross (and of a *T*) flanked by angels (color plate 6).

Any reader who contemplates the figure of this *T* as crucified Christ is directed by its composition to Christ's face and especially to his large-eyed stare centered over a cruciform halo. Inside a lesser initial of a ninth-century manuscript of Jerome's *Epistles,* one finds a much cruder version of Christ's face revealed in the letter, once again centered on a cross, but with alpha and omega hanging from its crossbar to identify the roughly schematic face by recollecting Christ's alphabetical figures for himself ("I am the Alpha and Omega") (fig. 35). On the chi-rho page of the Book of Kells (color plate 1), which begins the account of Christ's human lineage and marks the first appearance of Christ's name (written in Greek letters) in the Gospel of Matthew, a relatively realistic depiction of Christ's frontal face, atop curving trumpet patterns that suggest his shoulders, appears above the lithe limbs of the great letter chi (also a symbol of the cross),[52] and a slightly different version of Christ's face tops the rho at the point where it crosses the iota (which gives the iota the human face of Christ as well).[53]

Yet as we shall see in more detail in chapter 6, by no means all faces in the letters of religious manuscripts were intended to be the face of Christ. As early as the sixth century, in two *P*s beginning the word *Paul* in a manuscript of the Pauline epistles, frontal and profile faces would seem to be those of the author or the scribe.[54] The expressive face of a poorly shaven monk—the scribe?—forms part of the extender of an uncial *d* in the late eighth-century Sacramentary of Gellone (fig. 1). Whereas the scribal exegete of the Book of Kells represented Christ's face atop the first letters of the Gospel of Matthew to show Christ as incarnate in the letter of the Gospel text (which at this very spot begins to narrate his human lineage) (color plate 1), and the scribe of Jerome's *Epistles* depicted Christ's face in initial letters to suggest that these were inspired by Christ, the scribes of the Pauline letters and of the Gellone Sacramentary would seem to have been acknowledging ordinary human agency with their depictions of the faces of human writers in or as or supporting letters.[55]

In addition to evoking the spiritual sense of the letter by the relatively obvious method of depicting Christ's face in it, eighth- and ninth-century Insular scribal exegetes (as well as Continental ones influenced by them) elaborated a number of more deliberately enigmatic figures of revelation. One of the most conspicuous of these figures of a hidden divinity was the knot or the tangle, which was combined in later Continental visual exegesis with the vine, as in the page immediately following the "Te igitur" page of the Drogo Sacramentary, where golden vines knot around and tie up a series of lesser initials (fig. 36), and also, as we have seen, on the "Te igitur" page of the Sacramentary of Figeac (color plate 3), where a knotwork vine forms the figure of the cross as Tree of Life. A knot was a crossing, a "crux"—inevitably, then, a figure of the cross. Furthermore, a knot called for "explication," unfolding or straightening out.

In his commentary on the Book of Psalms, Origen used the knot as a metaphor for the visible aspect of the mystery hidden in divine letters, which required spiritual inspiration to explicate or "untie" it.[56] Gregory the Great, in his much-read *Moralia in Job,* compared the act of revelation and enlightening—Christ's and the exegete's—to the untying of knots: "When we untie the mystical knots of allegory by explication, we express clearly what we have heard obscurely." In a figurative comparison that may have encouraged Insular artists' adaptation to manuscript art of earlier pagan animal interlace motifs, Gregory described as a knot the Book of Ezekiel's enigmatic opening vision of the four tetramorphs (combining features of lion, eagle, ox, and man): "We will discuss the beginning of the book of the prophet Ezekiel, which is closed [to understanding] by great obscurities, as if it were bound by the knots of mysteries."[57] In his exegesis of John the Baptist's statement that he was unworthy to untie Christ's shoelace (Luke 3:16), Gregory, followed by Bede, explained the knotted lace as

FIG. 36. "Clementissime" page with letters knotted in golden vines. Drogo Sacramentary. Paris, B.N.F., MS lat. 9428, fol. 16r. Photo Bibliothèque nationale de France.

a figure for the mystery of the incarnation,[58] as did John the Scot, who elaborated upon its "inextricable tangle": "If then the sandal of the Word is the flesh of the Word, it is logical to think that the lace of His sandal designates the subtlety and the inextricable tangle of the mysteries of the incarnation. The precursor judges himself unworthy of untying this profound mystery."[59] Elsewhere, without specifically using the term *knot,* John the Scot described the order of Scripture in terms that evoke a labyrinthian knotwork: "a linking of sinuosities, a tissue of ingenious detours." He believed it impossible to understand the complex meaning of Scripture without following a tortuous path: "[T]he complex connection of divine thoughts in the holy prophets cannot be discerned otherwise than through very frequent transitions and the most secret and hidden returns from one sense to another, not only within the clauses, but even within the parts of the same phrase and even smaller units." Such complexity, John argued (following

Augustine and other exegetes), was the form the Holy Spirit took "out of desire to exercise our intelligence and to recompense zeal and discovery."[60]

The "interlace" designs of eighth- and ninth-century Insular and Merovingian manuscript illumination are pictorial realizations of the exegetical metaphor of the "knots" of Scripture, that is, the multiplex, associative, "intertextual" ways divinity was supposed to reveal (but still partially conceal) itself in writing. In effect, interlace patterns are "loosened" knots, knots that reveal to varying degrees the way they are tied. If we were able to pull on the ends of these traces, they would tighten into hard knots whose tying patterns would become much more impossible to decipher. Loosening and untangling the knots of the letter seems to be the activity engaging the monk figured, in the eleventh-century Bible of Saint Martial of Limoges, as part of the extender of the initial *Q* beginning the opening phrase of the Gospel of Luke (fig. 37). To picture the letter as itself a knotwork pattern or the container for one was a way of suggesting the awesome intricacy of scriptural revelation.

According to Christian theologians, Scripture could not be truly understood if read in a linear, literalist fashion. Medieval scribes contested this kind of conventional reading and tried to demonstrate the complexity of scriptural intertextuality pictorially, by means of initials that were filled with or that themselves formed ever different, ever new knotwork patterns. Just as the exegete, even in the smallest units of Scripture, discovered extremely complex linkages with all the rest of Scripture and shuttled back and forth continually between different levels of meaning, so the reader confronted with an initial such as the great chi of the chi-rho page of the Book of Kells has to stop linear, literalist reading in order to examine the knotwork within the body of the letter, to follow a yellow trace in the central lozenge, for example, as it twists and turns and redoubles back on itself (color plate 1).

Frequently such knotwork is made of one continuous strand or trace that repeatedly changes colors, such as, for example, from red to blue and back again in the interlace forming the crossbar-as-cross of the initial *N* in the Lindisfarne Gospels (fig. 31). On closer examination, what appears to be a wide braid of many strands of different colors turns out to be mostly a single strand that changes colors, as inside the base of the initial *I* supporting

FIG. 37. Man examining (to untangle?) the knots of an initial *Q*. Bible of Saint Martial of Limoges. Paris, B.N.F., MS lat. 8 (pt. 2), fol. 192v. Photo Bibliothèque nationale de France.

the human figure labeled Mary in the Sacramentary of Gellone (color plate 5). Color was one of the traditional figures exegetes, including John the Scot, used to suggest the supraliteral and multiple senses of Scripture; thus, the scribal depiction of the letter itself or the interior of the letter as a single strand changing colors to create a multicolored "text" suggests the fundamental oneness that links the apparent multiplicity—and suggests also the necessity, if the reader is to follow the sense of divine writing, of shifting back and forth between different supraliteral senses.

The variety of interlace or open knotwork patterns in medieval manuscripts is seemingly infinite. In some, usually facing the opening of a new scriptural or exegetical text, multicolored knotwork designs cover an entire page, which modern scholars conventionally designate as a "carpet" page (with reference to the complex interwoven designs of oriental carpets, an anachronistic and inappropriate analogy). In these cases, the knotwork patterns introducing the text of Scripture are a figural representation of its complexities and often also, by the designs that emerge (the figures woven into the text), a sort of prefiguration of the spiritual sense of the scriptural text that follows. The trace of the knotwork in these carpet pages is a figure for the trace of writing. Thus it serves as a pictorial revelation of the interlocking and multiplex structure of Scripture and also of the exegesis that both would loosen or untie the "mystical knots" of Scripture by following the trace of the Spirit and would, in the words of John the Scot, by "very frequent transitions and the most secret and hidden returns from one sense to another" even within the smallest units, discover "the complex connection of divine thoughts in the holy prophets."

Approximately contemporary with Gregory the Great's rhetorical figure of the "mystical knots of allegory" to be untied by exegesis, the earliest surviving carpet page, an added leaf from the sixth or seventh century, appears on the verso facing the opening of an eighth-century copy of Augustine's Gospel harmony *De consensu evangelistarum* (color plate 7). The page is composed of five different kinds of multicolored knotwork strips grouped together into a rectangular block (or, if we focus especially on the central knotwork strip and the two horizontal ones running along the top and bottom of the page, we may see the figure of an *I*—short for Iesus). By considering the number of strands interwoven in different strips and their shapes and colors, we could elaborate many symbolic meanings out of this knotwork.

The scribal exegete who used such a knotwork page as a preface prepared a contemplative, multivalent reading experience by putting in front of our eyes, just before we confront alphabet inscription, an enigmatic tracery whose patterns, as we try to penetrate them and follow the course of a single strand, quickly challenge our capacity to follow the trace and thereby impress us with the continuity and complexity of the textual patterns. Yet the knotwork of this sixth- or seventh-century carpet page seems regular and simple compared with the virtuosities of later Insular Gospels, where the knotwork is usually depicted as a living strand formed out of the infinitely ductile bodies of stylized animals, where the pictorial animation of the strand itself, as well as the figures formed by its tying patterns, are made to suggest, or enigmatically reveal, divine presence.

The Gospels of the Book of Durrow, probably written in Ireland in the early seventh century, present several carpet pages that, through their knotting patterns, form different figures of the cross. All of these carpet pages feature multicolored, inanimate knotwork, except for one, and even here inanimate strands form the circular knots within the central medallion (whose cruciform pattern is emphasized by the small central figure of an encircled cross) (fig. 38). On this one carpet page, rectangular bands of knotwork beasts that seem to be devouring one another frame the central knotwork medallion. Art historians have remarked that these interlaced animals recollect the ribbon-style animal interlace of nearly contemporary secular metalwork on buckles, clasps, sword hilts, and the like; in such places knotting might express a need for fixity, closure, or protection, and a pictured knotting of animal bodies might be intended to harness animal forces magically to this end.[61] The scribal exegetes of the Book of Durrow would seem, on this carpet page, to be adapting and appropriating to Christian ends two nonalphabetic forms of "writing": animate interlace designs and the knotting of colored or uncolored strands (the latter an ancient way of recording and remembering).[62]

The Durrow illuminator relegated a pagan form of pictorial writing (the tracing of interlaced ribbon-style animals) to the position of border framing a central circle composed of knots that reveal (and conceal) the cross and thus may figure the "mystical knots of allegory" of Scripture. By contextualizing the pagan picture-writing of interlaced beasts in this way, the illuminator of the Book of Durrow makes viewers see it differently (much as Paul did with the "outmoded letter" of the Old Testament); the central medallion presents the elucidating "key" of the cross, which may enable the viewer to perceive as crosses even the crossings of these biting and struggling bestial bodies. In perceiving the spiritual in the carnal, the viewer mentally transforms a pagan picture-writing into a Christian picture-writing and appropriates its magic force as an expression of divine power.[63]

The increasingly complex knotwork designs of the carpet pages intro-

FIG. 38. Animated interwoven page prefacing the Gospel of John. Book of Durrow. Dublin, Trinity College, MS 57, fol. 192v. Photo courtesy of the Board of Trinity College Dublin.

FIG. 39. Animated interwoven page preceding the Gospel of Matthew. Lindisfarne Gospels. London, British Library, MS Cotton Nero D.IV, fol. 26v. Photo by permission of the British Library.

ducing the different evangelists' accounts in the early eighth-century Lindisfarne Gospels are almost entirely formed of the elongated bodies of beaked and muzzled creatures. For example, in the page preceding the Gospel of Matthew (fig. 39), these interlaced animal bodies form, by their different colors and orientations, the figure of a large cross on a ground of interlace. As in the figural poems of Porfyrius (fig. 11) and, later, Rhabanus Maurus, the bold red outline around this cross pattern "reveals" it. The Lindisfarne illuminator provides keys to the cross patterns of his page also in the form of tiny crosses drawn within light, bright circles, which are, in this case, aligned within the rubricated cross pattern to form another figure of the cross within the figure of the cross. Whereas the animal interlace on the carpet page of the Book of Durrow is limited to a marginal frame, in the Lindisfarne Gospels animal interlace makes up the figures and grounds of the carpet pages (as well as filling initial letters of the Gospel text).

Eadfrith, the scribal exegete of the Lindisfarne Gospels, went a step fur-

ther than the scribe of the Book of Durrow in depicting the immanence of
the spiritual in carnal forms by making his interlaced animals evoke the
different animal forms (man, eagle, lion, ox/calf) through which the Holy
Spirit inspired the different evangelists. These animal symbols of divine
revelation were invented by exegetes in their effort to harmonize and explain two biblical visions: Ezekiel's (1:5–12) of the four four-winged creatures under the throne of God, each with the faces of man and lion on the
right side and of ox and eagle on the left, and Christ's, as related to John in
the Apocalypse (4:7–8), of the four six-winged and eye-covered creatures
around the throne of God—one resembling a lion; another, an ox; another,
a flying eagle; and another with the face of a man.

Jerome correlated these beasts with the different evangelists according to
the opening themes of their Gospels so that the figure of a man represented
Matthew (because his text began with an account of Christ's human lineage); the lion, Mark; the calf (or ox), Luke; and the eagle, John. In his homilies on Ezekiel, Gregory the Great followed Jerome's identification and
went on to explain how each of the four beasts, through its different qualities, also symbolized Christ and the elect.[64] Bede recommended suppleness
of interpretation concerning these correspondences, because very early exegetes such as Irenaeus had identified the eagle with Mark and the lion
with John.[65]

In the vision of Ezekiel each beast is, in fact, a tetramorph (part man, lion,
ox, and eagle), as the illuminator of the early eighth-century Trier Gospels
tried to show, in his version of what art historians call an "evangelists
page," by giving talons, claws, hooves, and feet to one human torso (fig. 40).
Insular Gospel books made much of these animals as symbols of divine
revelation by devoting whole pages to grouping them around the quadrants of a cross and depicting them separately, often in the act of inspiring
a human figure of an evangelist, in preface to different gospel accounts. Although patristic verbal exegesis and modern scholarship have tended to
treat each animal figure as a sign or symbol of a different evangelist, medieval illuminators visually authorized the texts of the Gospels by depicting
the animal as a figure of the Spirit inspiring the evangelist.

In the Durham, Lindisfarne, and Echternach Gospels and the Book of
Kells, not only the extreme stylization but also the fantastical combinations

FIG. 40. Tetramorph evangelists page. Trier Gospels. Trier, Domschatz, Codex 61, fol. 5v. Photo courtesy of the Bischöfliches Generalvikariat.

of morphological features in the bestial and human forms that make up the knotwork interlace of the carpet pages, the interiors of large initials, and the very bodies of lesser ones have hindered us from recognizing that older, pagan forms of ribbon-style animal interlace have been transfigured here into traces of the Holy Spirit carnally revealed through the animal forms the Spirit took in inspiring the evangelists. Just as southern scribes revealed Christ or the Holy Spirit in the letter by animating letters with the pictorial forms of fish or doves or vines (or combinations of all of these), northern scribes revealed the Spirit incarnate in Scripture, and especially in the texts of the Gospels, by depicting the trace of writing as the designs formed by the elongated and stylized bodies, interlaced in infinitely various combinations, of the man, eagle, ox, and lion.

Wayne Dynes hinted at this transformation of the shapes of the "evangelist symbols" into the shapes of the initial letters of Gospel texts when he so finely observed the formal similarities between the rampant lion on the "imago leonis" page of the Echternach Gospels (fig. 41) and the opening letters of Mark's Gospel text on the facing page (fig. 42):

> In a reciprocal fashion, the construction of the monogram INI echoes the lion, for it consists of two wide parts, corresponding to the lower and upper body of the beast, connected by a sinuous isthmus, rendering the beast's "waist." Moreover, the INI monogram is filled with repeating decorative designs and flanked by a series of black display letters which are in part enveloped with yellow coloring [like that of the lion]. The monogram has four flaring terminals echoing the four paws of the animal. In this harmony of beast and monogram one is tempted to see a kind of pun, with the vigorous movement of the beast initiating the narrative (and by implication the act of reading from left to right and the turning of the pages) and so providing a concrete embodiment of the word *initium*.[66]

This pictorial pun is fraught with sense. The rampant lion of Mark, that is, the Spirit in the form of a lion on the verso of one page, motivates and inspires quite literally—by taking the shape of and shaping—the initial letters of the opening of Mark's Gospel on the facing recto. We may imagine the Spirit-as-lion leaping to the right and, after the hiatus between the two pages, reemerging transformed into the enlivened curves of the opening letters of the Gospel of Mark.

Whereas pagan ribbon-style ornament turned the bodies of nonhuman

FIG. 41. "Imago leonis" page prefacing the Gospel of Mark. Echternach Gospels. Paris, B.N.F., MS lat. 9389, fol. 75v. Photo Bibliothèque nationale de France.

animals into interwoven strands, Insular scribal exegetes, who imagined Matthew to have been inspired by the Spirit in the form of a man, also represented the human form becoming a trace. On the "imago hominis" (image of a man) page of the eighth-century Echternach Gospels, Matthew's divine inspiration is represented by an extremely abstract human figure who holds open before his chest an inscribed book (fig. 43). The body of

FIG. 42. Opening letters of the text of Mark's Gospel. Echternach Gospels. Paris, B.N.F., MS lat. 9389, fol. 76r. Photo Bibliothèque nationale de France.

this human figure is formed by three sets of loops, the lowest of which resembles the shape of the letter *m* in the rubric above and is filled with the same triple-dot pattern as the letter. The strands and curvilinear shapes of the "body" of this image of the Spirit as man (or Matthew's inspiration) make the human form seem already well on the way to becoming writing. In an interlace-filled initial *M* opening the exegetical "argument"

FIG. 43. "Imago hominis" page prefacing the Gospel of Matthew. Echternach Gospels. Paris, B.N.F., MS lat. 9389, fol. 18v. Photo Bibliothèque nationale de France.

prefacing the Gospel of Matthew in the Book of Kells, the Spirit's incarnation in material forms (first of the man, then of the letter) seems to be revealed through pictorial designs. A human bust appears above the crossbar of the letter, while the man's feet seem to emerge from the central upright, which has replaced most of his body (fig. 44).[67]

The innovative designers of the late eighth-century Sacramentary of Gellone also formed letters out of the bodies of "evangelist symbols"; but they did so specifically in passages explaining the spiritual meaning of the different features of these animal figures, so that the pictorial figures serve to illustrate the literal sense of the text they help to form. On one page, the initial *L* of the name Luke is formed by the haloed head of a surprisingly long-horned "calf" atop an abstract interlace of cloven-hooved legs (fig. 45). Both the "horns of the two Testaments" and the "four feet of the four Gospels" are mentioned in the adjacent text explaining Luke's symbol; the calf (*vitulus*) has two horns because Scripture is made up of two parts, and four feet because there are four Gospels. The physical features of the ani-

FIG. 44. Human form emerging from an initial *M*. Book of Kells. Dublin, Trinity College, MS 58, fol. 12r. Photo courtesy of the Board of Trinity College Dublin.

mal figure of the Spirit are transformed into script by the verbal commentary of the exegete and also by the designer of the letter, who transforms the features of the calf quite literally into writing. Just below this *L* is an *I* (beginning the name John), formed by a haloed eagle's head atop a human body holding an open book and gesturing toward the text to the right, where it is explained that John's likeness is the eagle.

To a modern mind it might seem that, instead of the tangles of metamorphic animal bodies we encounter in Insular manuscripts of the Gospels, only the animate form the Spirit took in inspiring a particular Gospel should form the initial letters of that Gospel. This was the case in some later Continental manuscripts such as the tenth-century Evangelary of Metz, where the Carolingian scribe's desire for clarity and regularity manifests itself also in the classicized shapes of the letters. A winged, long-tailed calf embodies the initial *Q* opening Luke's Gospel (fig. 46); a

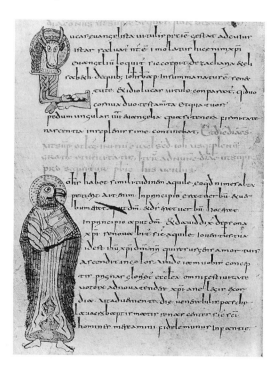

FIG. 45. Initial *L* of "Luke" and initial *I* of "John" as calf and eagle evangelist symbols. Sacramentary of Gellone. Paris, B.N.F., MS lat. 12048, fol. 42v. Photo Bibliothèque nationale de France.

kneeling angelic figure pointing with quill pen to the text opposite forms the *L* opening Matthew's Gospel (fig. 47), and so forth. It might seem more appropriate to us that the avian forms be eliminated from the interlacing of man and eagle in the central lozenge of the great chi on the chi-rho page of the Book of Kells (beginning the text of the Gospel of Matthew) (color plate 1) and that a carpet page introducing a particular Gospel text should feature only the relevant carnal form of the Spirit—that, for example, the Lindisfarne carpet page introducing the Gospel of Matthew (fig. 39), made up of the interlaced bodies of long-beaked and muzzled creatures, should picture only interlaced men. Insular scribal exegetes usually did not, however, make such simple and exclusive identifications, but rather they tried to depict the unified diversity of the Gospels by means of images of conflict or difference that were at the same time images of oneness: images of animals devouring and wrapping themselves around each other, thus becoming one; and metamorphic, "monstrous"-looking

FIG. 46. Initial *Q* opening the Gospel of Luke as a winged calf. Evangelary of Metz. Paris, B.N.F., MS lat. 9388, fol. 99v. Photo Bibliothèque nationale de France.

combinations into one body of the different animal figures through which the Holy Spirit was manifest to the evangelists.

That such amalgamation and knotting of animal forms was supposed to demonstrate the harmony and essential unity of the Gospels is suggested by the mixed morphology of the "evangelist symbols" over and under the arches of the Eusebian canon tables of the Book of Kells. The function of these introductory canon tables is to list all the concordances among the four different texts of the Gospels, to demonstrate that the sense is one, even though expressed through different words. In the first canon table of the Book of Kells (fol. 2r), which tabulates the similar passages in all four Gospels, under the same arch appear representations of the four different "evangelist symbols." The canon table on folio 5 recto (fig. 48) harmonizes passages from Matthew and Mark, Matthew and John, and Mark and Luke. As our eyes move down this page from top to bottom, we seem to observe the bodies of the animal figures of the Spirit gradually turning into knotwork traces. Above the great arch, on the left, the Spirit assumes the form of a winged man (an angel) and, on the right, of an eagle holding up a closed book with a human hand. Centered under the large arch are more obviously mixed creatures: on the left, a lion with clawed paws and, on the right, a horned ox with hooves, but both the lion and the ox here have winged and tail-feathered hind parts.[68] The heads of lions with knotwork manes bite and fasten onto the two smaller arches to form separate compartments within which intertwine the elongated bodies of men and eagles with leonine paws and hind parts. Farther down the page, in the interlace

FIG. 47. Initial *L* opening the Gospel of
Matthew as a winged man. Evangelary of
Metz. Paris, B.N.F., MS lat. 9388, fol. 17v.
Photo Bibliothèque nationale de France.

that fills the two outer columns supporting these arches, the bodies of eagles are even more fully subsumed into the tracery of knotwork. Such a
canon table presents, in the upper (heavenly) register of the page, forms in
which the Spirit appeared to the evangelists; on the lower (increasingly
earthly) levels of the page, these carnal forms become more "mixed" and
unrecognizable as they disappear into the trace of interlaced strands of
knotwork.

Although art historians have identified the "evangelist symbols" in and
above the arches of the Kells canon tables, no modern scholar has yet identified these (that is, the different carnal figures in which the Holy Spirit
supposedly was manifest to the different evangelists) in the knotted animal
interlace that fills the "carpet" pages, borders, and great initials and that
forms the bodies of lesser initials in so many Insular manuscripts of the
Gospels. Part of the problem lies in the names earlier scholars have given
to particular pictorial patterns, names that define and limit the way later
viewers see them. The so-called carpet page is just one case in point, in that
the term *carpet* suggests oriental tapestries and the ostentation of "sheer
decoration" and thus hinders our thinking of such designs as having other
functions—such as to protect (discussed in the next chapter) or to serve as
a pictorial analogy to and a figural commentary on the immediately facing
text of Scripture. Were the "evangelist symbols" called, more appropriately, symbols of the Holy Spirit (manifestations of the divine in animal
and human form), it would be easier to see why scribal exegetes would
want to incorporate these into the shapes of letters of the Gospels, which
are also manifestations of the divine. Indeed, in depictions of different

FIG. 48. Canon table featuring mixed forms of the animal symbols of evangelical inspiration. Book of Kells. Dublin, Trinity College, MS 58, fol. 5r. Photo courtesy of the Board of Trinity College Dublin.

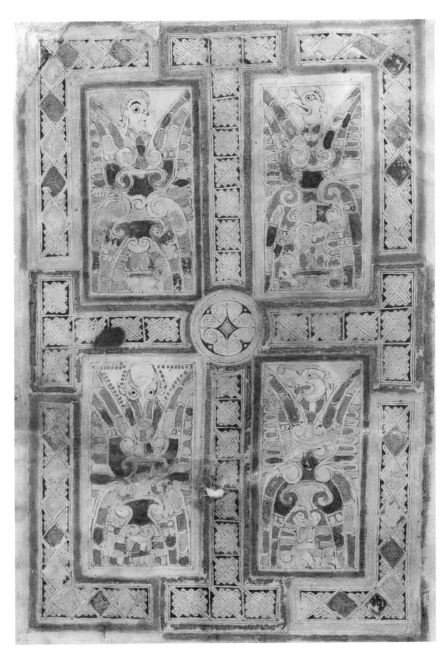

FIG. 50. Stylized ox's head (*lower left*) and lion's head (*lower right*) of the evangelist symbols cross page. Macdurnan Gospels. London, Lambeth Palace Library, MS 1370, fol. 1v. Photo by permission of His Grace the Archbishop of Canterbury and the Trustees of Lambeth Palace Library.

FIG. 51. Magnified detail of serpentine creatures emanating from the ends of the initials *IN* opening the Gospel of Mark. Book of Kells. Dublin, Trinity College, MS 58, fol. 130r. Photo courtesy of the Board of Trinity College Dublin.

evangelists as writers receiving inspiration, these animal symbols hold open in the heavens books or rolls from which the evangelists copy, so that these scenes of inspiration—and authorization—involve a double manifestation of the divine, in the forms of the animal and of the writing. Insular scribal exegetes conflated these two manifestations by picturing the script of the Gospels as a writing *by* or *of* the various bodies—often all intertwined—of the Spirit.

To the modern reader, the tangled animal bodies that form the knot-writing of the Book of Kells, as for example in a series of intertwined lesser initials (fig. 49), tend to look monstrous, serpentine, and diabolical, more like a deadly trap and a representation of the Pauline "letter that kills" than like a representation of the mystical knots of allegory or of the Holy Spirit assuming physical, written form. On careful examination of the shapes of the "evangelist symbols," as for instance on the "evangelists page" of the ninth-century Macdurnan Gospels (fig. 50), we see that they are highly stylized, especially in the case of the frontal ox's head and the profiled lion's head. In the aforementioned tangle of Kells initials (fig. 49), it is not very difficult to identify the lions and eagles (one of which grasps a fish, symbol of Christ); but what should we make of the spotted serpentine creature with the curling horns directly below the fish? Would the stylized "ox" head of the Macdurnan Gospels' "evangelists page" not look rather like this if seen from above? Similarly, in the animate interlace emanating from the ends of a great letter *N* beginning the Gospel of Mark in the Book of Kells (fig. 51), the serpentine-looking creatures whose teardrop-shaped horns elongate into knotting patterns may be the Spirit-as-ox, seen from above, turning into the trace of writing.[69]

In ways that disorient a modern viewer, Insular scribal exegetes, who knew that how we identify and interpret something often depends on the angle or perspective from which we see it, deliberately changed and combined different perspectives (frontal, aerial, profile) in their pictorial representations, probably to suggest, as by the different colors and shapes of the figures of the letters, the complexity and *totality* of Scripture's meaning. The incongruities and "monstrous" forms of the animal bodies that make up or fill the bodies of the letters of eighth- and ninth-century Insular Gospels, just like the complexity of the knotwork designs they form, are obfuscations of the conventional forms of letters intended to hinder conventional, literalist reading, and to reveal—enigmatically, mysteriously—the presence of divinity incarnate in this writing, of the Spirit in the letter.[70]

# 4

# SACRED LETTERS AS
# DANGEROUS LETTERS
# AND READING
# AS STRUGGLE

That a written text does not merely represent or tell about the divine but *is* the divine, and also that the divinity residing in the text makes it dangerous when not treated with proper respect, were ideas already present in the Hebrew religion and further elaborated by medieval Christians. The tablets of the Ten Commandments written by God's hand, which Moses brought down from Mount Sinai, were enshrined in an elaborately designed ark, and accidental contact with even this enclosure of the divine word caused death. On one occasion, when the oxen drawing the ark stumbled and Uzzah grabbed at the ark to steady it, he was struck down for this sacrilegious contact (2 Samuel 6:6–7).[1] But it was not only the tablets of the law inscribed by God's own hand that participated in divinity; the Pentateuch and other biblical texts given to patriarchs and prophets through divine inspiration, when copied by human hands in ink on parchment in formal Hebrew letters (called "Assyrian"), were also considered to be filled with divine power so that they "defiled" the naked hand of anyone who touched them, and thus had to be handled with covered hands.[2] According to a third-century Jewish teaching, the casings, wrappings, straps, or thongs attached to these texts and in constant contact with them participated in their power to defile the hands (and presumably participated also in their divinity): "The thongs and straps which one sewed onto a book . . . impart defilement to hands. A container of books, and a box of books, and the wrappings of a book, so long as they are clean, impart defilement to hands."[3]

Martin Goodman has tried to suggest the general outlines of how these divine texts would have been handled in synagogue services in the first century A.D.: "A crowd of worshippers, perhaps after special ablutions, gathered at a special place or building. Psalms were probably chanted in praise of the deity. From an adjoining room or other hidden place was brought a chest. An object was reverently extracted from the chest and from its special wrappers, all present trying to avoid touching it directly. At the end of the ceremony [during which the scroll was read] the object was carried back to its hidden place."[4] Goodman goes on to suggest that, to all appearances, this Jewish religious service would have differed from contemporary pagan cults only in that the "object of reverence was neither the god nor a representation of the god, to which the sacrifices and libations were to be offered, but a scroll, whose sole function was to be read."[5] Goodman's own analysis might lead us to quibble with his use of the word "sole" here, for he suggests that the material object of Holy Scripture, the inscribed scroll, also functioned as an idol.[6]

In the Christian church, codices of the Holy Scriptures, often enshrined between covers of precious metal and jewels, were placed on the altar (or in Eastern Orthodox ritual, on an empty throne), and they were presented or received with veiled hands.[7] Used in this way, the divine writing of the Holy Scriptures was not merely an "emblematic portrayal of the divine presence" but a permanent trace or relic of that presence.[8] Indeed, Eastern defenders of religious images took the offensive against their Western critics in the late eighth century to point out that Westerners were turning a blind eye to their own adoration of Holy Scripture: "They say in effect that one must not worship anything made by human hands, as if the codex of the Gospels that they adore and kiss daily weren't made by human hands. Certainly, they cannot deny that a Gospel Lectionary is more venerable than a dog, which is not the work of human hands."[9] Scripture was the earthly manifestation of divinity; displayed on altar or throne, the codex of Holy Scripture functioned even more obviously as an "idol" than had the Hebrew scroll.[10]

The motif of veiled hands, suggesting the divinity present in the material object of the Holy Scriptures, appears as early as the end of the sixth or the beginning of the seventh century in a Syriac Bible. At the beginning of the Book of Proverbs, Wisdom is represented by three figures framed in a rectangle: King Solomon, holding a codex in his bare hand and making a didactic gesture; the incarnate Christ, whom the Virgin holds before her in an oval mandorla; and the Church, holding in her veiled left hand the codex of the Holy Scriptures with a cross on its cover.[11] This image represents the historical embodiments of divine wisdom through time, which the viewer can read from left to right along the horizontal axis running through the center of the picture; Christ's presence in the enlarged codex that Ecclesia bears, the Old Testament fulfilled by the New, is signaled by the cross on its cover and Ecclesia's veiled hand.

By the late seventh century, the motif of veiled hands appears in a Western manuscript, the famous Codex Amiatinus written at the monasteries of Wearmouth or Jarrow and taken by Abbot Ceolfrid to Italy for presentation to the pope. In a full-page frontispiece to the Gospels (fig. 52), Christ is represented "in Majesty": he is encircled and set off by a series of roundels representing heaven; he is haloed, enthroned, and flanked by angels; and he holds up a codex. Not only does Christ hold up a closed codex with his veiled left hand, but he gestures with his right, extending his first two fingers horizontally to point at the book. In the four corners of this same frontispiece, standing on ground lines that represent earthly existence, are the four evangelists, three of whom, like Christ, use the cloth of their outer garments to cover their hands as they hold up codices of the Gospels, while the fourth, John, holds his codex in his naked hand. It is unclear why John's hand should be uncovered, when even Christ-in-Majesty offers a respectful example and covers his hands to present the Gospels to the reader or viewer.

There is a nearly contemporary representation of the handling of Holy Scripture with veiled hands in the Lindisfarne Gospels, which, according to a colophon inscribed therein, "Eadfrith, bishop of Lindisfarne Church,

FIG. 52. Christ-in-Majesty frontispiece to the Gospels. Codex Amiatinus. Florence, Biblioteca Medicea Laurenziana, MS Laur. Amiatino I, fol. 796v. Photo by permission of the Ministero per i Beni Culturali e Ambientali.

FIG. 53. Matthew's inspiring angel holding a codex in his veiled hand. Lindisfarne Gospels. London, British Library, MS Cotton Nero D.IV, fol. 25v. Photo by permission of the British Library.

originally wrote . . . for God and for St. Cuthbert and—jointly—for all the saints whose relics are in the Island."[12] Eadfrith, who probably also directed the illuminations, prefaced the Gospel of Matthew with a full-page picture of the evangelist's inspiration. As a seated, haloed Matthew writes in a codex on his knee, directly over his head an angel labeled "imago hominis" blows a trumpet and holds in his veiled left hand a closed codex (fig. 53). This is an image of Matthew's inspiration by the Holy Ghost in the shape of a man, that is, of a trumpeting, book-holding angel. In the mid-eighth-century manuscript of the Gospels thought to have been made in Canterbury and known today as the Codex Aureus, the full-page depiction of Matthew's inspiration also shows the Spirit over the evangelist's head as a haloed angel holding up a closed codex with his draped left hand. (See fig. 54.) In the Lindisfarne Gospels, however, the Holy Spirit inspiring Matthew takes a second manly shape in addition to that of the book-holding angel. There has been much dispute over the identity of the bearded, haloed (but not cross-nimbed) figure who holds a book with a

FIG. 54. Matthew's inspiring angel holding a closed codex in his veiled hand. Codex Aureus of Stockholm. Stockholm, Kungliga Biblioteket, Codex Aureus MS A.135, fol. 9v. Photo courtesy of the Kungliga Biblioteket.

covered hand and whose bust seems to materialize from behind a drawn curtain, with no feet showing below (much as the angel's torso materializes from behind Matthew's halo). Perhaps the figure is Christ—the face of divinity revealed—who was depicted as bearded and holding a codex in his veiled hand also in the Christ-in-Majesty frontispiece to the Gospels of the contemporary Codex Amiatinus (fig. 52).[13]

It may seem paradoxical that Christ or the Holy Ghost should present the Holy Scriptures with covered hands—for how can divinity be defiled by contact with divine presence? Surely their veiled hands cannot be meant to protect them from defilement, but rather to serve as a sign of awe and respect that both identifies the codex so handled as Holy Scripture and suggests a hierarchy of sacredness, with priority given to the written Word. Held by divine figures with respectfully covered hands in heavenly spaces, the divine prototype of Scripture extant "from the beginning" seems even more holy than its bearers or than its inspired copy, made by the naked hand of the evangelist-scribe. The heavenly, preexisting Word is power-

FIG. 55. Inspired evangelist holding
with a covered hand the Gospel
codex he writes. Maaseik, Belgium,
Church of Saint Catherine, Codex
Eyckensis A, fol. IV. Photo
Museactron, Maaseik.

fully valorized—even "idolized"—when Christ enthroned in Majesty is
represented holding up the codex of the Scriptures with a covered hand.

Although most early Insular images of the divine inspiration of an evangelist show the evangelist-scribe touching with naked hands the book or
scroll he inscribes or holds up, there are examples of evangelists who take
divine dictation more respectfully (and unrealistically) by covering the
hand with which they hold the book in the act of writing. This is the case,
for example, in a full-page illustration of the inspiration of an unidentified
evangelist that would have prefaced his Gospel in a now fragmentary codex of the Gospels probably made in northern England in the early eighth
century (fig. 55). The haloed scribe's wide-eyed stare suggests he is seeing
and hearing a text invisible to us and copying this into the open codex he
holds with his veiled left hand. In the roundels at the top of the arches of
the canon tables prefacing this same Gospel Book, busts of the evangelists
and of their spiritual symbols (lion, calf, eagle, man) all hold codices with
covered hands. Whereas the evangelists make gestures of admonition with

FIG. 56. Historiated initial with a religious figure holding a codex in his veiled hand. Saint Petersburg, National Library of Russia, Cod. Q.v.I.18, fol. 26v. Photo courtesy of the National Library of Russia.

their free hands, which are bare, the animal symbols of their inspiration hold codices with both paws, hands, claws, or hooves covered.[14]

The motif of veiled hands appears also in what has been thought to be one of the earliest surviving historiated initials, that is, an initial enclosing an illustration of a person or event mentioned in the adjacent text. In an early manuscript of Bede's *Historia ecclesiastica* made at the monasteries of Wearmouth or Jarrow in about 746, the letter *H* beginning the second book of Bede's history contains a haloed, half-length human figure bearing a cross in his right hand and holding up a codex in his veiled left hand (fig. 56). He has a very short beard and appears to be wearing a kind of skullcap. The identification "Augustinus" written on this figure's halo is a later addition reinterpreting the figure, who was probably meant to represent Pope Gregory, the end of whose life is the subject of the beginning of Bede's second book. The saintly figure within the letter handles and controls two extremely powerful forces for saving souls and fighting demons: the cross and the Word. Christ bears these same two objects in an early scene of the Last Judgment.[15] Gregory's covered hand, like that of Christ, signals the identity of the codex as *Holy* Scripture and signals its power.

In all of the examples so far discussed, divine or holy figures (Christ, saints, evangelists) present Scripture, either to us as readers or to other figures in the same pictorial space, with covered hands. There is, however, a famous mid-ninth-century example of somewhat more ordinary people veiling their hands to present a Bible. At the end of the large Carolingian Bible long known to art historians as the Vivian Bible, there is a full-page image of the Bible's presentation to Charles the Bald, who sits enthroned in

FIG. 57. Monk with covered hands presents the Bible to Charles the Bald. First Bible of Charles the Bald. Paris, B.N.F., MS lat. 1, fol. 423r. Photo Bibliothèque nationale de France.

the upper register under a hand of God.[16] While the heavenly hand streams down golden rays of divine sanction upon him, Charles himself gestures acceptance of the large codex, which three tonsured monks hold out to him with veiled hands (fig. 57). The presentation of this Bible to Charles is accepted also, with a hand gesture similar to that of Charles, by an untonsured figure on the right: Count Vivian, the lay abbot of Saint-Martin-de-Tours.[17] To offer Charles a codex filled with the divine presence is to invest him, just as the heavenly hand does, with power. (If we were to imagine this scene a few seconds later, with Charles still enthroned in the upper register and now holding the codex, it would echo representations of Christ-in-Majesty.) In these early representations, Holy Scripture is nearly always depicted in the veiled hands of those who are holy themselves, never in the hands of laymen. Contact with Scripture, as the veiled hands suggest, was not to be taken lightly.

The power of Holy Scripture and the potential danger of physical contact with it—even visual contact[18]—was also suggested by images, usually at the symbolic "thresholds" of the text, its points of entry: awesomely designed cover pages and initial letters. E. H. Gombrich has proposed that, in general, interlace, knotwork, mazes, tangles, and other figures of "indeterminability" depicted on objects may be a kind of "protective animation . . . endowing artefacts with the potential to ward off evil" because they are impossible to grasp visually—in effect, impenetrable. Gombrich goes on to speculate about the apotropaic function of animated knotwork:

> If it could be shown that there also exists a widespread disposition to attribute to hostile powers a dread of confusion and indeterminacy, we would come closer to an interpretation of the tangled dragons of Northern art. . . . The "dragon tangle" can best be understood as an animated interlace. The ribbons or ropes are endowed with heads and are thus seen to twine and writhe, sometimes "tying themselves into knots." Maybe this combination offered another source of protection. Able to resist disentanglement by evil eyes and filled with dragon power, the fabulous beasts are yet held in the maze of their own making.[19]

Other art historians have applied this general theory of protective animation to images covering books. Lawrence Nees, for example, notes: "[C]onsiderable evidence indicates that in the late antique and early medieval period the images both outside and just inside of books could also serve a more profound function, being designed to protect the sacred book against demonic penetration."[20] In elaborating on the apotropaic function, Jürgen Gutbrod has called attention to the way in which monstrous figures are incorporated into and made to "serve" the initial letters of Holy Scripture: "With the help of visualization, with the sign of the cross and the sacred word, evil was forced into service of the holy and made to assume the form of a letter. The meaning of this confrontation of the unholy with the holy text in manuscripts cannot be emphasized enough, for the power that inhabits the word in the Middle Ages is to be grasped herein. For the understanding of the initial, this point of view is of the greatest importance."[21]

Protective, apotropaic animation is usually thought to be addressed to evil spirits or evil eyes. This notion would seem to be too reductive when applied to the figurative animation of cover pages and initials of holy texts, which awe the mortal, human viewer as well. Perhaps it would be more accurate to say that such protective animation is a warning addressed to the evil intentions—or the potential sinner—in any viewer. Holy texts such as the Lindisfarne Gospels were made "for" saints and were to be handled and read not by just any layperson or monk but only by the initiated, the priestly class, in liturgical contexts, with ritual precaution.

It was not only depictions of knots and interlace that served to empower the codex to fend off evil spirits, according to Nees, but also, and especially, the figures of the cross and of the four evangelists.[22] This is one reason they appear on elaborately designed outer covers or cases like the eighth-century Lough Kinale and the eleventh-century Soiscél Molaise book shrines[23] and on cover pages of early biblical texts, such as a cover page of the Book of Durrow (fig. 58) or of the ninth-century Macdurnan Gospels (fig. 50), with their interlace-filled crosses in the center and "evangelist symbols" in each of the four quadrants.[24] The wonderfully elaborate animated knotwork designs surrounding and filling the various cross patterns of the so-called carpet pages preceding and covering each Gospel text in the Lindisfarne Gospels (fig. 39), as also in those of Lichfield, might also be perceived as powerfully indeterminate or enigmatic figures threatening to ensnare the overbold, announcing the danger of trying to penetrate such a text—in short, making it seem "sacred."

The knotwork of seventh- through ninth-century Insular Gospels is an adaptation to manuscript pages of the snake-dragons and animated interlace conventional in secular metalwork. Yet as I have argued in chapter 3, Insular artists reinterpreted and Christianized the old secular motif, tried to harness it to empower Christian writing. They present us with a text that literally "contains" and transforms demonic forces into Spirit. With relatively few changes of detail—here and there an emergent claw, talon, horn—they turned intertwining snake-dragons into the highly stylized bodily traces of the "evangelist symbols" (man, eagle, calf, lion), which might more properly be called symbols of the Holy Spirit. Understood in this way, the dangerous power of fascination demonstrated by such animate knotwork is no longer diabolical but divine. The viewer is faced with a manifestation of the power of the Holy Spirit.

One might say that illuminated Insular Gospel books "fight demons" quite demonstratively in the way they tie the pagan, diabolical figures of snake-dragons and other serpentine forms into knots and contain them by and train them into the shapes of letters of Holy Scripture. The spiritual-

FIG. 58. Cover page with an interlaced cross flanked by evangelists. Book of Durrow. Dublin, Trinity College, MS 57, fol. 2r. Photo courtesy of the Board of Trinity College Dublin.

ization of pagan forms is complete if we see these living letters not as coiling, struggling snake-dragons but as the Spirit—in the forms of lion, eagle, calf, or man—motivating and "becoming" Scripture. It is doubtful, however, even in the case of Gospel books, much less Psalters and other collections of religious texts, whether viewers would take this further interpretive step. Highly stylized and ribbonized though they may be, the intertwining bodies of predatory beasts locked in struggle (even with men, from the turn of the ninth century on) and seeming to devour or strangle one another are quite hard to spiritualize entirely; so the impression remains of diabolical forces held in check by Holy Scripture, contained within and trained into the shapes of letters, but not entirely transformed.

This is the effect of the large initials on the opening page of the Gospel of Mark in the Book of Kells (fig. 59). The great, semiattached letters *INI* tightly contain within their cloisonné-like compartments various stylized, struggling birds and beasts of prey, which spill out the ends of these same letters into loose, patterned knots that serve as finials to finish or close the letters. But in the upper-right-hand corner of this page is a troubling image of predation. The figure of a man, with interlace patterns filling his legs and torso, is caught in the jaws of a lionish creature whose "body" is the abstract border filled with stylized, interlaced predators. The man pulls the tongue of the lion with an arm that weaves through the lion's head, while he pulls at the knotwork pattern of his own beard with his other hand, and his legs weave through the "neck" of the lion. The meaning of this border scene is far from clear. Can the lionish creature be the lion of Mark, symbol of the evangelist's divine inspiration, thus an image of the evangelist in the "grip" of inspiration? Even if intended as a depiction of the divine motivation of the trace of Scripture, this image of a human figure in the maw of a lionish beast may also suggest diabolical assault, and the dangers that the first words of the Gospels, in particular, were supposed to protect against. Seen in this light, the much enlarged initials *INI*, like the following *TI* combined into a cross, are as if brandished (like a monstrance) in the face of the devil. These initials demonstrate their control of predatory forces both by compressing them into geometrical compartments and patterned finials and by capitalizing on the apotropaic power of fascination—the threat of visual ensnarement—raised by labyrinthian interlace.

Figurative representations of entanglement and struggle incorporated into the initial letters through which the reader/viewer must "enter" the different sections of many Insular and northern Continental Gospels,

FIG. 59. Opening page of Mark's Gospel, with a man and a lionlike beast interlocked in struggle (*upper right*). Book of Kells. Dublin, Trinity College, MS 58, fol. 130r. Photo courtesy of the Board of Trinity College Dublin.

Psalters, prayerbooks, and other compendia of holy texts from the eighth through the twelfth centuries not only animate and empower these letters, but they may also suggest the difficulties—even the dangers—of approaching Holy Scripture.[25] Reading the Scriptures, like handling them, was challenging—and the same might be said of copying them, which involved both handling and reading.

Cassiodorus set the tone when he wrote that "each word of God, calligraphed by the scribe, is a wound inflicted on Satan."[26] To copy the divine word was to do battle with the devil; likewise, to read it (which involved pronouncing the words). This is why, in representations of the conquest of the devil, the victor may hold up a codex representing Scripture (and the reading or other active uses of it) as one of the forces whereby the devil is vanquished. In a long series of Psalter illuminations representing Christ trampling on the lion and asp—from the Carolingian Stuttgart and Utrecht Psalters to the eleventh-century Insular and northern Continental Bury Saint Edmunds, Crowland, Tiberius, and Winchcombe Psalters— Christ holds up an open codex, presumably a Psalter, in his free hand, while at the same time treading underfoot the diabolical beasts and stabbing them with a crosier topped by a cross.[27]

Along with the Gospels, it was the reading and recitation of the Psalter that was believed to engage the devil most fiercely of all biblical texts. We know this in part from the evidence of surviving Anglo-Saxon charms, wherein certain psalms and the openings of the Gospels were pronounced or written, in conjunction with other measures, to drive away the diabolical forces that caused illnesses. For example, in a collection of medical charms in the eleventh-century manuscript known as the Lacnunga Book, there is a recipe for a "holy drink against tricks of elves and against every temptation of the fiend." The complex recipe begins with writing on a paten (the plate upon which bread is transformed into the real body of Christ through the religious ritual of the mass). To be inscribed on the paten are several Gospel texts, beginning with John 1:1, "In principio erat verbum," and three of the prayer psalms: "Deus in nomine tuo salvum me fac" (53:3, O God, save me in thy name), "Deus misereatur nobis" (66:2, God have mercy upon us), and "Domine deus in adjutorium" (a variant of 69:2, the "lorica"). These texts are supposed to be washed from the paten into a drink composed of herbs and consecrated wine, which is then rendered even more potent by having masses sung over it, as well as other prayers and precatory charms (chiefly psalms), before finally being imbibed.[28]

The Psalter's power against diabolical forces is also testified to by early Christian writers. Already in the sixth century, the Greek John Moschus reported the following advice from Abbot Marcel of Scete to his monks: "Believe me, sons, nothing so disturbs, arouses, annoys, wounds, destroys, saddens and arouses against us the demons and Satan, that author of perdition, as continual meditation on the psalms. In effect, all of holy scripture torments the demons, but nothing torments them like the psalter."[29] The abbot went on to explain why this is so—"For when we meditate upon the psalms, we pray for ourselves on the one hand, and on the other we curse the demons"—and he concluded by citing several especially tormenting psalms, such as 7:16–17, "He has made a pit and dug it deep, / and he himself shall fall into the hole that he has made. / His mischief shall recoil upon himself, / and his violence fall on his own head."[30]

Indeed, early medieval Psalters were often prefaced by a text—the *Dicti Sancti Augustini,* erroneously ascribed to Augustine—that presented the singing of psalms as a highly effective way of fighting and defeating Satan: "The singing of psalms . . . drives out demons. It disperses shadows. . . . It exposes the Lord and offends the Devil and extinguishes illicit desire. . . . It destroys evil. . . . It is solicitude from all vices. Daily it is the good battle. It tears out the root of all evil, just as the breastplate covers, just as the helmet defends. . . . He who loves singing psalms zealously cannot sin."[31] Certain psalms were perceived as having even more protective power than others, as for example the cry for divine aid of Psalm 69:2 ("Deus in adiutorium meum intende"; "O God, make haste to help me"), which became known in the Insular church as the "lorica" or impenetrable "breastplate."[32] Already in the fifth century, Cassian recommended the constant internal repetition of this psalm for its prophylactic effect: "Meditate on it, never stop turning it over within your breast. Whatever work or ministry you are undertaking, go on praying it. While you are going to sleep, or eating, or in the last necessities of nature, think on it. It will be a saving formula in your heart, will guard you from the attacks of demons."[33]

Given the power over diabolical forces ascribed to the Psalter, it is not surprising that copying the Psalter was a favorite form of monastic penance in the Insular world. For example, the Irish abbot of Ratisbon, Marianus Scottus, who died in 1088, is reported as having written "many portable Psalters for poor widows and clerics . . . for the good of his soul."[34] The abbot was presumably writing not only as his own personal penance or spiritual battle against sin but also to give others, the recipients of his Psalter copies, a powerful weapon with which they in turn might engage the devil. For this very reason, the Psalter was the most common "private" devotional manual at this time, only later to be replaced by Books of Hours.

As we shall see, monstrous figures of the demonic are, for the most part, held at bay and relegated to the blank or open spaces surrounding the holy text in fourteenth-century Books of Hours, thus demonstrating the danger of distraction from—or of not reading—the holy letters. In the earlier Psalters, however, figures of the demonic are entangled with the very shapes of Holy Scripture in the initials whereby the reader "enters" the text, which suggests that the locus of struggle with sin is the very act of reading and performing the letters and words of the Psalter.[35] From about the ninth century, the figural shapes of initial letters of the Psalter included human forms doing battle with or trying to escape from the jaws of monstrous beasts or from the ensnaring tendrils of the letter. In ways the reader might identify with through the human forms involved, such initials figuratively dramatized the struggle involved in the "spiritual battle" of reading this particular text, a struggle against the devil *also* in the form of the "letter" of carnal or literalist understanding.

This is the point of an initial *N* in the early ninth-century Corbie Psalter, whose innovative scribal exegete has left us what may be one of the first surviving examples of an initial dramatizing the "spiritual battle" of reading Scripture (fig. 60). The outlines of the letters *No* are greatly obfuscated by the fact that they are formed by struggling animal and human shapes: a lion, a dragon, and a warrior form the three strokes of the initial *N,* and the warrior's round shield forms the following letter *o.* The lion and dragon are conventional figures for the devil; these are the creatures Christ tramples underfoot with such apparent ease while holding up an open text of the Psalter in the aforementioned Insular and northern Continental Psalters. But in the Corbie initial, the warrior is having a harder time of it. Al-

FIG. 60. Initial *N* as a man fighting beasts. Corbie Psalter. Amiens, Bibliothèque municipale, MS 18, fol. 67r. Photo Bibliothèque municipale d'Amiens.

though the lion and dragon are locked in struggle, biting each other's necks, the dragon's serpentine tail coils around and ensnares one of the legs of the fleeing warrior, who has turned his back on the beasts and tries to free himself by raising his sword to strike the dragon. The warrior may represent David (who was understood as a figure for Christ and was often depicted in Psalter illumination fighting against the devil in the forms of a lion or of the giant Goliath). However, the medievalized attire of the Corbie Psalter's warrior, as well as the direction of his movement, suggests that he may also serve as a figure for the Christian reader, that is, a figure with whom the reader may identify. Although he has turned his attention momentarily to freeing himself from diabolical forces, this warrior-reader is clearly trying to "put the devil behind him" in his movement toward or into the text. This initial *N* shows that the point of textual entry is a difficult one, but the following letter of the psalm, the *o,* is depicted as a shield.

Paradoxically, the initials of the sacred text are pictured as sites of both peril and protection. The reader as warrior cannot enter the text without battling the demonic forces of the "letter" that try to entangle him, but he is provided with the offensive weapon of his sharp sword and the defensive ones of helmet and shield.

The initial letter is made up of figures representing opposed forces, both of which may illustrate early medieval understandings of Pauline doctrine. In his famous extended metaphor of the Christian as warrior in Ephesians 6:13–17, Paul urged Christians to fight the devil with the shield of faith and the "sword of the Spirit," which he explained as "the word of God": "Therefore take unto you the armour of God, that you may be able to resist in the evil day, and to stand in all things perfect. Stand therefore, having your loins girt about with truth, and having on the breastplate of justice. And your feet shod with the preparation of the gospel of peace: And in all things taking the shield of faith, wherewith you may be able to extinguish all the fiery darts of the most wicked one. And take unto you the helmet of salvation, and the sword of the Spirit (which is the word of God)." In his Epistle to the Hebrews 4:12, Paul again compared God's word to a sword: "The Word of God is alive and active. It cuts more keenly than any two-edged sword."[36] As we have seen from their martial metaphors and images of psalms as offensive weapons and protective armor (such as the impenetrable breastplate or lorica of Psalm 69:2), early medieval monks used the word of God in the way Paul had recommended, that is, as a spiritual sword (rather than a material one) to fight diabolical forces.

The spiritual sword of the word of God, in Paul's and later interpreters' understanding, was not so much the literal words of Scripture as their spiritual sense as revealed to Christian interpreters by the Holy Spirit. For example, rather than understanding the Book of Psalms objectively as a historical text spoken by and referring to the life of David or Solomon, Christian interpreters from as early as Tertullian rejected a literalist reading in favor of a spiritual one, understanding David as a figure for Christ. Jerome explained that David sang the psalms in the role of Christ or the church or of a prophet.[37] Surviving interpretive rubrics (*tituli psalmorum*) in medieval Latin manuscripts of the Psalter from the eighth through the twelfth centuries, rubrics that function rather like modern stage directions to clarify which character speaks a particular part, show that medieval Christians understood the psalms to be sung largely in the voice—or persona—of Christ.[38] Furthermore, the medieval Christian performed the psalms in a highly subjective manner, identifying with Christ, and praying for his own deliverance through Christ's prayers of supplication to God-the-Father.[39]

The Pauline "sword of the Spirit" was not just a metaphorical sword as opposed to a material one, the word of God used as a "weapon" against diabolical forces; the "sword of the Spirit" was also the trenchant, spiritualizing interpretation that cut through the "killing letter" of Old Testament texts to liberate their spiritual sense. The maker of the Corbie Psalter initial under consideration (fig. 60) adapted Paul's figurative description of the Christian's battle against diabolical forces to the act of reading or performing the Psalter, which he depicted as a wielding of the sword (of the Spirit) against ferocious beasts (the killing letter of a carnal, literalist understanding) that would ensnare the warrior.

One might object that the human figure in this initial *N* is just as much a part of the letter as the beasts he fights. This is true; the human interpreter is part of the carnal world from whose "coils" he struggles to free himself. Significantly, it is the warrior's lower body, his leg, that is caught in the serpentine grip of the dragon's tail. Only the warrior's sword, raised on high, "surpasses" the letter by exceeding the bounds of the conventional shape of a letter *N*. With the sword of spiritual understanding, which surpasses the letter, the warrior-reader of the psalms must free himself from carnal, literalist understanding.

Like earlier Christian illuminators, the maker of this initial animated the letter with pictorial figures that serve to reveal the spiritual sense of the text. However, rather than simply suggesting the divinity immanent in the letter (by picturing a letter as a combination of doves and fish, for example), the pictorial figures of this Corbie Psalter initial suggest that the letter is a site of struggle between diabolical and spiritual forces. Indeed, such figures may suggest that the letter itself can be dangerous if not handled properly, that is, if not surpassed through spiritualizing interpretation.

In another Corbie Psalter initial representing the letter as a locus of struggle between spiritual and diabolical forces—David conquering Goli-

FIG. 61. Initial *P* as David slaying Goliath. Corbie Psalter. Amiens, Bibliothèque municipale, MS 18, fol. 123v. Photo Bibliothèque municipale d'Amiens.

ath with a stone from his sling—it may be significant that there is a visual equivalence between the shape of the letter and of the diabolical force (fig. 61). The upright of the letter *P* is also the body of the giant, while the figure of David moves freely in front of the loop of the letter, using the letter as a backdrop rather than being incorporated into it. The hand of God, which gives David the victory, violates rather than conforms to the shape of the letter. Finally, the small winged spirit escaping above Goliath's head at the moment the stone kills him is also free of the shape of the letter. In his combat with Goliath, David represents both Christ defeating the devil and the reader's spiritual battle against diabolical forces in general, and more specifically in the guise of the "letter" of the psalm text. Just as David slays Goliath and frees the tiny winged spirit, so the Christian reader engaged in spiritual combat overcomes the "letter" or literal sense of the psalm text to liberate its spiritual sense. The instrument with which David overcomes Goliath in this Corbie initial is not the "sword of the Spirit" but rather his slingshot. In initials from other Psalters, illuminators found a way to include the symbolic sword by depicting a later moment in the combat, the instant when David cuts off Goliath's head with his sword.

The spiritual combat to read texts other than the Psalter in a Christian way was also depicted in initial letters down through the twelfth century. For example, in a twelfth-century Latin manuscript from Canterbury of the Old Testament history of the first-century Jewish historian Josephus, there is a complex, embodied initial *A* depicting the combat of a man with a sword against the diabolical forces of a lion and a dragon (fig. 62). All the strokes of the letter are replaced by animated figures—even its crossbar, which is formed by the warrior's swordstroke penetrating the lion's belly. As in the Corbie Psalter initial created three centuries earlier, the warrior's lower body is most vulnerable. The lion claws him on the back as he encircles it with one arm, and the bare flesh of his leg is caught in the grip of the dragon's teeth, while a frond of its foliate tail ensnares the same leg. Nevertheless, the spiritual forces seem to have the upper hand, for the warrior's ensnared leg treads on the dragon, and his sword thrust has forced the lion to regurgitate, at the very apex of the *A,* a naked feminine body that probably represents a soul (Eve?), who grips by the claws a tiny dragon. On one level, then, we can understand this scene as a representation of Christ conquering the devil.[40]

The warrior saves not only the regurgitated soul but also the small man at the bottom right being crushed under the weight of the lion (just as the dragon is being crushed under the foot of the warrior). This little man looks back up over his shoulder at the combat, while at the same time moving toward and pointing with his outstretched index finger at the text of Hebrew history at hand. The direction of the warrior's gaze and the sword that pierces the lion's body and comes out between two lines of writing both serve to point our attention to the text. In addition to evoking Christ as Savior, the warrior may be a figure for the reader, a figure doubled by that of the more humble little man making his move toward the text. The import of the initial would seem to be that the Christian reader can escape the diabolical forces of the literal, carnal sense of the text by using the sword of the Spirit, that is, by spiritualizing and Christianizing the sense of Josephus's history. Reading the *Jewish Antiquities,* like reading the Psalter and other Old Testament texts, is spiritual combat.

FIG. 62. Initial *A* as struggle between man and beast. Canterbury Josephus codex. Cambridge University Library, MS Dd.1.4., fol. 220r. Photo by permission of the Syndics of Cambridge University Library.

Expanding on Paul's warnings of the mortal dangers of literalist reading ("the letter killeth"), Augustine explained in *On Christian Doctrine* that literal interpretation of Scripture is an enslavement to the flesh that kills the soul by reducing human intelligence to a bestial level: "That is, when that which is said figuratively is taken as though it were literal, it is understood carnally. Nor can anything more appropriately be called the death of the soul than that condition in which the thing which distinguishes us from

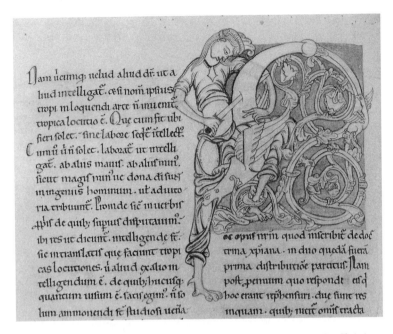

FIG. 63. Initial *H* as struggle between man and monster. Augustine, *On Christian Doctrine*. Cambrai, Bibliothèque municipale, MS 559, fol. 40v. Photo courtesy of the Centre culturel de Cambrai.

beasts, which is the understanding, is subjected to the flesh in the pursuit of the letter."[41] The problem of the reader's implication in the carnal world of the letter is suggested by an initial *H* introducing the fourth book of *On Christian Doctrine* in a twelfth-century manuscript (fig. 63). Here the human figure forms the symbolic upright of the initial, while the dragon's body forms the curves of the letter, and its tail sprouts into tortuous foliate coils.

The weakness of the "flesh" of the human figure is emphasized by his bared stomach and leg, which is being bitten at the knee by a dragon, while the other ankle is caught in the coils of the dragon's tail. Even more telling, this human figure, whose attention is entirely engaged by the body of the dragon, puts one arm around and "embraces" the dragon in the act of struggling against and piercing it with his sword, and he himself—as a result of the dragon's bite?—has diabolical claws and spurs instead of feet. The human figure's lower body is very much part of the carnal world against which he struggles by piercing the dragon with his sword, which seems to liberate from the coils of the dragon's tail the small bird (a dove figuring the Spirit?) that flies away to the right while looking back at the struggle. As a depiction of successful spiritual combat against the carnality of the letter, this image is almost more frightening than reassuring. What reader would be comfortable identifying with a spiritual warrior whose feet have turned to claws?[42]

In an earlier chapter we saw how vegetal embodiments and excrescences of initial letters, such as the golden vines enwrapping and knotting about the initials of the Drogo Sacramentary (figs. 34 and 36), suggested their spiritual life, or, more precisely, Christ's presence in the vine of the letter. The tendrils of such letters do not seem dangerous, as do the tentacular coils that impede and ensnare both human and bestial figures in some initials of religious manuscripts made in Normandy and Anglo-Norman England in the late eleventh and twelfth centuries.[43] Indeed, the foliage that sprouts from the bestial bodies making up these initials may represent folly (or sin), a visual equivalence based on a verbal one, the "serious" pun on the similar sounds of the Old French or Anglo-Norman nouns for "leaf" and "folly" and the verbs for "to sprout leaves" and "to act foolishly, or to mock or befool someone."[44]

In some twelfth-century Insular and northern Continental initials, foliage takes over the letter and begins to make it look like a leafy labyrinth, within or against which the spiritual combat takes place. For example, the "Beatus vir" page of one twelfth-century Psalter presents, within the upper and lower loops of the initial *B*, two scenes of combat (above, David forcing open the lion's mouth with his bare hands; below, David killing Goliath with his slingshot) (color plate 8). Figuratively, these two combats represent the spiritual struggle of psalmody. In the previously discussed initials *A* and *H* (figs. 62 and 63), the ensnaring foliage is an exuberant, luxuriant outgrowth of the tail of the dragon; in the *B* of this Psalter, however, the origin of the vines that both form and fill the frame of the letter is less clear. Perhaps they may be seen as originating in the monstrous mask that joins the upper and lower loops of the *B*,[45] in which case it is the forked tongue of the monster and its two horns that sprout into foliage and fill the loops of the *B* with a dense jungle forming the immediate context for the scenes of spiritual combat. In the upper loop neither David nor the lion seems to be hindered by ensnaring vegetation, but in the lower one Goliath's body is interwoven through the coils of the vine, while David is relatively unimpeded in his attack, merely stepping over one branch.

Although their tropes do not find pictorial expression in manuscripts of Scripture or its exegesis until centuries after their invention, Biblical exegetes from Origen on had imagined themselves as heroic hunters who chased in the "dense woods" of Scripture.[46] The "dense woods," the tangle of seemingly impenetrable vegetation and innumerable branchings, was another image, along with the labyrinth[47] and the knot, that figured the enormous complexity of Scripture and did so in a way that made reading and interpreting it seem to be a very challenging—even dangerous—activity.

To "surmount" the letter is a visual metaphor for victory in the struggle to achieve spiritual understanding.[48] This is the sense depicted on a full page of the early eleventh-century Pericope Book from Reichenau, where a man scales the upright of an initial *I* (fig. 64).[49] It would seem to be the sense of the human activity figured in many eleventh- and twelfth-century Insular and northern Continental "clambering initials" (Dodwell's term), in which human figures struggle to make their way upward through the coils filling the framework of the uprights or the loops of initial letters depicted as flourishing vines.[50] The degree of the human figure's entanglement in the coils of the letter tends to suggest the difficulties of "overcoming" the snares of the literal. For example, in an initial *G* from a manuscript of Augustine's *City of God,* two human figures within the letter exemplify different degrees of success in dealing with it (fig. 65). The figure at the bottom gazes toward the text while gripping a large, vined coil of the letter with both hands. His legs, spread wide as if he might be trying to jump through the hoops of the coil, are in fact interwoven through the spiral, so that it is not at all clear what his activity can accomplish. He appears to be caught in the letter's coils. On the other hand, a leaping human figure above him seems to move much more freely, his legs unobstructed by the coiled tendril of the letter (which if anything offers his foot temporary support), so that he has managed to catch a fish in one hand and a bird in another (symbols of Christ and the Spirit?), both depicted as above and

FIG. 64. Initial *I* scaled by a man.
Pericope Book. Wolfenbüttel, Herzog
August Bibliothek, Cod. Guelf. 84.5
Aug.2, fol. 41r. Photo courtesy of the
Herzog August Bibliothek.

outside the confines of the letter. In his upward course, this leaping figure keeps his eyes fixed on the text inscribed above him. A hunter successful despite the dense woods, a "clambering" figure who leaps gracefully upward, this little man may well evoke the Christian reader who is successful in avoiding the snares of the letter, successful in spiritual combat.

The initials whereby the reader entered Scripture were by no means always depicted as potential snares, even in twelfth-century Insular Psalters. For example, on the "Beatus vir" page of the Saint Albans Psalter from around 1123, the great initial *B* serves as a stage or backdrop before which the enthroned figure of King David receives the words and music of the Psalter via divine inspiration, represented by the huge dove poking its beak into his ear as he plays the psaltery with one hand and with the other holds up a codex inscribed with the words "Annunciationem sancti spiritus eructavit beatus david psalmista quem deus elegit" (The blessed psalmist David, whom God chose, poured forth the Annunciation of the Holy Spirit) (fig. 66). The inspired psalmist performs effortlessly, for he is a mere

FIG. 65. Initial *G* with one man entangled in the letter (*below*) and another surmounting it to catch a fish and a dove (*above*). Augustine, *City of God*. Florence, Biblioteca Medicea Laurenziana, MS Plut.12.17, fol. 5r. Photo courtesy of the Biblioteca Medicea Laurenziana.

conduit of the divine. On this page the idea of psalmody as spiritual combat is quite literally relegated to the margins.[51] In the upper right, completely separate from the initial letter, there is a drawing of two knights on horseback engaged in battle. A lengthy Latin marginal commentary by the illuminator explains this image as a figurative representation—to be understood by the eyes of the heart, that is, spiritually—of the battle against diabolical forces engaged by cloistered souls.[52] The knights' swords and lances are explained as the spiritual weapons of Christian faith and hope (and not, as Paul had done, in his image of the Christian warrior, as the "word of God" itself). Knightly combat here replaces earlier imagery of fighting or hunting diabolical creatures (such as the lion, dragon, or Goliath) and of avoiding ensnarement in the tendrils of the letter.[53]

From the mid-twelfth century on, in Psalters and prayerbooks made for pious laypeople, and made increasingly outside monastic scriptoria, figures of danger and struggle—of combat, pursuit, ensnarement, fascination, and folly or sin—were located *outside* the letter, in the margins of the page

FIG. 66. "Beatus vir" page. Saint Albans Psalter. Hildesheim, Saint Godehard's Church, fol. 36v. Photo courtesy of the Warburg Institute.

surrounding the text or in the blank spaces at the ends of lines.[54] The initial letter came to be depicted as a site of order, hierarchy, and stable authority, while struggle was marginalized. The spiritual was ever more clearly separated from the carnal or worldly, with the margins becoming the site of the "danger" of mundane distractions.

For example, in the late thirteenth-century combined Psalter and Book of Hours[55] made for Yolande of Soissons (fig. 67), the initial *D* has been tamed and regularized. There is nothing awesome or fearful about this letter. Framed by a square against a square, colored ground, the initial itself acts as a round frame through which we see the scene of Pentecost, with the dove of the Holy Spirit descending to the aid of the Virgin and Christ's disciples, who stand and gaze upward with dignified hand gestures of acknowledgement. The scene can be taken in and identified at a glance and does not require the reader to track down the figures in an interwoven space. This clear view of divine intervention, seen through the letter, accompanies the prayer for divine aid once known as the impenetrable breastplate or lorica: "Deus in adiutorium meum intende" (O God, make haste to help me). Whereas earlier monastic Psalter initials depicted the letter as a site of struggle between spiritual and diabolical forces (and thus suggested that reading and performing psalms—and especially the lorica—were a way of fighting off the devil), this initial from a Psalter made for a secular noblewoman depicts an act of grace happening within the letter (and would seem to suggest a much less problematic notion of what it means to read and perform psalms or other religious texts).

In Yolande of Soissons's Book of Hours, reading the text presents no danger, which arises instead from distraction, from letting one's eyes wander to the borders of the page.[56] Here, in the margins of the page, we risk visual and mental ensnarement. We may be fascinated by the equivocal incongruities, impossible to resolve into any one natural shape, of a series of chimerical creatures composed of different body parts of birds and beasts, one with two different bodies to a single head, another with two heads to a single body.[57] It is impossible, for example, to identify or attach a name for any natural bird we know to the avian creature in the right margin, which has webbed feet, a falconlike body, bat wings, and two almost vulturelike heads on two thin necks. The same is true of the composite creature nose

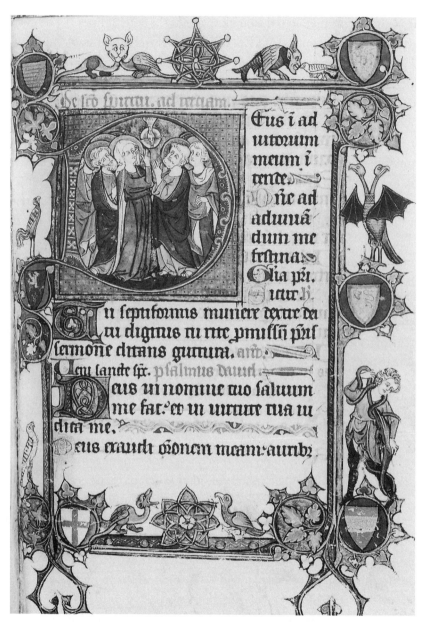

FIG. 67. Initial *D* historiated with a scene of Pentecost; dove and chimera nose to nose (*upper right*); man entangled in the knots of a serpentine dragon (*lower right*). Psalter of Yolande of Soissons. New York, The Pierpont Morgan Library, M. 729, fol. 273r. Photo courtesy of The Pierpont Morgan Library.

to nose with a small bird in the upper right margin. Shall we call it a satyr because it has a man's face with a goat's horns and cloven hooves? But this would ignore the fact that the creature has the torso and tail of a fish and the wings of a bird. There is no way to resolve the permanent, formal equivocation of such creatures, which makes them traps for the eye and mind.

In addition to figures of indeterminability that work to ensnare our attention, there is a figure of entanglement in the lower right margin of this Psalter page, where a man struggles to free himself from the serpentine coils of a winged dragon wrapped around his neck, both arms, and one leg. Were it not for the thickening of the dragon's body and the hint of folded wings at the level of the man's waist, we might take its elongated neck and tail for a rope. Lilian Randall has suggested that the man tangled in serpentine knots here might represent the classical hero Laocoön,[58] but it seems more likely that the figure's origin is closer to home, that is, to Insular and northern Continental traditions of manuscript illumination. In the initial letters of many such manuscripts, beginning in the ninth century and reaching a high point in the mid-twelfth, human figures are entangled in the coils of flourishing vines or dragons' tails, which are, in turn, embodiments of or contained within initial letters. Rather than removing it to the outer margin of the page, as did the secular illuminator of the Psalter of Yolande of Soissons, a monastic illuminator two centuries earlier would have included this scene of entanglement within or as part of an initial letter.

In the Salvin Hours, a private prayerbook from around 1270, the hours of the Virgin open with a great initial *D,* the first letter of Psalm 50:17, "Domine, labia mea aperies" (Lord, thou wilt open my lips) (fig. 68).[59] With its regularized geometrical interlace patterns, the outlines of this initial emanate from the several tiny, vestigial-looking monster heads that appear at intervals around its circumference; only at the upper and lower left do the outlines of the letter take on a certain life as they terminate in spiral coils. The two spirals may be seen as elongated tongues emerging from the mouths of the tiny monster masks at the corners of the letter's upright. Densely interwoven through these spirals are blue and white lionish creatures and figures of men who seem to be chasing them. Whereas earlier

FIG. 68. Initial *D* historiated with a Tree of Jesse. Salvin Hours. London, British Library, MS Add. 48985, fol. 1v. Photo by permission of the British Library.

Psalter initials were often filled with coiling vines and foliage and predatory beasts to suggest the toil and struggle involved in reading and understanding Scripture, in the *D* of the Salvin Hours these figural motifs appear, instead, as offshoots or excrescences of the letter pushing out toward
the margins of the page (but still contained within the rectangular frame
of the initial, which in this case detours around them).[60] Two dragonish

creatures with tails that elongate into vined coils appear outside and just above the rectangular frame of the letter; although they appear against an extension of the colored grounds that underlie the initial and other letters on this page, these monstrous creatures have been relegated to a more marginal and irregular space, outside the bounds of the rectangular frame.

Within the enclosure of the *D* there is a vine, but a very different sort of vine from those threatening entanglement that had conventionally appeared in initial letters. This vine has been carefully trained and transformed into a tree of Jesse sprouting not from the letter but from the sleeping Jesse's groin. The vine is here used as a framing device to order and hierarchize the depictions within its symmetrical scheme. Within its central, mandorla-shaped loops, the vine frames depictions of the human lineage of Christ from David on up; on each side of this central column, its loops frame scenes from the life of Christ.

Many other things might be observed of this initial and of the *D* of the Psalter of Yolande of Soissons, and many other examples might have been pressed into service to demonstrate how motifs that were once part of or contained within the animated body of the initial letter were, in the thirteenth and fourteenth centuries, pushed into the margins. Several scholars have noted this general trend and tried to explain it in different ways. According to Carl Nordenfalk, the reduction in the size of religious manuscripts made for private owners (instead of for religious institutions such as monasteries or cathedrals) caused the marginalization of "decorative elements," thus enabling their proliferation in available border space:

> Since there could be no question of abandoning entirely the accumulated wealth of decoration inherited from the past, a compromise solution was arrived at; the initials were relieved of a portion of their burden by shifting the decorative elements from the letter itself to the margin of the page, with the result that both the foliage and the zoomorphic forms inhabiting it enjoyed a new, less restricted field of action. This drastic change opened the way to a new development in the decoration of manuscripts and while, to begin with, the marginal rinceaux took the shape of short stems, little by little they proliferated, invading all the open space along the borders. This development, however, properly belongs to the Gothic period.[61]

Like Nordenfalk, Hélène Toubert remarks the displacement of "ornament" from the letter itself to the margins: "[T]he initials of the thirteenth century bore in themselves the seeds of future ornamentation. Soon the projections of the letter would defurl into the margins, beneath the text, and they would be filled, little by little, with men, animals, and monsters playing on the page." The motivation Toubert offers for this displacement is "the need for legibility and clarity [of the letters of the text] . . . imposed by the imperatives of the more massive production of the [secular] ateliers." Nevertheless, as Toubert points out, "rationalization and simplification did not signify uniformization."[62] Nor, in most cases, did the reduction in manuscript size or the need for legibility motivate the illuminators of manuscripts for wealthy laypeople to leave initial letters "naked" by entirely disassociating from them any pictorial designs and images. Older pictorial motifs were marginalized as new ones were invented to empower sacred writing differently.

Both Nordenfalk's and Toubert's explanations for the displacement of figures of the letter into the manuscript pages' margins assume that these figurative designs are purely ornamental—in other words, that they are devoid of any intention with respect to the inscribed text. In short, "pure" tends to mean "devoid of meaning"—which is, of course, only theoretically possible and not really so, for readers fill the void and project meaning even where none may have been intended. It has been my contention throughout this book that the pictorial figures embodying the letter in early medieval religious manuscripts are nearly always "impure" decoration, because they are designed, in various ways, to enliven, empower, and sacralize religious writing, to make it seem awesome.

A changing attitude toward religious writing and the reading of it, which accompanied the growth of lay literacy and the demand for private prayerbooks and other religious texts, must have helped motivate the displacement into the margins of the inscribed text of pictorial designs that had once formed part of the body of initial letters. No longer was the act of reading made to seem so challenging; the initial letter—the point at which the reader's eye entered and his or her mind began to grapple with a new section of text—was no longer depicted as a site of struggle. The proper place for this was the margins.

Recognizing that the pictorial marginalia of later medieval manuscripts originated in the figures of earlier medieval initials ("in its first phase marginal decor develops less through the invention of new themes as through the liberation of a Romanesque fauna and humanity, most of which earlier inhabited spirals and letters"), Jurgis Baltrušaitis attempted to explain this displacement in semiotic and symbolic—rather than economic—terms; he described it as a "liberation" and the creation of an "antiuniverse . . . set up opposite to regular order and exemplary figures."[63] Yet the "liberation" of this "antiuniverse" by moving it from the letter to the margins might also be understood as a kind of exorcism and expulsion of diabolical forces from the body of the initial letter. The effect of this displacement was to reduce the apparent risks of reading the sacred text by keeping the dangers of the "antiuniverse" at bay on the borders of the text, so that it was not absolutely necessary to confront them if one kept one's eyes piously trained on the center.[64]

The marginalized "antiuniverse" became, with respect to the pious central text, a locus of distraction or diversion in the sinful, "errant" sense. The antic figures of the margins are obviously looking elsewhere than at the central text; they are otherwise engaged, involved in secular and impious activities in which we also partake as we gaze at them and away from the central text. For example, the margins of the Rothschild Canticles from around 1300 are especially rife with figures of distraction by erotic desire: a horse (symbol of lust) plays phallic-looking bagpipes (45v); male heads grimace at coquettish women rather than looking up at what the clerical figure beside the text points to, that is, the text itself and a full-page image of Christ as the fountain of life (33v).[65] The lower margins of the verso of two consecutive pages of this same manuscript turn our erring eyes to good by presenting for our instruction visualized fables on the positive and negative uses of distraction. On 181v, we are instructed how to distract the devil and save our own souls by denying our sexuality as the male beaver does, for he escapes from the hunter by biting off and abandoning his own testicles, which the hunter covets.[66] On 182v, we are warned lest the diversion of self-pride lead to the loss of our souls, just as the female tiger loses her cubs because she is distracted by the image of herself in mirrors thrown down by the thieving, fleeing huntsman.[67]

In Gothic religious manuscripts made in secular workshops for wealthy laypeople, the marginalized "antiuniverse" came to be elaborated as a distraction or diversion from the central text, and sometimes even in a playful sense, rather than a frighteningly dangerous or admonitory one.[68] Of course, what is funny and what is frightening depends on the viewer's own propensities, then as now, as Madeline Caviness has demonstrated with respect to the marginal figures of the Hours of Jeanne d'Evreux.[69] Yet however one chooses to interpret late medieval marginal figures, the general point of this chapter remains: the initial letters of certain early medieval sacred texts were depicted as living and highly challenging, and the very act of reading them was figured as a struggle with diabolical forces; such texts were to be handled by a restricted group with ritual precaution. A late medieval reader of the same sacred text in a contemporary manuscript version made for him or her in a secular workshop would be likely to encounter figures of struggle only in the margins, especially in the form of visual distractions from reading. This shift in the locus of "danger" on the page, as well as in the apparent seriousness of the threat, suggests a major change in attitudes toward the reading of sacred texts as their readership expanded.[70] As we shall see, this change was accompanied by new figurative ways of empowering and authorizing the sacred letter.

# 5

# ENIGMA AND AUTHORITY

## *Early Medieval Gospels*

T hus far, although we have not put it in these terms, we have been exploring a number of pictorial solutions medieval Christian scribes found to the problem of how to fix or "close" a text so that it would be respected and preserved and, if copied, changed as little as possible. Merely to write the text down was not enough, because the writer would not be able to "defend" his text into eternity against those who would deliberately or inadvertently change and adapt it to their own interests or understanding in transcribing it.

A legal document of a contractual nature (of which there were a finite number of copies, two for many contracts) might actually be closed and sealed to prevent invalidating change. For example, Roman contracts at the time of its republic were sealed codices formed of several wax tablets bound together so as to present the same text written on the inside and on the outside of the codex. The inner text was authenticated twice: by the seals of the parties and witnesses to the contract, which were visible only once the codex was opened, and by these same people's seals attached to the thongs that closed the codex in such a way that the inner text could be seen (or changed) only by breaking the outer wax seals.[1] When papyrus replaced wax tablets for contracts, the inner writing was "closed" by rolling the sheet(s) and attaching the ends with a string fixed to the outside of the roll by the waxen seals of the witnesses, so that the roll could not be unfurled without breaking these seals. Medieval charters, written on animal skins, could be closed and sealed in much the same way; sometimes the tying of knots validated the legal action described in the charter, symbolically closing the deal with the literal closure—or tying up—of the text.[2]

In the Vulgate Apocalypse (5:1), the book ("librum") in the right hand of the Almighty, which is described as having writing inside and out and as being sealed with seven seals, seems to be imagined in terms of a contemporary Roman legal contract. The authority of this sacred book's contents is guaranteed by its divine origin, but also by its closure from the time of its inscription, for no one could later have tampered with or changed it.

Closure by means of seals and knots that are never opened is not a workable way of validating a text such as the Gospels that needs frequently to be read. Doctrinal texts with a proselytic goal had to be produced in multiple copies "open" to adaptative interpretation, yet "closed" to changes in the letter of the texts. The great difficulty of obtaining such closure, as well as the desire to do so, is suggested by verbal prefaces and epilogues attached to copies of Holy Scripture to authorize them by explaining aspects of their transmission history. Thus, for example, the "admonition" at the end of the first volume of Abbot Stephen Harding of Citeaux's early twelfth-century Bible (originally bound in three volumes, now in four) relates how, in this particular manuscript, accumulated errors and unauthoritative additions to the Latin Bible have been eliminated by comparing versions and questioning Jewish experts on the Hebrew texts (following Jerome's methods).

With his closing warning to future readers not to fill up the blanks in this manuscript (blanks made by erasing unwarranted earlier additions) and not even to annotate it, Stephen Harding tried to "close" the text of the Bible whose making he had supervised:

> [W]e have entirely erased all the superfluous additions, as will appear in many places of this book, and notably in the Book of Kings, where a great number of these errors were found. And now we beseech all those who will read these volumes not to add anything to this work, and by no means the aforesaid superfluous verses and parts. We also forbid, by the authority of God and our congregation, that any person

should treat this book, prepared so laboriously, disrespectfully or presume to annotate it in any way with his own hand [literally, "fingernail"], either in the text or the
margins.[3]

With this account of his conscientious labors at critical editing, Stephen
Harding tried to authorize his text with human effort. But he apparently
did not believe this persuasive enough, for he did not stop there; he explicitly forbade future readers, "by God's authority," to make the slightest
change, thus adding the dissuasion of fear of divine punishment for trans-
gression against the text.

In this first Old Testament volume of an early twelfth-century Bible, the
English abbot supplemented verbal attempts to assure textual closure with
the visual ones of intricately animated and interlaced initial letters. In the
original second Old Testament volume, initial letters are sometimes
formed by the bodies of the human authors of actions and stories (the divine author being God). For example, the Book of Esther begins with an
initial *I* figured as a queenly Esther trampling on a dragon and holding up
and pointing to a small closed codex. Initial letters can also be historiated
in this volume; that is, they may frame and participate in the pictorial representation of the action of the story. The initial *A* of the Book of Judith,
for example, forms the sides of a tepeelike tent wherein we see Judith in
the act of cutting off the sleeping Holofernes' head.[4]

In the original third volume of this same Bible, Stephen Harding's designers sanctified the Gospels and other New Testament texts with visual
representations of their divine inspiration. In the opening initial *I* of the
Gospel of John, for example, the evangelist's inspiration by the Holy Spirit
is represented by a huge eagle literally seizing John's tonsured head in one
of its talons (with claws penetrating his eye, ear, and mouth) (fig. 69). With
the other talon the eagle holds an unfurled scroll inscribed with the Gospel's first words, "In principio erat Verbum et Verbum erat apud deum,"
which are repeated in the adjacent text column of the twelfth-century
copy, to which John points with one hand, while another scroll (whose
writing is illegible) floats upward from his groin. By pictorially linking the
Gospel text under our scrutiny to the very text John received through his
visionary contact with the divine, the designer of this figurative initial tried
to authenticate and sanctify his copy.[5]

FIG. 69. Inspiration as seizure in the initial *I* opening John's Gospel. Bible of Stephen Harding. Dijon, Bibliothèque Municipale, MS 15, fol. 56v. Photo F. Perrodin.

A century and a half later, the designer of an initial *A* opening a French prose translation of the Apocalypse would even more boldly equate—or elide—the text originally revealed to John and the text before our eyes. Inside this opening initial, an angel stands at the seated John's back pointing a directing finger toward the column of writing, which John leans out of the initial to inscribe with his pen on the page before us (fig. 70).[6] Such bold pictorial elision might make us think the Holy Spirit spoke French!

Before printing made it possible to produce texts in multiple identical copies, with every letter in exactly the same place in every text and every

FIG. 70. John inspired, leaning out of an initial *A* to write the text of this French prose Apocalypse. Paris, B.N.F., MS fr. 403, fol. 2v. Photo Bibliothèque nationale de France.

letter shaped exactly as others of its kind, accomplishing such a paradoxically open closure was a feat achieved in large part by the ways in which writing was represented pictorially. For example, a written text that was "open," being allowed to circulate through multiple copies (and even translations), might be validated and symbolically or magically "closed" by depicting initial letters as knots and writing in general as a form of interlace or knotwork. Instead of, or in addition to, picturing the letter itself as a knot, the text could be enclosed in knotwork borders. To hedge the inscription with knots was to provide a visual equivalent for the knots that closed and validated a medieval charter, a symbolic closure in lieu of a real one.

How successful such pictorial techniques were in preventing textual destruction or change must be judged from a medieval, rather than a modern, perspective. The gap between the two is enormous. To readers used to print, even the most sacred texts copied in medieval manuscripts present an enormous variability. We are finely attuned to the fact that no two manuscript copies are ever completely alike and to the innumerable instances where medieval scribes erred or deliberately intervened to improve even the most holy texts. Modern readers, many of whom do not permit themselves to "deface" the printed page by writing in the margins of costly books, tend to be shocked by what they perceive as disrespect for the authority of the written word on the part of medieval readers, who left interlinear and marginal traces of many sorts. Because we are accustomed to contemporary standards of conservation, which suppose that no printed text should ever be lost (for each is now stocked in a national library to preserve it in perpetuity), we are also acutely aware of the loss and destruction of medieval manuscripts, of the relatively small number that have come down to us intact, especially from the early Middle Ages. Yet the accumulated evidence of so much change and destruction does not mean that the medieval makers of sacred texts did nothing to try to prevent it. Indeed, if we consider the number of illuminated, pictorially designed—as opposed to plainly inscribed—texts that have survived from the early Middle Ages, we would have to admit that the image given to writing in particular manuscripts aided their survival.

Before the age of print, the most effective way to "close" a text (short of sealing or locking it away from human eyes forever) was to make it seem awesome. From an early medieval point of view, the most authoritative text of the Gospels was not necessarily the most correct or scholarly, but it was the one perceived to be a relic imbued with divine presence, for such a text inspired viewers with fear of transgressing against divine or saintly powers if they presumed to change its letters or words. A relatively large number of the earliest surviving codices of Holy Scripture seem to have been taken for relics of particular saints who copied or owned them, as Patrick McGurk has remarked: "The association is chronologically improbable in the cases of the seventh-century St Chad with the eighth-century Lichfield Gospels and of the seventh-century St Columbanus with the fourth-to-fifth-century *Codex Bobiensis;* but it is plausible or, at least, acceptable palaeographically, in the cases of St German with the beautiful sixth-century purple Old Latin Psalter, and of St Eusebius († 371) with the fourth-to-fifth-century Vercelli Gospels, and of St Marcellinus, bishop of Ancona from 550, with the sixth-century Ancona Gospels."[7] Oral traditions about the reliquary status of certain codices were sometimes preserved in written form and compiled or associated with the text. However, to make it even more impressive, verbal testimony needed supplementation by visual testimony. The enshrinement of the text in an elaborately figured reliquary book cover or casket, or beneath cover (or "carpet") pages, or in an ornately designed script witnessed—explicitly or implicitly, mimetically or symbolically—to its divine alterity.[8]

To increase its visual impressiveness and hence its authority, the script of a sacred text was sometimes partially written in a deliberately archaic way. The scribal exegetes of the great initial pages of Insular Gospels occasionally imitated Greek and runic letters thereon to suggest the antiquity of the text. Even more important, the script was animated, as we have seen, with pictorial designs incorporated into the shapes of letters, which gave them the appearance of mobility and life and enriched their signifying power. The living knotwork of the letter visualized the enigma of divine intention; it was the mysterious trace of the Spirit, fraught with meaning but closed to the uninitiated, not to be changed or tampered with lightly.

We might go so far as to say that early Christian scribes, to create the impression of divine presence in sacred writings, used pictorial designs to *fetishize* letters. A fetish is a thing enchanted, divine, or oracular (from the Portuguese word *fetisso,* derived from the Latin words *fatum, fanum, fari* ). Originally a derogatory name given by Western Europeans to cult objects of civilizations they considered to be "primitive," the fetish was a concept Charles de Brosses explored in 1760 in *Du culte des dieux fétiches.* Although cultural chauvinism prevented him from making the comparison, Brosses's description of how West Africans treated their chosen material "fetishes" might also describe medieval Christian devotion to elaborate reliquaries containing saints' relics—or to elaborately designed Gospels and other texts of Holy Scripture: "These are so many Gods, sacred things, and also talismans for the Negroes, who pay them a precise and respectful devotion, addressing their vows to them, offering them sacrifices, parading them in processions if possible or carrying them on their own persons with the greatest signs of veneration, and consulting them on every occasion of interest, considering them in general to be as tutors to men and as powerful protectors against all sorts of accidents. They swore by them, and this was the only sermon these perfidious people did not dare to violate."[9] The African fetish and the European saint's relic are transitional objects, that is, objects also imagined to be subjects, signifiers imagined to be Signifiers. The same is true of the fetishized medieval letter of a sacred text, which may be designed, for example, with eyes all over it (fig. 23) or as a combination or tangle of living creatures, all imagined to be material embodiments of the divine, writing as being. To endow inanimate objects—bodily remains, alphabetic inscriptions—with the power of a living presence is a work of imagination, an illusion created, in part, by means of fetishizing verbal and visual representations.

Just as monasteries and other groups in the early Middle Ages relied on the power of saints, whose bodily traces they possessed, to protect them against all sorts of dangers, so also they relied on the protective power of holy books conceived as incarnations of divinity (and relics of their saintly scribes). To turn the letter into a kind of fetish or amulet, the medieval scribe designed and knotted it, emphasizing the "ligatures" of writing. *Ligatura* ("something knotted") is a common late classical word for amulet (used by Augustine, for example, in *On Christian Doctrine* 2.20.30). Furthermore, to the extent that image magic is based on the belief that a being's image (in the sense of a visual manifestation of some sort, not necessarily a visual likeness) is part of that being, people might hope to ensure access to its presence and power by trying to chain down or permanently fix (by, for example, sculpting or drawing) images of a divinity that had been revealed to them. Such revelations may have come in visions and dreams or in the shapes of natural objects. As Charly Clerc speculated long ago, using second-century Greek texts on the subject, "The primitive idea would have been this: the image of any being gives a hold on it. If the image is bound, the being, even if a god, will likewise be bound."[10] Writing imagined as an incarnation of divinity—as Holy Scripture was imagined—was depicted as alive and also as knotted and "bound" in various ways. Such pictured closure may express the enigma of the text's infinitely complicated sense ("bound by the knots of mysteries," as Gregory put it),[11] and also the human desire to capture and control the power of a supernatural being.

If the Gospel Book of Kildare survived long enough for Gerald of Wales, in the twelfth century, to see and describe it and its miraculous inscription, this was because the text had the status of a sort of relic of divinity, for its enormously complex pictorial designs were believed to have been invented by the Holy Spirit, who revealed them to the scribe in a dream and later guided him in reproducing them exactly. Although not a direct imprint of divinity (as relics such as the Veronica were believed to be), the intricate tracery of the Book of Kildare was noted by Gerald to resemble an imprint or "erasure" (today called a "rubbing"). The first image he marveled over, in terms that recollect the Veronica, was "the face of Majesty, divinely drawn." The legend of the scribe's inspiration and direction by the Holy Spirit in the design of this Gospel text brought it close in category to the relics of Christ and the Virgin "made without human hands" (*achiropiites*), images such as the Veronica supposedly produced by an imprinting contact with the divine face, which left permanently a revealing trace of divinity.[12]

The pictorial "signature" of the Gospel Book of Kildare is, according to the legend, not the scribe's but God's, for the Holy Spirit directed the text's design, borrowing a human hand, in effect, to draw divine designs. Despite its scribal inscription, it is an "autograph" copy every bit as valid and authoritative, every bit as much a vestige of divinity, as those (no longer extant) copies the Spirit had, centuries earlier, inspired the evangelists to inscribe. Given such beliefs, the veneration as miracle-working relics of the hands of another monastic scribe, Ultan, is hardly surprising, because his were the human hands that signed for God in producing the intricate pictorial designs of the letter; they were the instruments whereby divinity assumed a material form, the instruments of an incarnation.

In addition to being an act of devotion, the extremely intricate and original designing of the letter of religious texts seems to have been a way to higher office and even to saintly reputation in the early medieval Insular world, because extreme virtuosity was "proof" of divine inspiration—proof that the draftsman was the chosen, sanctified instrument of divine revelation.[13] The inspired Columba, reputed scribe of the Psalter known as the Cathach and of over three hundred other books, achieved saint-hood;[14] and Eadfrith, scribe and illuminator of the gorgeously designed Lindisfarne Gospels, became bishop of Lindisfarne.[15] Nor is it surprising, given the equation between scribal virtuosity and divine inspiration and sanctity, that even intellectually outstanding individuals with extensive exegetical training inscribed and illuminated relatively lengthy texts as acts of devotion (and perhaps also as bids for saintly reputation).[16]

As legend had it, the sacred texts Saint Columba copied were miraculously "closed." It was impossible to wash out any of the letters of any of the three hundred books inscribed by Saint Columba, no matter how long these were immersed in water.[17] The supernatural permanence of such letters could be due only to a divine presence holding them in place, making it impossible to recycle the skins (as was often done) by washing out the ink of the outdated or redundant text and reusing the parchment for a new inscription.

A similar story about miraculous imperviousness to immersion was told of the Lindisfarne Gospels, which supposedly fell overboard during a storm in the Solway Firth on the way to Ireland when the monks were trying to move to safety the relics of Saint Cuthbert, as well as the bones of Bishops Eadfrith and Aethelwald (one the writer, the other the binder of the Lindisfarne Gospels). When the Gospels fell overboard, the monks prayed to the saint; the waters stilled, and they returned to land with a fair tailwind. Then Saint Cuthbert appeared in a vision to one of the men and told them to look for the manuscript when the tide was low: "Accordingly they go to the sea and find that it had retired much further than it was accustomed; and after walking three miles or more they find the sacred manuscript of the Gospels itself, exhibiting all its outer splendour of jewels and gold and all the beauty of its pages and writing within, as though it had never been touched by water." The early twelfth-century narrator of this account, Simeon of Durham, went on to attribute the miracle to the "merits" of Saint Cuthbert "and of those who made the book, namely, bishop Eadfrith of holy memory, who wrote it with his own hand in honour of the blessed Cuthbert, and the venerable Aethelwald, his successor, who caused it to be adorned with gold and precious stones."[18] Although Simeon's inflection of the story gives credit to holy men for the miracle, the miraculous permanence of the writing of the Lindisfarne Gospels might also be taken as proof of its divinity. For another occasion, the events of the story might have been explained differently, with the Gospel text itself credited with stilling the waters into which it fell.

Just as sixth-century Byzantine miraculous imprints of Christ's face "made without human hands" were carried into battle to place God on the side of the possessors of these permanent physical traces of Christ,[19] so also medieval rulers and lords tried to ensure divine aid by including in their baggage—or even displaying in the face of the enemy[20]—religious texts believed, because of their ornately designed, enigmatically animated letters, to be inscribed by the Holy Spirit via a human hand. A late sixth-century Psalter with dove and fish initials, long attributed to Saint Columba, was called "Cathach" ("Battler") because, as a holy relic, it was carried into battle to guarantee the victory of its possessors.[21] Ornately illuminated religious manuscripts lost with the baggage of defeated nobles and rulers were regularly ransomed and bought back. That such precious books should have been exposed to the dangers of war (rather than more utilitarian copies) suggests that their pictorial designs increased the impression of divine presence and hence their value as talismans or amulets capable of protecting their possessors. Many an early medieval battle was, in effect, a battle of the books, with each side protected by its relics of divinity, its book-fetishes.

The elaborately decorated, protective-gem-encrusted covers and clasps of the Lindisfarne Gospels, and of many a later illuminated religious manuscript, "closed" the text by enclosing it outwardly, just as did the reliquary shrine of the golden casket (*cumdach*) of the Book of Kells (stolen at the beginning of the eleventh century—such rich enclosures put sacred texts in peril by tempting thieves). Yet a "secular cover," as the *cumdach* was called with reference to its merely human origin,[22] could never be as effective a closure as the divinely inspired designs of the writing itself.

The pictorial figures of the initial letters of early medieval religious texts—hieroglyphs of the Spirit or of Christ, intricate knotting, vivifying vegetal and animal forms—perform this role of "closing" or "tying up" the text by manifesting enigmatically the plenitude of life and sense incarnate in the letter. Paradoxical as it may seem, by taking legibility-obscuring

Christian liberties with conventional letter shapes—by continually making initials different and new to create the visual impression of a living, divinely empowered, and infinitely meaningful writing—early medieval scribal exegetes actually worked to limit changes to the letters and words of the texts they copied and transmitted. The pictorial figures of the letter, by animating and rendering it enigmatic and awesome, warded off change.

A designed letter such as the great chi of the chi-rho page of the Book of Kells (color plate 1) is meant to be a revelation or an epiphany, not a mere object among a host of other objects in the world, as Renaissance illuminators would later depict letters to be—mere marks in ink and paint on the fragile support of parchment or glass, or incisions in stone monuments. Whereas all of creation seems to be symbolically contained and tied up *within* the initial letters of certain eighth- and ninth-century Insular Gospel books, the illuminator of a fifteenth-century Book of Hours might reify the text and reduce it to an object in the context of a surrounding world by depicting the page bearing the letters of the sacred liturgical text as literally "chained" into a window frame, and partially blocking the reader's view of a realistically depicted world (fig. 71). Such a mise-en-scène provokes the desire for a "transparent" text that will allow us to read right through it to the underlying, earlier reality that the writing is supposed to represent.

The same might be said of a late fourteenth-century manuscript of the secular romance of *Giron le courtois,* whose text columns the Lombard illuminator has turned into flaps partially masking our view of underlying depictions of scenes from the story, which include a spectator who points to the pictured action (rather than to the letters of the text, as the hand of a conventional *nota* sign would do) (fig. 72). On the chi-rho page of the Book of Kells there is, on the contrary, nothing underlying or behind the great chi; it blocks nothing from our view but rather gives the impression, owing to its magnification, of moving toward us off the page and revealing the enormous complexity and seeming incongruity of forms that make up its interior. The opacity of the great chi is the effect of presenting *too much* to see, of revealing mystery.

Even in the case of a text economically inscribed (with no elaborate pictorial designs helping to suggest richer, nonliteral senses), our perception in

FIG. 71. Text page with an initial *D* depicting the Annunciation chained into the window frame. Hours of Charles of France. New York, The Metropolitan Museum of Art, Cloisters Collection, 1958. MS 58.71b verso. Photo Metropolitan Museum of Art.

FIG. 72. Text columns as flaps covering a realistically depicted scene. *Giron le courtois*. Paris, B.N.F., MS nouv. acq. fr. 5234, fol. 34r. Photo Bibliothèque nationale de France.

the text of a plenitude of possible meanings that seem to surpass ordinary human signifying ability or comprehension tends to increase its value for us and to make it begin to seem oracular. Although a text whose meaning is enigmatic is "open" in that it seems to support multiple and differing interpretations, it is "closed" by our reverence for its complexity. Precisely because the "letter" of such a text is not transparent, refusing to let us read straight "through" it to a singular message, we are incapable of fully translating it into other letters and words, and so, if we do not want to destroy this wealth of meaning, we must preserve the letter as is—and record our own interpretations elsewhere, in the enclosing, enshrining "margins" of the enigmatic text.

Prophetic, divinely inspired texts might manifest themselves initially as supernatural inscription (from the marks on the liver of a sacrificed animal to the divine writing on the wall) or be revealed orally and translated by a human scribe into alphabetic inscription (as with the oracles of Apollo[23] or the books of the Old Testament prophets, still supposedly under the influence of inspiration) to permit study and decipherment of hidden meanings and eventual retrospective elucidations or confirmations of prophecy.[24] Any text with prophetic potential called for conservation in writing exactly as it had been received, without any change to its letter. Indeed, the claim that a text was divinely inspired or potentially portentous justified the expense of writing it down and attempting to close and preserve it unchanged.[25]

Augustine advised Christian teachers to valorize Scripture by discovering hidden, enriching allegorical senses when they taught it to lettered pagans, who might be disappointed with the simplicity of the Bible's literal sense.[26] Analogously, eighth- and ninth-century Insular scribal exegetes exercised extreme ingenuity in complicating the forms and figures of the initial letters of the Gospels, especially in ceremonial codices for display on altars and at religious celebrations, to prevent "reading through," to make the text seem more opaque and enigmatic (and suggest the mysterious presence of divinity). Visual incongruities, as well as complexity and intricacy of design and color, were ways of suggesting multiple, simultaneous meanings, of creating the impression of the supernatural. As I have earlier argued concerning the Book of Kells, the traces of its initial letters are also those of animal bodies that recollect the animal symbols of evangelical inspiration (grouped together on separate pages of the Book of Kells or over and in the tympana of the arches of its canon tables); these enigmatically interlaced, incongruously combined animal bodies as letters figuratively manifest the Spirit in the letter and the unity of the four different Gospels as inspired, inhabited texts. The pictorial designs that animated and mystified the initial letters of sacred texts in various ways evoked a supernatural presence, which powerfully authorized the writing and thus worked to "close" these texts.

The ambitious scribal exegete Eadfrith of Lindisfarne was not, however, content to suggest the divinity of the Gospels he copied solely by animating their initial letters, by depicting the animal symbols of evangelical inspiration grouped together around the quadrants of a cross, and by suggesting the patterned richness of meaning of Holy Scripture through the analogy of the intricate cruciform tracery of "carpet" pages. For the first time in the

FIG. 73. Luke inspired, writing his Gospel. Lindisfarne Gospels. London, British Library, MS Cotton Nero D.IV, fol. 137v. Photo by permission of the British Library.

Insular world, Eadfrith valorized and made the Gospel texts more awe-inspiring by also representing the very act of transmission of the divine exemplar to the human scribe.[27]

On separate pages prefacing the different Gospels, Eadfrith depicted the different animal forms of the Spirit floating in the sky behind the evangelists, sometimes blowing upward-curved trumpets, and holding up the closed codices of the Gospel exemplars just over or beside the haloed heads of the evangelists (figs. 53, 73, and 74). With the exception of John, each evangelist writes in a bound codex, on a scroll, or on an unbound page. Mark, for example, writes with one hand on a single sheet, while holding up with his other the finished, closed codex of his Gospel (fol. 93v).[28] All write in an apparently supernatural ink, for no lettering shows, and there is no mundane inkpot in sight.[29] Eadfrith's evangelists are inspired scribes copying the divine exemplar; they write by means of a mystical vision of the exemplar, and possibly also a mystical hearing of it signified by the trumpeting. In no case do the evangelists look either at the exemplar

FIG. 74. John inspired.
Lindisfarne Gospels. London,
British Library, MS Cotton
Nero D.IV, fol. 209v. Photo
by permission of the
British Library.

(which is closed) or at what they are writing; instead, their hands write automatically, while they stare into space, their attention riveted on an inner revelation. Modern observers have often commented on the unrealistic aspect of such images. Medieval techniques of writing required the strictest attention to quill and parchment during the process of inscription; no scribe, however skillful, could write while gazing into space. Furthermore, there was no such thing as direct redaction into codices. Medieval scribes wrote on parchment sheets that were later bound into books. This pictorial elision of the intermediate stages of mundane textual production emphasizes the supernatural character of the divinely inspired text. The evangelists' "automatic" writing demonstrates that they are mere instruments of the Spirit, and that the texts of the Gospels they produce are entirely authoritative, for they are very nearly *achiropiites,* divine autographs.

With the image prefacing John's Gospel, Eadfrith makes an even more striking visual statement (fig. 74). As with the other evangelists, the Spirit, this time in the form of an eagle, holds the closed codex of the divine exemplar over John's head. But John is not engaged in the act of copying divine revelation with a pen. Instead, he displays a blank, unfurled scroll and motions with his free hand in the direction of the text of his Gospel inscribed on the facing page, as if to show his finished work, as if this text were the one he had copied under divine inspiration. John's gesture toward the text on the facing recto authorizes this particular copy of his Gospel: the richly and enigmatically designed text of the Lindisfarne Gospels. As we shall see later, Eadfrith's subtle, fictional conflation of the evangelist-scribe with himself is repeated in various ways by other illuminators attempting to confer the authority of divine inspiration on their particular copies of the Gospels.

There are several partial precedents for the iconography of Eadfrith's evangelist pages, but none witnesses as effectively as Eadfrith's to the divine authority of the transcribed text. For example, in the Gospels of Saint Augustine, written in Italy at the end of the sixth century and sent to England with Pope Gregory's missionaries, there is a page depicting the evangelist Luke as a philosopher in an antique pose, seated on a chair under an arch with his head pensively resting on his hand, while he displays an open codex turned toward the viewer and inscribed with the Latin words from the Gospel of John (1:6): "Fuit homo missus a deo, cui nomen erat Ioannes" (There was a man sent from God, whose name was John) (fig. 75). The codex in Luke's hands would thus appear to be a compilation of all four Gospels and not only the Gospel according to Luke.

Among the many novelties of this frontispiece is the combination of the classicizing author portrait of evangelist-as-philosopher with the image of the winged bull (a relatively early pictorial occurrence) holding a closed codex in its front hooves in the tympanum directly over Luke's head, but separated from the evangelist's space by a thick lintel. Framed between the columns supporting this lintel are a series of literal illustrations of events of Christ's ministry narrated in the Gospels. Despite the supernatural incongruity of a winged bull holding a book in the heavenly register of the page, the artist's intention in this frontispiece seems to be to show us what the Gospels actually say, rather than to mystify; the book Luke displays is clearly inscribed, and the writing is translated into narrative pictures at the side (with each picture labeled in the margins in a later, eighth-century,

FIG. 75. Portrait of Luke prefacing his Gospel. Gospels of Saint Augustine. Cambridge, Corpus Christi College, MS 286, fol. 129v. Photo by permission of the Master and Fellows of Corpus Christi College, Cambridge.

hand), thus putting into practice Gregory the Great's view that pictures should translate writing for the illiterate.[30] Luke's open codex is presumably a transcription of the closed book that the mystic bull holds in the heavenly register, but how Luke knows the contents of the divine exemplar is not the subject of the picture.

Nor is inspiration the sole focus of a depiction of Ezra copying the Old Testament prophets in the late seventh-century English Codex Amiatinus (fig. 76), which Eadfrith imitated in his own "portrait" of Matthew (fig. 53), taking care to eliminate all signs of mundane textual transmission. According to early exegetes such as Irenaeus and Clement of Alexandria,[31] God inspired Ezra with miraculous remembrance of all the previous words of the prophets so that he would be able to correct the Scriptures corrupted during the Exile. Although his halo suggests divine inspiration, as does the fixity of his wide-eyed stare into space, Ezra in the Codex Amiatinus is also represented after the tradition of a Jerome: as a scholar in his library with a volume he has consulted open on the floor and an impressive cabinet of books at his disposal (perhaps of Scripture already corrected) to assure, by means of critical comparison, the correctness of the text he is in the act of inscribing.[32] This scholarly depiction of Ezra in his study writing—in legible ink from an inkpot so worldly as to cast a shadow, although a golden one—attempts to reauthorize the texts of the Old Testament prophets by witnessing to the erudition and meticulousness of their scribal transmitter (and perhaps also, by implicit analogy, to the erudition and meticulousness of the medieval makers of the Codex Amiatinus).[33]

The divine inspiration of a Gospel text is first depicted, among surviving examples, in the early sixth-century Greek Rossano Gospels, written in silver and gold on purple-dyed pages. A seated Mark writes at the dictation of a female figure standing before him and draped in blue from head to toe, with only her face showing. As both gaze off into space in different directions, the female figure closely directs Mark's writing hand with her extended fingers, which nearly touch the unfurled scroll that supernaturally floats above Mark's knees, as does his inkwell and other writing equipment (fig. 77). In an innovative adaptation of classical iconography, representing the inspiration of a poet or philosopher by his muse, this draped female figure would seem to embody the evangelist's inspiration

FIG. 76. Portrait of Ezra. Codex Amiatinus. Florence, Biblioteca Medicea Laurenziana, MS Laur. Amiatino I, fol. 5r. Photo courtesy of the Biblioteca Medicea Laurenziana.

FIG. 77. Mark writing his Gospel at the Spirit's dictation. Rossano Gospels. Rossano, Museo Diocesano di Arte Sacra, fol. 241r. Photo courtesy of the Museo Diocesano di Arte Sacra.

by the Holy Spirit or divine wisdom.[34] What is striking here is the scribal exegete's attempt to authorize the Gospel text with a picture of its supernatural origin, its transmission, through the scribal agency of Mark, from the veiled figure of divinity to the page.

This new visual way of insisting on a divine origin for the different Gospel texts supplemented earlier visual demonstrations of their unity: most fundamental, from about the second century on, their enclosure within the bounds of a single codex; their visual concordance from the late fourth century on by means of prefacing canon tables; and, as of the sixth century, the depiction of each of these canon tables as an architectural structure, a temple supported by the differently designed columns of the different Gospels, a tabernacle housing and enshrining the Word.[35]

The Gospels presented a serious problem of instability and lack of "closure"—and not solely because they had to circulate in multiple copies open to reading and interpretation. The fundamental problem was that the Gospels were too many and too different. A unique text relating the story of the one life that was supposed to reveal God's intentions would have been much tidier. Already in the second century, Tatian had woven the different accounts into the improved, unified, "composite edition" of his *Diatessaron,* which in a sense competed with and threatened to replace the different Gospel accounts.[36]

The most effective prohibition against changing the literal texts of the Gospels was their reputation for being divinely inspired, although this reputation was not based on a self-authorizing verbal introduction such as John provided for the Apocalypse:[37] "This is the revelation given by God to Jesus Christ. It was given to him so that he might show his servants what must shortly happen. He made it known by sending his angel to his servant John, who, in telling all that he saw, has borne witness to the word of God and to the testimony of Jesus Christ." The Gospels were, at best, implicitly authorized as divinely inspired by an account of Pentecost written elsewhere (and not usually collected in the same codex as the Gospels): the second chapter of the Book of Acts, which relates how the Holy Spirit entered the apostles and enabled them to bear witness to Christ in languages they had not previously known. Although the emphasis in Acts is on inspired verbal preaching, the writing of the Gospels was apparently considered to be an extension of this (and in many medieval depictions of Pentecost, codices of their own Gospels—instead of scrolls representing speech—have already materialized in the hands of the evangelists).

In the century preceding the making of the Rossano Gospels, which recycle a classical muse as the Holy Spirit to authorize a Gospel text, Jerome had provoked much controversy over his comparative method of establishing one correct text out of many and his questioning of the story of the divine inspiration of the seventy-odd Greek translators of the Old Testament and, consequently, of the authority of their translation, the Septuagint. Augustine, for example, accepted the divine inspiration of the Greek text of the Old Testament that had been used, and thus "approved," by the apostles of the primitive Christian church, and he considered this text to be just as authoritative (indeed, even more so for Christians) as the "original" Hebrew versions on which Jerome relied. In Augustine's view, expressed in *The City of God* and elsewhere, differences in divinely inspired versions marked the progressive stages of divine revelation and were to be understood in terms of divine will (not of human error or intentional, politically motivated change, as Jerome had posited in order to explain and dismiss parts of the Septuagint that diverged from "original" Hebrew versions).[38] Indeed, Augustine denounced the hubris of a single translator's setting up his own authority against so many.[39]

The designs that valorize Christian religious texts with increasing frequency and ingenuity from the sixth century on—and even Jerome's own Vulgate Gospels—demonstrate the ineffectiveness of Jerome's criticism of the superfluous "ornamentation" of Scriptures and his questioning of the wisdom of believing stories or claims of inspiration that might mask tendentious aims and sanction illegitimate textual changes. The visual enigmas of intricately knotted, animated letters; depictions of evangelical inspiration; monumentalizing, harmonizing canon tables—all such pictorial designs witnessed to or suggested the divine origins and unity of the Scriptures and thereby authorized biblical texts more powerfully than could Jerome's own verbal prefaces. Jerome, for example, in his letter to Pope Damasus (beginning "Novum opus"), tried to authorize "his" edition of the Gospels both by human agency—that is, by his own conscientious scholarly labors at establishing a single Latin version ("corrected against the oldest Greek manuscripts")—and by the orders of the ruler of the church (for Jerome claimed to be serving Pope Damasus's desire for an improved Latin text of the Gospels).[40]

That all of these pictorial and verbal methods, with numerous variants, could be and often were put to use in the same manuscript suggests how hard it was to authorize and "close" the letter of a circulating text in the Middle Ages. Even the early Rossano Gospels combined several of these visual and verbal "closing" devices: compilation of the Gospels into one codex, unifying canon tables (although not yet depicted as temples), full-page depictions of evangelical inspiration, verbal prefaces by Jerome (his letter to Pope Damasus, his general preface to the Gospels), and Eusebius's letter explaining the canon tables—not to mention the splendor of silver and gold letters on purple-dyed pages (a sheer material valorization of the letter that would, in later and more northern manuscripts, be replaced or supplemented by the fetishizing animate interlace designs of the initial letters themselves). Richly illuminated late antique and early medieval religious manuscripts have survived in disproportionate numbers, even if only in a fragmentary state, precisely because their pictorial designs gave them reliquary status as traces of the divine—and of a scribal hand rendered saintly by divine direction.[41]

The early sixth-century Greek Gospels of Rossano show the Holy Spirit with a darker blue halo against a lighter blue ground, and Mark with a discrete halo suggested by a thin white line (fig. 77). A halo is necessary to transform the muse into Holy Spirit here and thus to authorize the text Mark inscribes by demonstrating its divine inspiration. In addition, Mark's own halo beatifies him for serving as the instrument of the Spirit. In the nearly contemporary Latin Gospels of Augustine (fig. 75), the Spirit is represented by a figure impossible to confuse with a muse, a figure so incongruous and evidently supernatural that it requires no identifying halo: a bull holding a closed codex in its front hooves in the tympanum over Luke's head. Nor is Luke haloed in this contemplative image of him displaying the Gospels. Eadfrith of Lindisfarne, on the other hand, sanctifies Matthew with a bold, banded halo in his depiction of a moment of textual transmission (fig. 53). From the Spirit in the manly image of an angel above Matthew's head, but in the same space, Matthew receives the revelation of his Gospel, which he copies onto a blank codex on his lap as he gazes elsewhere. Eadfrith's full-page depictions of inspired evangelists in the act of writing authorize the letter of the different Gospel texts and beatify their writers as instruments of divinity. At the same time Eadfrith's representations, by implicit analogy and elision, tend to sanctify the medieval scribe (himself) and the specific copy of the Gospel text before us (the Lindisfarne Gospels).

The analogy between medieval scribe and evangelist is emphasized in certain other Gospel manuscripts by means of visual incongruities suggesting the conflation or copresence of different figures. For example, in the later eighth-century Codex Aureus of Stockholm, both the seated Matthew holding an unfurled scroll and his look-alike inspiring angel (Spirit in the image of a man), who holds a closed book in the arch over Matthew's head, have tonsures like medieval monks (fig. 54). This tonsure may not be an inadvertent anachronism but a medieval scribe's way of authorizing his own particular copy by suggesting that he too has been visited by the Spirit in the act of rewriting, re-"incarnating" the Scriptures. The highly stylized "imago hominis" page in the early eighth-century Echternach Gospels is one of the more striking examples of how a conflation of pictorial figures authorizes and sanctifies on several levels at once (fig. 43). The unhaloed human figure displaying the open Gospel of Matthew and labeled "imago hominis" ("image of man") suggests at least three concurrent "people": the Spirit becoming the letter (as I suggested in chapter 3); the evangelist Matthew in a state of inspiration (inhabited by, conflated with the Spirit); and, because of the human figure's monastic tonsure, the medieval scribe of the Echternach Gospel of Matthew (inhabited by the Spirit).

Before the advent of printing, each new copy of an authoritative text such as a book of the Bible—not to speak of each new translation—needed to be sanctioned anew by the text's originator. His trace or seal, some visible vestige or relic of him, was necessary to empower the text by reaffirming his presence and denying difference. To this purpose, the animating, enigmatic pictorial designs of the letter were supplemented with ever more explicit pictorial testimonies to the divine direction of the human scribal hand. Like the verbal account of the divine inspiration of the Book of Kildare's designs, relatively realistic pictorial representations of evangelists as scribes receiving divine inspiration from marvelous animal forms of the Spirit (as on the Lindisfarne Gospels' evangelist pages) testified to the Spirit's presence in the letter, but they did so in the third person, so to speak. They did so more "objectively" than did the mystically designed letters themselves or than more enigmatic pictorial testimonies to evangelical and scribal inspiration, such as the incongruously (implying miraculously) conflated image on the "imago hominis" page of the Echternach Gospels (fig. 43) of the Spirit as the evangelist Matthew as medieval monk—or, facing the opening of the Gospel of Matthew in the Book of Kells, centered on the page and surrounded by lions, eagle, and calf, the even more incongruously conflated human figure with mismatched hair and beard colors, one open eye and one blank one, one hand hidden in his bosom, and the other bearing a closed book, whom we can only identify as an image of divine inspiration, as a copresence within Matthew of the Spirit in the image of man, and of God (fig. 78).[42]

Manuscripts of the Gospels were by no means the only medieval texts to

FIG. 78. Portrait of Matthew inspired. Book of Kells. Dublin, Trinity College, MS 58, fol. 28v. Photo courtesy of the Board of Trinity College Dublin.

be valorized and mystified by pictorial representations of their divine authorship, as well as by designed writing whose intricacy suggested supernatural direction of the human hand. According to one of Aldhelm's students at Malmesbury in the seventh century, all of the many volumes brought back from Rome were inspired; his awestruck description suggests that inspiration was extended in the early medieval period to many Christian texts that were not parts of the Bible, strictly speaking, but commentaries on it and other Christian writings: "Lo, they brought back many rows of volumes composed by manifold and mystic rules, whose author is known to have been aided by the Holy Spirit, volumes which prophets and apostles of the wise-speaking oracle, inspired by the Holy Spirit, set down on parchment."[43] In copying these same texts, Insular artists used pictorial figures of the letter and visual representations to testify to their divine authorship. Mystification of the origins of texts helped to render them sacred.[44]

The divine inspiration of Old Testament writers and patristic commentators was most commonly figured by the dove of the Holy Spirit in various stages of descent or even poking its beak boldly into the writer's ear, such as David's in the Beatus initial beginning the twelfth-century Saint Albans Psalter (fig. 66). A late ninth-century missal containing the Gregorian canon of the mass depicts Gregory the Great with a dove at his ear as he displays an open book (Paris, B.N.F., MS lat. 1141, fol. 15r),[45] and an eleventh-century illuminator sanctifies Jerome's text (despite Jerome's own insistence on the authority of good scholarship) by showing him seated like an evangelist under an arch and taking divine dictation from the dove at his ear (Cambridge, Corpus Christi, MS 389, fol. 1v).[46] When Augustine is depicted writing biblical exegesis, he is visited by an inspiring angel (another form of the Holy Spirit) who proffers him a codex with veiled hands.[47] In another case, Augustine's inspiration is imaged as aural (divine dictation) rather than visual (from a written text). In an eleventh-century manuscript containing his work (Brussels, Bibliothèque Royale, MS 10791, fol. 2r), a tiny angel appears just behind Augustine's head as he writes in a bound codex. Rather than being shown as visited by a dove or an angel, the writer might also be pictured as the target of rays of inspiration descending toward his head from a divine hand.

As we have seen, early medieval scribes worked to fetishize and empower the writing couched on the pages of the Gospels and other religious texts. By means of the animating and mystifying designs of initial letters and by depictions of their writers as mere "secretaries" receiving divine dictation, they implied that these letters were physical traces or relics of divinity.

Holy Scripture became the model for "potent" writing and was used to caution other Christian—and even secular—writing, not only in the practical sense, as when secular charters were inscribed in empty spaces of the Book of Kells[48] or when the Bible or Gospels were physically present to "witness" the drawing up of written contracts, but also in a more abstract way. For example, in a famous dispute in 1101 between Anselm of Canterbury and Henry I of England, as recounted by Eadmer of Canterbury, Henry's bishops preferred to trust the evidence of their own ears (from an earlier papal audience) over the sealed papal letters produced by Anselm's side, which Henry's bishops dismissed as "the skins of wethers blackened with ink and weighted with a little lump of lead." Anselm's side retorted, "Shame on you! Are not the Gospels written down on sheepskins?"[49]— thereby using the power of the writing of the Gospels to guarantee that of other writing.

# 6

# ARCHAEOLOGY OF
# THE AUTHOR FUNCTION

In his inaugural lecture at the College de France, Michel Foucault suggested that eighteenth- and nineteenth-century literary historians invented, and individual writers subsequently took upon themselves, what he termed the "author function" and defined as a way of drastically limiting the nearly infinite possible meanings of a text or a series of texts by accrediting only those meanings supposedly intended by the author. Foucault proposed that we study in more detail "how the principle of the author was put into play."[1] In certain respects, that is what my preceding chapters have been about, although at a period far earlier and in a broader sense than Foucault suggested. Already by the late fourteenth century, self-conscious poets such as Guillaume de Machaut and John Gower took upon themselves and fully assumed the "author function" by collecting, compiling, commenting on, supervising the rubrication and illumination of, and in other ways trying to fix and stabilize—to maintain control over—their own oeuvres.[2] Centuries before them, as we shall see, readers and interpreters who did not themselves presume to be authors had already invented the transfer of power over the text that Foucault called the "author function."

Medieval grammarians' very explanations of the multiple etymological origins and spellings of the word *author* (*auctor, actor,* or *autor* in Latin) suggest earlier attempts to empower and enliven the figure of the author. A. J. Minnis has summarized these various etymologies:

> [A]*uctor* was supposed to be related to the Latin verbs *agere* "to act or perform," *augere* "to grow" and *auieo* "to tie," and to the Greek noun *autentim* "authority." An *auctor* "performed" the act of writing. He brought something into being, caused it to "grow." In the more specialised sense related to *auieo,* poets like Virgil and Lucan were *auctores* in that they had "tied" together their verses with feet and metres. To the ideas of achievement and growth were easily assimilated the idea of authenticity or "authoritativeness."[3]

At the beginning of the thirteenth century, Hugutio of Pisa identified the spelling *auctor* with the notion of an author as one who augments or amplifies something, making it grow; on the other hand, he argued that the spelling *autor* might mean *ligator,* someone who ties something together or knots it.[4] Evrard de Béthune distinguished between the spellings *auctor* (from *augendo* and *agendo,* "augmenting" and "acting") and *actor* (from *autentim,* Greek for "authority").[5] In all these instances the author, not the reader, is imagined as having creative, transformative powers over the material of the written text. Nor can it be sheer coincidence that these particular authorial powers—to act, to grow, to tie—are visually represented by the figures animating and empowering the letters (as complicated knots, as burgeoning plants, as moving and acting creatures) of so many medieval manuscripts, first sacred then secular.

Of course, it was—and is—ultimately impossible to restrict or fix the meanings of any text, but that does not curtail the desire to do so by maintaining authorial power over it. Furthermore, in a manuscript culture one could not hope to control the sense of a written text without first succeeding at another chimerical task: fixing or maintaining control over the text's letter—that is, the sequence of alphabetic characters, grouped into words and larger units of sense, that compose the text. The complaint against writing Plato attributed to Socrates was that it could not "defend itself" against "unfair abuse" (either misinterpretation or falsifying change to its letter). After the invention of printing and copyright laws, writers have had to worry less and less about falsification of the letter of their texts. It is hard to imagine, for example, that someone could quote this paragraph in print changing half the words and still attribute it to me. I can be fairly certain that my words will be quoted or reprinted correctly. Print has fixed the letter of my text; only its sense remains mobile, for anyone is capable of making what he or she wants of it. That we no longer have to worry about the fixity of the letter of what we write is probably the major reason Foucault conceived of the "author function" narrowly, as a way of restricting possible interpretations and trying to fix the *meaning* of a written text or series of texts.

The "principle of the author" as a way of trying to close and maintain control over a written text's sense, as well as its letter, was established long before the eighteenth century. It was called into play—even in the elementary form of personalizing imprints of fingernails or mantle fringes on cuneiform tablets—almost with the very invention of writing. The apparent impersonality and impotence of the inscribed text, such as a contract of donation or other material engagement, called for personalizing, empowering supplementation. The impression of personal presence was conveyed by adding imprints of the contracting parties: on Mesopotamian clay tablets, imprints of the fingernails or the fringe of the robe or of another personal marker; on medieval charters, imprints on wax of the beard hair, the fingerprints, the seal ring, or other cachet—and once, even of the donor's toothy bite! Such impressed bits or marks of people, "by materializing the presence of the contracting parties and witnesses, perpetualizes the currency, hence the validity, of the contract," in the words of Elena Cassin.[6]

In order to replace a person (or the "person" of God), a written text had to be mythologized as, made to seem to *be,* a person. That textual interpreters did engage in such imaginative projection is suggested by the many examples, already in the exegetical writings of the early Christian fathers, of the attribution of voice (and human personality) to letters, pages, and texts, as Joseph Balogh has pointed out: "[F]or ancient man, even the page of a book, indeed, even an isolated, dead letter had . . . a voice: the book or the letter 'spoke' or 'fell silent.'"[7]

Part of the history of the author function is the story of the various attempts to personify writing to empower it and make it seem more capable of replacing a person, that is, doing what a person in the act of speaking might do (defend himself, persuade, enforce). One way early Christian

FIG. 79. Author portrait of Terence. Plays. Vatican, MS lat. 3868, fol. 2r. Photo courtesy of the Biblioteca Vaticana.

scribes helped to personify writing was by supplementing and combining it with depiction: at first they imitated classical portraits of secular authors on papyrus rolls, where the image of the author presided directly over the column of writing in which his text began.[8] With the invention of the codex, Christian scribes began to place an image of the author on a separate page (or frontispiece) preceding—indeed, directly overlying—the pages of the following written text.[9]

Probably from a third-century original (now lost), a Carolingian scribe faithfully copied one classical author portrait as a frontispiece to the plays of Terence in a manuscript from around 820–30 (fig. 79). The frontal bust of the author appears to have been painted on a framed square canvas, which rests on a low pedestal and is supported upright for our viewing by two men wearing actors' masks. The only writing on the page is the name Terence above the depicted picture. In fact, this frontispiece copy of a classical author portrait does not depict Terence as a living person, but rather it depicts his framed portrait, a memorial image, which would seem to be less effective at creating an illusion of authorial presence than other types of depiction (such as, for example, a full-length, unframed image of a person engaged in an action or—even livelier—a person who overlaps or steps out of his frame, as was so common in later medieval vignettes of authors).

Although most of the earliest and most authentic (by today's standards) Greek texts of the Gospels—the Vaticanus, the Sinaiticus, the Alexandrinus—have no pictorial supplementation at all, some very early collections of Scripture do present author portraits. The late sixth-century Rabula Gospels, written in Mesopotamia, depict the evangelists beside the canon table arches preceding the texts of their Gospels proper.[10] The makers of a sixth- or early seventh-century Syriac Bible (Paris, B.N.F., MS Syr. 341) relied even more heavily on author portraits to give a human face to Scripture. Each book of the Old Testament (and probably also of the New Testament section of this codex, now lost) was introduced with a standing portrait of its human author or chief character.[11] Each portrait was unframed on the bare surface of the vellum page, and each appeared right above the beginning of the new text, so that the person seemed to attest to and preside over his or her words.[12]

As we have seen, classical author portraits also lie behind the first evangelist "portraits" in Latin Gospels. The early sixth-century Rossano Gospels appropriate a classical portrait of a poet inspired by his muse to depict Mark writing under inspiration (fig. 77); the late sixth-century Gospels of Saint Augustine, made in Italy, present Luke in the antique pose of a philosopher (fig. 75); and Eadfrith of Lindisfarne modeled his Matthew (fig. 53) on the classicizing author portrait of a writing Ezra, which Eadfrith found in the late seventh-century Codex Amiatinus (fig. 76), made in Italy and probably itself modeled on Cassiodorus's lost sixth-century Calabrian Codex Grandior. Perhaps the most successful and long-lived adaptation of a classical author portrait of the medallion type (like that copied in the Terence manuscript) is the Christ-in-Majesty frontispiece to the Gospels in the Codex Amiatinus (fig. 52), which was imitated in many versions, even in stone tympana. The spatial arrangement of this page clearly subordinates the human authors of the Gospels to the divine author. Holding codices, the four evangelists stand on ground lines in the four corners of the page, while Christ-the-Word sits in the center of a medallion-mandorla signifying heaven and holds up the "original" text with a covered hand while pointing to it with the other. Mediating between the heavenly source and the evangelists standing on their ground lines are the flying figures of the Spirit. With this visual preface, the Amiatinus illuminator authorized the following Gospel texts as inspired versions of the same divine source.[13]

As we have seen, early Christian scribes had to revise classical types of author portraits to emphasize that Scripture's true author was divine. Holy Scripture was, like any other writing, a replacement for its writer, but in this instance the true writer—God or the Holy Spirit—composed and signed through the instrument of a human hand and mind. In the preface to his *Moralia in Job,* Gregory made the mere instrumentality of the human writer perfectly clear by comparing him to the "pen" with which the Holy Spirit authored the text:

> It is very superfluous to inquire who wrote the work, since by faith its author is believed to have been the Holy Spirit. He then himself wrote them, who dictated the things that should be written. . . . If we were reading the words of some great man with his epistle in our hand, yet were to inquire by what pen they were written, doubtless it would be an absurdity, to know the author of the epistle and understand his meaning, and notwithstanding to be curious to know with what sort of pen the words were marked upon the page. When then we understand the matter, and are persuaded that the Holy Spirit was its author, in raising the question about the writer what else are we doing but making inquiry about the pen as we read the epistle?[14]

Medieval depictions of evangelists pointedly examining their quill pens may allude to Gregory's analogy and evoke the human writer's merely instrumental role in transmitting a text authored by the Spirit.[15] Other, earlier ways of accomplishing the same task were discussed in the preceding chapter: frontispieces depicting evangelists writing under the inspiration of the Holy Spirit in animal or human form (as in the Rossano or Lindisfarne Gospels) or the pictorially incongruous conflation of figures—God, the evangelist, the monastic scribe (as in the Echternach Gospels, from the ultimate to the immediate causes of the text)—so that God or the Spirit appears to show through the evangelist, who may also have certain features of a medieval monastic scribe.

The classical author portrait attempted to control the text from the outside, for it literally presided over the writing, either directly above the text column or overlying it on a separate page. Although early Christian scribes and designers of codices of Holy Scripture did resort to this kind of control, northern ones, especially, seem to have preferred—or to have found it more effective for doctrinal reasons—to animate and authorize sacred letters from within, by combining them with pictorial figures so that the letter itself was formed by a living shape or "contained" life in its interior spaces (as do the historiated initial letters of so many sacred texts all the way up to the Renaissance).

Scripture was God's writing, and if it was to have coercive power (if the clergy were to derive power from their contact with and custody of Scripture), it had to contain the presence of God. The signifier had to be perceived as the signifying subject (the Signifier). Early monastic scribes in the north harnessed the power of image magic to this effect. In previous chapters, I have demonstrated at some length how Christian scribes from the sixth century on—and perhaps most creatively in eighth- and ninth-century Insular Gospels—enfleshed words, designed initial letters so that God might seem to be immanent or incarnate in these letters. As we have seen, eighth- and ninth-century illuminators did not shy away from depicting the human form of God in or as the letter: on the chi-rho page of the Book of Kells (color plate 1), where Christ's head tops two letters; on the chi-rho page of another Gospel (influenced by Insular models, although local legend at Tours would identify its scribe as Saint Hilarius), where the lower limb of the letter chi terminates in a "human" hand, presumably that of Christ, the "Word made flesh" (fig. 2); on the "Te igitur" page of the Sacramentary of Gellone, where the crucified body of Christ incarnates the letter $T$ (color plate 6), to name but a few examples. In the tenth-century Evangelary of Metz, the initial $L$ beginning Matthew's Gospel (fig. 47) is formed by the kneeling body of a very human-looking, haloed angel—the Spirit inspiring Matthew—who points with a quill pen to the text materialized in writing at his right.

COLOR PLATE 1. Chi-rho page. Book of Kells. Dublin, Trinity College, MS 58, fol. 34r. Photo courtesy of the Board of Trinity College Dublin.

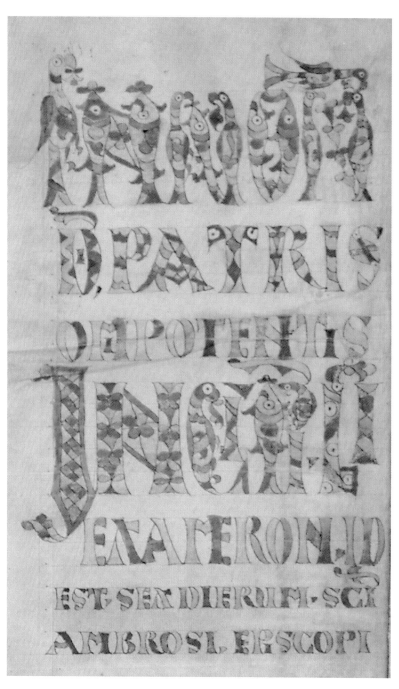

COLOR PLATE 2. Eagles and fishes forming letters. Ambrose, *Hexaemeron*. Paris, B.N.F., MS lat. 12135, fol. 1v. Photo Bibliothèque nationale de France.

COLOR PLATE 3. Cross-patterns of an initial *T*. Sacramentary of Figeac. Paris, B.N.F., MS lat. 2293, fol. 19v. Photo Bibliothèque nationale de France.

COLOR PLATE 4. Multicolored figural letters and grounds. Augustine. *Questiones in Heptateuchon.* Paris, B.N.F., MS lat. 12168, fol. 1r. Photo Bibliothèque nationale de France.

COLOR PLATE 5. Letter *T* (*end of the third line*) heightened and surrounded by red dots. Sacramentary of Gellone. Paris, B.N.F., MS lat. 12048, fol. IV. Photo Bibliothèque nationale de France.

COLOR PLATE 6. Initial *T* of the "Te igitur" page as Christ crucified. Sacramentary of Gellone. Paris, B.N.F., MS lat. 12048, fol. 143v. Photo Bibliothèque nationale de France.

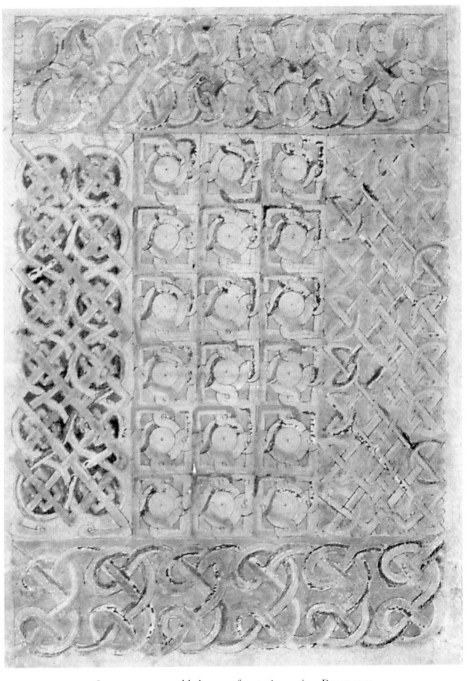

COLOR PLATE 7. Interwoven page added as a preface to Augustine, *De consensu evangelistarum*. Paris, B.N.F., MS lat. 12190, fol. ov. Photo Bibliothèque nationale de France.

COLOR PLATE 8. Initial *B* of "Beatus vir" with David harping (*left*), fighting a lion (*above*) and Goliath (*below*). Psalter. Evreux, Bibliothèque municipale, MS 131, fol. 1r. Photo courtesy of the Bibliothèque municipale d'Evreux.

FIG. 80. Portrait of Paul. Epistles.
Munich, Bayerische Staatsbibliothek,
MS Clm. 6436, fol. 2r. Photo
Bayerische Staatsbibliothek.

The "body" of the letter might also be figured as a part of the body of a human writer, especially a writer imagined to be particularly powerful because touched by divinity, inspired, saintly.[16] An exceptionally early example of a writer depicted as contained within his letter is a sixth-century initial *P* beginning the name Paul in a manuscript of Paul's Epistles (thought to be of North African or Spanish origin); the loop of this initial encloses a laurel-wreathed human head in profile, which would seem to be an image (a "portrait") of Paul (fig. 80).[17] From the late eighth century on, a human hand or head sometimes emerged from an initial, as, for example, in the Sacramentary of Gellone, where a hand grasping a cross replaces the crossbar of an uncial *e* (fig. 81), or in a ninth-century Greek manuscript of Gregory of Nazianzus's sermons in which the initial *e* is regularly depicted with a pointing hand as its crossbar (fig. 82), thus turning it into a kind of embodied *nota* sign and restoring to writing the emphatic gesture of a body in the act of speaking.[18] The scribal illuminators of the Sacramentary of Gellone were remarkably inventive and clever in their embodiments of initial letters (figs. 27, 29, 45, 81, and color plate 5), and they even pictured the hands and tonsured, shaven heads of medieval monks, perhaps the scribes of the manuscript, as letters (fig. 1). In this latter instance, the inspiration (if not merely the piety) of the human writer may be suggested by the upward stare of the monk whose arm and hand "form" the extender of the uncial *d* and uphold the loop of the letter (the first letter of the word *deus,* "God").[19]

When an image of Christ is visible on the page, the gaze and index finger of the human author-as-letter may point in Christ's direction (rather than

FIG. 81. Initial *E* with its crossbar as a hand holding a cross. Sacramentary of Gellone. Paris, B.N.F., MS lat. 12048, fol. 123v. Photo Bibliothèque nationale de France.

upward off the page) to signal the true source and sense of the text, as is the case in a twelfth-century manuscript of a Latin translation of the Jewish historian Josephus's *Antiquities,* which was understood by Christians, like the historical narrative of the Old Testament, as prophecy of Christ (fig. 83). Here the figure of the author, identified by a very large Jew's hat, forms part of the letter (the upright) and "upholds" part of it (the loop of the *P* as scroll announcing the title "Antiquitatum"); but instead of looking or gesturing toward and testifying to the letters that follow this initial *P* beginning the word *principio,* the human author points backward to the initial letters of the first word of the text, *IN,* which are superposed to form a monogrammatic cross shape against a cross-shaped gold ground. The initial *I* is the standing figure of Christ (identified by a cruciform halo), who rests one hand on and supports the *N* on which are depicted the different phases of the Creation. Josephus gestures toward this illustration of the literal sense of his history, which begins with a narrative of the Creation; but Josephus (the human author depicted as the first initial of the second word) also points to a prior, superhuman author: Christ figured as the first letter of the first word. It is no coincidence that the Christian designers of the initial letters of this manuscript have managed to ground the text of Josephus's *Antiquities* in the body of Christ.

Figures of the author as letter were also used to authorize or empower, and thereby to help fix or limit changes to, certain kinds of medieval secular writing. For example, in a tenth-century Vergil manuscript, the first book of the *Aeneid* begins with a standing figure of the author, who forms the upright of the initial *P* and reads from a scroll that forms its loop.[20] Sur-

FIG. 82. Hand of an initial *E*.
Sermons of Gregory of Nazianzus.
Paris, B.N.F., MS grec 510, fol. 104v.
Photo Bibliothèque nationale de France.

prisingly, the device of depicting the author as initial letter survived until the end of the fourteenth century in certain French royal charters (which were empowered also by signatures or seals that assured a permanent testimonial presence).[21] Just as a sixth-century scribe drew the head of Saint Paul within the circle of the *P* beginning the name Paul (fig. 80) in order to suggest the presence of Paul within the letter of his Epistles, so the scribal illuminator of a charter of Charles V dated 1366 concerning the inheritance of the duke of Orléans depicted the crowned Charles V within the circle of his name's first letter, an initial *C* figured as a dragon firmly closing the letter by the ferocious grip of its tail and teeth upon a scepter (fig. 84). This bust of Charles V in the first letter of his name, looking toward and witnessing to the following letters of the text of the charter he grants, is also a portrait in the modern sense of the term; it is the depiction of an individual (reproducing his or her peculiar features to make the individual recognizable) and not merely a general likeness, as are most author "portraits" connected to medieval letters.

Another portrait of Charles V occurs in a slightly later charter, an act founding the Chapel of the Holy Trinity at Vincennes in 1379 (fig. 85). Here the upright of the initial *R* beginning the text is formed partly by the king's body itself as, crowned by two angels, he stands upright on a dais behind a long, narrow tapestry and gazes toward the Holy Trinity (depicted on the curve of the top loop of the *R*) while handing the sealed charter of donation (which forms the crossbar of the *R*) to a group of monks (kneeling in the right leg of the *R*). Although this animated initial does illustrate the literal sense of the words of the charter, it does more

FIG. 83. Initial *P* with a figure of Josephus pointing to a figure of Christ forming an initial *I*. Josephus, *Antiquities*. Paris, B.N.F., MS lat. 5047, fol. 2r. Photo Bibliothèque nationale de France.

than that. The conflation of pictures with the shapes of the letter serves to suggest the source of the letter's—the written charter's—power to enact a transfer of property: the person of Charles V, empowered by God (for Charles's action of bestowing a gift upon the monks "through" the letter—

FIG. 84. Portrait of King Charles V of France in an initial *C* of a royal charter. Paris, Archives nationales, J.358, no. 12. Photo Archives nationales.

the charter/crossbar—is divinely authorized by means of the angelic crown bearers who bestow divine power upon the king).[22]

By the late fourteenth century, the conflation of human bodies with the shapes of letters was old-fashioned, while such carefully detailed mimesis of the individual features of the human author or writer was new. Ernst Kris and Otto Kurz, in *Legend, Myth, and Magic in the Image of the Artist,* have suggested that "where the belief in the identity of picture and depicted ['effigy magic'] is in decline, a new bond makes its appearance to link the two—namely, similarity or likeness."[23] Whereas the only image capable of creating an impression of presence on most viewers today is the perfectly exact likeness obtained by means of a photographic imprint, mimetic painting may have given late medieval viewers the illusion of the presence of the person depicted. For a late fourteenth-century viewer who had actually seen him, the strikingly "realistic" (for the times) likenesses of

FIG. 85. Charles V as an initial *R* of a royal charter. Paris, Archives nationales, AE II 401 A. Photo Archives nationales.

Charles V incorporated into the initial letters of these charters may have revived the "magic" of earlier, generic author portraits, which had faded into the status of mere representations. As Kris and Kurz point out, "whenever a high degree of magic power is attributed to an object— whether this be the fetish of primitive men or the miracle-working ritual image of civilized man—its resemblance to nature is rarely of decisive importance."[24] (Indeed, when image magic was most powerful, the picture usually did not resemble outward appearances at all, for a divine author was believed to reveal his presence in enigmatic ways, so that Christ's incarnation in the letter, for example, was first signaled by depicting the letter as a grape-bearing vine or a fish, and not as a human body.) The relatively high degree of likeness of the drawing of Charles V incorporated into the initial letter of his charter (fig. 85), to the extent that it created a magical

FIG. 86. Saint Hilarius holding up the initial *C* of his text. Paris, B.N.F., MS lat. 1699, fol. 3v. Photo Bibliothèque nationale de France.

effect of the king's perpetual presence (stronger than that of the waxen figure impressed by his seal), could be an effective way of guaranteeing and empowering the writing.[25] When the king's body forms the letter, surely the writing embodies his will.[26]

In a twelfth-century manuscript of Saint Hilarius's *De Trinitate,* the human body of the saintly author depicted to the left of the initial letter no longer forms or is the letter. Instead, the writer, robed and mitered as a bishop, stands to the side of the letter holding it up, guaranteeing it with the power of his presence as he tramples a dragon underfoot and stabs it down with his crosier (fig. 86).[27] In this particular instance we may read, to the left of the base of the initial, the following inscription: "savalo monacus me fecit" (Savalo the monk made me). Is such an inscription merely a clever way for a medieval scribe to identify himself by showing that he, like the saintly author, has had a part in the writing of this text? Or is it also an act of pious devotion (like his copying of the saint's text), which the scribe hopes will assure, through the continuous presence of his own name near a letter inscribed by himself and upheld by the saint, his own proximity to and protection by the saintly presence? Half a millennium earlier, in the late seventh-century Valerianus Codex of the Gospels, in an act that would seem presumptuous if not intended to function as an ex-voto, another scribe, Valerianus, placed his own name at the center of a cross topped by a bust of Christ (fig. 87).[28]

It is impossible to tell where image magic ends (when the image no longer seems to convey a presence) and representation begins (when the image is conceived as a substitute standing for someone or something absent), for the border lies in the mind of the individual viewer. Letters pictorially animated to create an impression of authorial presence might be understood by some medieval viewers, even from the beginning, as mere representations.[29] Acquisition of the technical means to fix the letter of a text ever more permanently—critical editing procedures, printing, copyright laws—eventually rendered obsolete and redundant earlier efforts to fix the letter by image magic (designing letters to give the impression of the continuing presence of the writer *in* or *as* the letter) or by representation (picturing the writer's physical presence near the letter to guarantee it by recollecting that presence).

As readers in a long-established print culture, we tend to see the pictorial designs of medieval manuscript pages either as "decoration" or as illustrations of the literal sense of the words; we have become impervious to image magic in the realm of alphabetic inscription (although certainly not in many other contexts), and we find it difficult to imagine the possibility that letters designed as living forms might ever have done more than represent the life that is really absent from the letter. Yet ex-voto scribal "signatures" and donor or owner "portraits" in close proximity to sacred letters[30]—and the treatment of such letters and the codices in which they are inscribed, in general, as though they were divine or saintly relics imbued with supernatural powers—suggest that some medieval people viewed them quite differently.

In *Medieval Theory of Authorship,* A. J. Minnis has stressed the changing attitude toward Scripture manifest in commentaries written by thirteenth- and fourteenth-century scholars. Biblical exegesis before the thirteenth century did not emphasize the literal, historical sense (which was attrib-

FIG. 87. *Valerianus scripsit* (Valerianus wrote this) inscribed in the center of the cross. Valerianus Codex. Munich, Bayerische Staatsbibliothek, MS lat. 6224, fol. 202v. Photo Bayerische Staatsbibliothek.

uted to the human author), but instead pursued the supraliteral senses put there by the divine author. Divinity and extreme complexity of intention—authority and enigma—were supposed to go hand in hand. This view of Scripture is reflected in the extraordinary figural complications and pictorial animation of the initial letters—the writing—of sacred texts. However, in the early thirteenth century, with the movement of theological study to the universities, the secular influence of Aristotelianism and the adaptation of the Aristotelian prologue to study of the Bible, "It became fashionable to emphasise the literal sense of the Bible, and the intention of the human *auctor* was believed to be expressed by the literal sense."[31] During the same period, and well before, there is a resurgence of the "portrait" of the human author of Scripture, whose body is no longer merged with the shape of the letter but exteriorized so that he either presides over the column of letters in the manner of a classical author over his text or uses the letter as a backdrop or stage.[32]

As we have just seen in a twelfth-century manuscript of a work on the Trinity, its human author, Saint Hilarius, stands to the side of the first initial of his text to "uphold" it (fig. 86). Even earlier, in the second half of the eleventh century, in a Bible made in Rome or central Italy, a figure of Solomon stands with an unfurled scroll directly over the column of letters of his text. As in a classical author portrait, Solomon is depicted on the bare ground of the vellum, and he is not incorporated into an opening initial; instead, his feet are firmly planted between the letters of his text's opening rubric.[33] When David is pictured as harping in late medieval Latin Bibles, although he is still very often represented within the enclosures of the Beatus initial, there is no dove poking its beak into his ear, no obvious sign of divine inspiration to turn the human author into a mere instrument.[34] Likewise, the evangelists are increasingly represented without any sign of divine inspiration (no animal symbols of the Spirit dangling scrolls or holding codices of the divine exemplar before their eyes). Instead of copying automatically under the mesmerizing influence of the Spirit, they more often appear to labor diligently, bent over their writing tables with their eyes on their scripts.[35]

Later medieval representations of John, the evangelist who made the strongest explicit claims to divine inspiration, illustrate the growing emphasis on the human author (and his intentions). By the end of the tenth century and the beginning of the eleventh, Insular Gospel manuscripts begin to draw attention to John's position as a human witness to Christ's life by means of crucifixion frontispieces wherein John, standing beside Christ on the cross, busily records the experience in a codex.[36] Compared with earlier frontispieces representing the divine inspiration of John's Gospel as he copied it, the focus in these crucifixion scenes is very much on the human author. By the mid-thirteenth century, a French translation of the Apocalypse that amply represents John's divine inspiration in its historiated initials as well as in framed vignettes nevertheless also places considerable emphasis on the human author by opening with a series of pictures of the life of John (Paris, B.N.F., MS fr. 403, fols. 1–3). Above the initial *A* (which reveals an inspired John reaching out of the interior of the letter to write the manuscript before our eyes) is a framed narrative depiction of an event from John's life, his exile by the emperor Domitian (fig. 70). As suggested earlier, images of John examining his pen in late fourteenth-century French translations of the Apocalypse may well evoke the inspired writer's instrumentality, but it is not improbable that these visual allusions to Gregory's metaphor are made with a certain ironic wit, for a scribe would examine his pen when there was a problem with it, when it—or he—wasn't writing smoothly, when the words stopped flowing. As Suzanne Lewis has pointed out,

> John no longer [as in earlier Apocalypse illumination] gazes at the visions or listens to their voices and sounds but instead busies himself at his desk writing, staring intently at his pen, biting his nails, and scratching his head. Perhaps responding to the increasing self-awareness and cultivation of the authorial persona by such contemporary writers as Froissart, Fr. 13096 confronts the reader with an unsettling series of author portraits cataloguing the contorted agonies of authorship in unprecedented detail. Only rarely does John look up from his work to acknowledge the presence of an angel or even the Lord himself. Even when the seer is included as a protagonist within the illustrations of the visions themselves, he is inevitably still seated at his desk with the tools of the writer's trade at hand.[37]

In her study of twelfth- and thirteenth-century French and Insular manuscripts of Paul's Epistles, which most often show Paul in the interior of initial letters of his text, Luba Eleen demonstrates a similar tendency.

Although there is an occasional dove of the Holy Spirit at Paul's ear as late as 1200, the illuminations increasingly focus on human authorship: "[T]he scenes most frequently used as illustrations for the Epistles [are] author portraits, messenger and preaching scenes."[38] Paul is shown behaving as an author: attesting to his text (standing or seated, holding a scroll or book); in the act of writing it; and transmitting it (sending it by messenger, or presenting it orally to an individual or a community).

Secular, vernacular authors were depicted inside or presiding over the letter of their texts in much the same way as sacred ones—which is not surprising when one considers that the scribes and illuminators working in the ateliers of the later Middle Ages produced both religious and secular manuscripts. Nor is it surprising that some of the earliest representations of medieval vernacular authors are those of poets who wrote in the first person and stressed themselves and their subjectivity, such as the troubadours.

In certain late thirteenth- or early fourteenth-century manuscript collections of troubadour verse such as the A, I, and K songbooks, wherein texts by different authors are grouped together and introduced by a rubricated vernacular *vida,* or "life of the poet," an image of the troubadour performing or explaining his work often appears within the initial letter beginning the first poem of his collected "corpus." The body of the poet is not confounded with or contorted into the shape of the letter, but it overlays or rests on the letter while remaining distinct from it, as though using the letter (which is "framed" or set off against a rectangular ground of a contrasting color) as a backdrop or stage (fig. 88). With gestures of oral communication—upraised forearms and hands and directed gazes—these generically portrayed troubadours perform or explain their songs from the stage of the initial letter; indeed, if we judge from the direction of their gazes, they often seem to be reading the adjacent text. For example, Marcabru in the K songbook manuscript (fig. 89) stands in a frontal position and gestures straight ahead toward an undepicted audience (whose position we occupy as readers) while at the same time turning his head and eyeballs sharply to the side toward the adjacent text, as though reading and performing or explaining it to us.

From occupying the interior of the medieval letter, the figure of the ver-

FIG. 88. Marcabru in the initial *C* of his lyric. Troubadour songbook A. Vatican, MS lat. 5232, fol. 27r. Photo courtesy of the Biblioteca Vaticana.

nacular author turned to taking charge of it from a position outside and above—for the figure of the author rested on the column of his text, as if the very function of the written text were to "support" the author.[39] In the M songbook manuscript, the image of the troubadour author presides over the letter of his text by figuring in a square frame the width of a column; this framed author "portrait" rests on the base of the much smaller square enclosure of the initial letter (which is depicted as a sprouting vine) and on the text column itself (fig. 90). The author "portraits" in this songbook tend to illustrate the motivation for each troubadour's verse as extrapolated from it (and explained in his *vida*): many troubadours ride fine horses to suggest their nobility and refinement or aspirations thereto; Jaufre Rudel embraces his lady; Giraut de Borneil, seated at a lectern, reads or lectures from an open book in academic robes. By means of these images of authors performing or explaining or generally presiding over and controlling "their" texts, the makers of the troubadour songbooks tried to fix the letters of lyric texts by recollecting an authorial presence, and, even more boldly, they tried to determine and delimit the letter's meaning with reference to an authorial intention. The contextual supplementation of the letter in these songbooks by a written (and even rubricated) "life of the poet" and by a figure of the poet demonstrating his aspirations and activities are implementations—and very precocious ones—of the attempt at textual closure Foucault called the author function.

In their essay studying iconographic models for the portrayal of authors

FIG. 89. Marcabru in the initial *C* of his lyric. Troubadour songbook K. Paris, B.N.F., MS fr. 12473, fol. 102r. Photo Bibliothèque nationale de France.

in frontispieces or prefatory pictures drawn mainly from fourteenth- and fifteenth-century manuscripts of English and French vernacular literature, Elizabeth Salter and Derek Pearsall have effectively demonstrated the late medieval tendency to supplement a vernacular text with an image of its author; they summarize the different types of author portrayal thus:

> 1) the author as teacher, lecturing from a textbook before students who follow his discourse in their own books . . . ; 2) the author as writer, usually represented as writing at an upright writing desk . . . though occasionally as holding his completed book . . . ; 3) the author as reader, represented as reading from his book which he has before him on a lectern . . . ; 4) the author as reporter, writing as events unfold . . . ; 5) the author as preacher . . . ; 6) the author as dreamer . . . ; 7) the author as protégé of a patron, usually in the form of a presentation picture, where the author kneels before his patron holding out to him a copy of his book . . . ; 8) the author as protagonist, represented in a famous scene from his life.[40]

In this essay, Salter and Pearsall did not explore at length the function of author portraits in general or the significance of differences in the details and mise-en-scène of these, for their essay's main purpose was to put into comparative perspective the frontispiece "author portrait" of a famous early fifteenth-century manuscript of Chaucer's *Troilus and Criseyde* (fig. 91). Although wary of reception studies of medieval vernacular literary works based on minute interpretation of their pictures,[41] Salter and Pearsall would surely acknowledge the validity of interpreting the "larger picture" drawn by their study, which is that the late medieval vernacular literary text in manuscript tends to be presided over by an image (although usually not a true-to-life portrait) of its author.[42]

FIG. 90. Giraut de Borneil at a lectern. Troubadour songbook M. Paris, B.N.F., MS fr. 12474, fol. 1r. Photo Bibliothèque nationale de France.

In the Cambridge Corpus Christi manuscript of Chaucer's *Troilus* (a single-author codex because it contains only this one work, as is the case with at least eight other codices containing only the book of *Troilus*),[43] some ninety blank spaces were left for pictures never completed; an "author portrait" was the only illumination that the early fifteenth-century makers of this manuscript apparently considered too essential to postpone. According to Salter and Pearsall, we should understand the iconography of the *Troilus* frontispiece as an adaptation of the "preaching" type of author portrait (in which we see the author transmitting his work orally). Although this frontispiece has caused much controversy among Chaucerians, one point seems clear: it attempts to restore the person of the author to his writing by representing, at the outset (although not by means of a true-to-life portrait in the modern sense), the text's author physically presiding over and controlling the presentation of his work.

To modern eyes, accustomed to authors' photographs on their published books' jackets, there is nothing surprising about an image of the author accompanying his text—except, perhaps, that this is not the sort of true-to-life portrait we might expect. Concerning the author portraits in later medieval manuscripts of the *Roman de la Rose,* David Hult notes how "natural" they seem to us and consequently how easy it has been to ignore them: "The recourse to authorial designation would seem to satisfy a fundamental need to anthropomorphize the literary object. . . . One of the principal ways in which the *Rose* is partitioned within the manuscript is by means of the illustrations and, most especially, by the inclusion of an authorial portrait, a motif that has garnered virtually no attention either with respect to

FIG. 91. Frontispiece "author portrait" of Chaucer's *Troilus and Criseyde*. Cambridge, Corpus Christi College, MS 61, fol. 1v. Photo by permission of the Master and Fellows of Corpus Christi College, Cambridge.

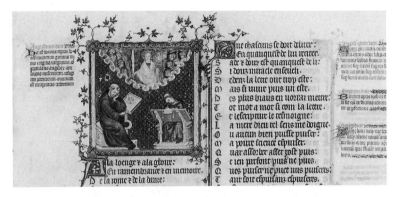

FIG. 92. Gautier de Coinci composing his *Miracles de Notre Dame.* Paris, B.N.F., MS nouv. acq. fr. 24541, fol. 3r. Photo Bibliothèque nationale de France.

its iconographic or to its literary significance."[44] Indeed, an author "portrait" of some type is the most common pictorial supplement to late medieval writing.

Given the late medieval tendency, as discussed, to emphasize the labors of the human author of religious texts, what is perhaps most surprising about vernacular author portraits is their subtle and not infrequent recourse to the iconography of supernatural inspiration and divine or royal authorization as a kind of reinforcement. Gautier de Coinci's vernacular verse compilation of *Miracles de Notre Dame,* in an early fourteenth-century codex of his collected works, offers one such example. In this single-author codex (Paris, B.N.F., MS nouv. acq. fr. 24541, fol. 3r), the authorial prologue to Gautier's *Miracles* is preceded by an image of a reflective author, his head leaning on his left hand and an open book on the table before him, addressing with his right hand and dictating to another monk who writes on a sheet of parchment on a table (fig. 92). In a semicircular heavenly register above the author's head, the crowned and enthroned Virgin holds a book in one mantle-covered hand and a palm branch in the other. Although the Virgin does not lean out of heaven to offer the divine original to Gautier (as the animal symbols of inspiration so often did to the evangelists), we may suppose that the reflective Gautier sees the contents of the Virgin's book in his mind's eye or in an interior vision. By suggesting that Gautier's vernacular verse is inspired by the Virgin, this author portrait tries to authorize the following text more forcefully than can Gautier merely by claiming, as he does in his prologue, to be turning an earlier Latin book into French rhyme. On the folio following this image, Gautier is depicted at study (fol. 4r); beside a lectern of the sort that enabled comparative consultation of several codices, he reads a book (presumably the Latin source) while also holding it open to us at an awkward angle.

One of the boldest and best-known secular adaptations of the iconography of divine inspiration is a large miniature prefacing a codex of the poet Guillaume de Machaut's collected works, whose making Machaut is believed to have himself supervised in the late 1370s.[45] This codex, Paris, B.N.F., MS fr. 1584, contains a table of contents demonstrating, according to its introductory rubric, Machaut's own ordering for his works: "Vesci l'ordenance que G. de Machaut vuet qu'il ait en son livre" (Here is the order G. de Machaut wants there to be in his book). Furthermore, Machaut provided a versified general prologue to this codex, which explains his works in terms of his poetic vocation, for he claims to have been inspired by Love and formed by Nature to write verse. Two large author portraits occupy the top two-thirds of each of two text pages of this prologue.

In the first of these large miniatures (folio D), in a hilly country landscape Machaut sits inside his study at a lectern before an open book; he is pictured just at the moment when he turns from his reading to receive the visit, at his open door, of the crowned and winged angelic masculine figure of Love, who presents to the poet his children, Thought, Delight, and Hope, who will reveal to Machaut the matter whereof to write (fig. 93).[46] The second large miniature (folio E) shows Machaut standing before a house in a similar country landscape to receive the visit of Nature, personified as a queen, who introduces to him her children, Sense, Rhetoric, Music, the practical abilities with which Nature endows the poet.

Modern editors have preferred the reversed order of pictures, rubrics, and text—Nature before Love—in the only other fourteenth-century manuscript that opens with the prologue, Paris, B.N.F., MS fr. 22545, whose illuminations are less carefully ordered and less skillful. One suspects the main reason for this preference is the notion that natural gifts should come before love's inspiration.[47] Yet there is an even more compelling reason to prefer the pictorial and textual order of Paris, B.N.F., MS fr.

Text below image:

Commeat Amours qui a ouy nature
vient a Guillaume: & machaut et li
am ine trois de ses enfans est asanoir

E sup amours qui nient euer estat di
set son mener douce a toieuse vie
Si ai ony Guillaume se te di

FIG. 93. Guillaume de Machaut receiving the visit of the God of Love. Paris, B.N.F., MS fr. 1584, fol. D. Photo Bibliothèque nationale de France.

1584—the manuscript whose compilation and illumination Machaut him-self reputedly supervised—and that is the powerfully authorizing iconog-raphy of its first image. Even as it brings the angelic figure very much down to earth, this depiction of Love's visit to the poet recollects earlier images of evangelists or church fathers at their books being inspired by angelic vis-itors. There may even be a hint here of another late medieval image of inspiration: the angelic Annunciation to the reading Virgin (who is, how-ever, conventionally approached by her angelic visitor from the left, un-like Machaut).[48]

Their names suggest that the allegorical figures who visit the poet are as-pects of his own psyche; the "revelation" the poet is inspired to set down in words—in the material form of his writings gathered in this codex—is, in fact, self-revelation. Machaut's illuminator has adapted and diverted the iconography of divine inspiration here to sanctify a book of vernacular verse whose purpose (like that of Holy Scripture) is to reveal, although often obscurely through figurative and poetic language, the presence of the subject himself (God in the case of the Bible, Machaut in the case of his codex). Not only the full-page frontispiece author portrait, but also the many smaller framed miniatures of Machaut writing on a scroll or in a book, which punctuate his codices, help to perpetuate the myth of the Signifier—or, as Foucault might put it, to establish the "author function," the myth of the Author—that is, the presence of the subject controlling his writing, even though that presence is shown to be increasingly supervisory, commentatorial (external to rather than conflated with or immanent in the trace of the letter).[49]

Textual transmission always involves change, whether of the relatively minor sorts brought about by copying an exemplar or the major ones caused by translating it into a different language altogether. Just as each copy of a charter needed to be guaranteed and authenticated anew with the seal or symbol—an impression of the permanent presence—of its originators, so also each new copy of a handwritten text needed authentication, and the copying of an author portrait effectively materialized (or recollected) the physical presence of the text's author.

When the new copy was a vernacular translation of a more authoritative original, that is, being the trace of two men (its original author and its translator), medieval illuminators sometimes resorted to curious expedients to personify the new version. Such is the case, for example, in a late fourteenth-century manuscript of the *Cité de dieu*. Resting on the support of an initial *A* opening the prologue of Raoul de Presles's French translation of Saint Augustine's *City of God* (completed in 1375), an enshrining architectural frame contains relatively true portraits of Raoul de Presles and the French king. Raoul kneels to present his open book to a crowned Charles V, who grasps the book with one hand while looking directly into Raoul's eyes (fig. 94). In addition to the two courtiers standing behind the king, there are heavenly witnesses to this presentation: two angels, who hold up a tapestry behind the king to demonstrate his sanctity (for the king's power derives from God through his anointment). The haloed, mitered, crosier-bearing ecclesiastical figure who stands behind Raoul and presents him to the king with an encouraging hand gesture (just as patron

FIG. 94. Raoul de Presles presenting his French translation of *The City of God* to Charles V. Paris, B.N.F., MS fr. 22912, fol. 3r. Photo Bibliothèque nationale de France.

saints present their protégés to Christ or the Virgin in contemporary paintings) can only be Saint Augustine, the "original" author, who here sanctions the translation by presenting Raoul to the king, who sanctions the translation again with his gaze and touch.[50] Raoul de Presles apparently needed more than his own pictured presence—even "realistically" portrayed—to empower his vernacular translation.[51] The vernacular translator is here presented as an instrument of divine and saintly will, which author and authorize the text.

The relationship between a translator and the classical or patristic author he translated into the vernacular was somewhat analogous to that between a prophet or inspired evangelist and the divine author whose text he transmitted; both translator and prophet might be considered to be mere instruments, not authors, peripheral rather than central figures. However, in the later Middle Ages, as we have seen, the focus of exegesis was increasingly on the literal sense and on the human authors of sacred texts. Likewise, in late medieval presentation miniatures, the translator came to displace the original author as the focus of attention. In the Lindisfarne Gospels (fig. 53), the face of the divine author—the Word—peeps out from behind a

FIG. 95. Nicole Oresme presenting his French translation of Aristotle's *Ethics* and *Politics* to Charles V. Brussels, Bibliothèque royale Albert 1$^{er}$, MS 9505, fol. 1r. Copyright Bibliothèque royale Albert 1$^{er}$.

curtain to witness the human author Matthew receiving from the Spirit and copying down the text of his Gospel; in fourteenth-century French presentation miniatures, original authors sometimes peep out from behind curtains at translators presenting their works to the king.

This is the case in a presentation scene depicted directly above the prologue Nicole Oresme addressed to Charles V at the beginning of his French translation of Aristotle's *Ethics* and *Politics,* which the king commissioned from Oresme (fig. 95). Little notice has been taken of the white-haired and bearded old man who watches this act of textual transmission from behind the curtain at the king's back. In her study of illuminated manuscripts of Aristotle, Claire Sherman remarks that this miniature "identifies those who set in motion the translation contained in the volume presented," but she takes the white-bearded onlooker for an anonymous courtier and suggests that he does not disturb the intimacy of the foregrounded figures.[52] With respect to portraits of Socrates and other ancient writers, Sherman notes, however, that "authoritative doctrine and wisdom are embodied in mature, masculine figures characterized by their white hair and beards."[53] If Christ can look out from behind a curtain in the Lindisfarne Gospels, surely Aristotle can do likewise in a presentation miniature opening his *Ethics*—in a vernacular translation that serves to "reveal" Aristotle to a wider audience. The original author is not replaced but merely *displaced* by the translator—who occupies a more central space, along with the ruler—in such authenticating representations.

Presentation miniatures manifest a desire for textual conservation and closure by showing the human author placing his writing in the hands and protection of a powerful person whose contact with the text serves to sanctify and further authorize it. In the earliest Carolingian and Ottonian cases, this powerful figure is a saint or important ecclesiastical figure to whom the monastic scribe presents and dedicates his work, as for example in the early ninth-century frontispiece to the Codex Juvenianus (containing the Acts of the Apostles, the Apocalypse, and other Holy Writ, as well as the first book of Bede's *Expositio Apocalypsis*). In this frontispiece, a monastic figure labeled "Juvenianus subdeacon," presumably the scribe and designer of the pictured codex, hands the codex to an enthroned Saint Lawrence, while over them God's hand reaches down from the heavens in a gesture of benediction.[54] An Ottonian designer even went so far as to use a double-page spread of the codex to give the reader an active role in the book's presentation: on the verso he placed the giver, moving toward the right and stretching out his hands to offer the codex; on the recto he placed the powerful figure enthroned, reaching out his hand to the left to receive it. By turning the verso over onto the recto, the reader can bring the depicted book into contact with the depicted hand of the saint or ecclesiastical leader.[55]

In addition to the scribes of religious texts, their authors and exegetes were shown presenting codices to saints, popes, and even to divinely consecrated kings, as in the frontispiece to the Vivian Bible (fig. 57). Secular authors and translators soon followed suit, presenting their texts to kings and powerful lay rulers in framed miniatures and frontispieces to their works. Almost inevitably, the viewer elides the codex depicted in the presentation scene with the very manuscript in which the presentation scene is painted. The effect of this elision is to authorize and valorize the text in hand as a sort of relic, for we assume it has been in contact with and has been the property of the saint or anointed ruler shown receiving it. Furthermore, even if the manuscript in hand, and its presentation miniature, are merely copies of those in a codex originally given to (or intended for presentation to) the saint or king, we tend to honor the fiction of the presentation scene and to take it, as well as the text of the manuscript, for the one originally presented.[56]

Usually a book presentation scene in a medieval manuscript serves to authorize, or increase the authority of, the text—and thus works to encourage its conservation in that particular manuscript and also to discourage changes to its letter in copying. Directly above the inscribed text the presentation miniature depicts the body of its author (and sometimes also that of the original author, who guarantees or bears witness to a translation). But the presentation scene also shows an anointed king—or saint, pope, or bishop—presiding *over* the inscribed text in the very act of accepting the depicted codex, which he takes into his possession and protection. To the extent that we identify and elide the depicted codex with the inscribed text before our eyes, the ruler's gesture of acceptance serves to authorize the inscribed text anew—and to authenticate every copy of it in which the presentation scene is depicted.

# THE LETTER IN
# RENAISSANCE
# PERSPECTIVE

T his study of the ways alphabetic
inscription was combined with drawing and depiction in the Middle Ages,
while not denying the multiple functions of such figuration (marking and
mnemonic functions, enhancing material or aesthetic value, explicating or
illustrating), has concentrated mainly on the ways in which pictorial representations of writing—figures of the letter—have worked to empower
and authorize it by encouraging the illusion (an effect of image magic) of
the signifying subject's continuing presence in (or, later, near) the inscribed
text. Mere black marks on a surface did not seem capable of defending
themselves from alteration or of replacing effectively the person of their
speaker. In order to do that, the marks had to be animated by pictorial representation and color, had to be seen as a living trace, moving, changing,
*being.* Writing could be empowered only by fetishizing and mystifying it,
and this is exactly what early medieval Christian scribes and illuminators
did to "God's" writing (although they would not have characterized their
pictorial elaborations of the letter of Scripture in this way, for they pro-
fessed to be the mere instruments that made manifest divine designs).

The great chi of the chi-rho page opening the Gospel of Matthew in the
Book of Kells epitomizes the artful fetishizing of the letter (in this case the

first letter of Christ's name in Greek) as the living trace of God, as an incarnation of divinity (color plate 1). Had they been written in a continuous classical script, the initial letters of the Gospel of Matthew (on Christ's human lineage) would have done no more than commemorate Christ by verbal recollection of his past presence—and current absence—but the Kells artists designed these initial letters so as to produce the impression of living bodies whose limbs are divinely animated: letters that *are* God. Through its magnification and the energetic curves of its limbs, the great chi seems to spring forward at us, moving outward in an act of revelation. The intricacies of the various figural designs contained in the compartments of this letter's interior—from the interlaced men and birds in the central lozenge of its torso to the animate and linear interlace and geometrical dot and flower patterns in its limbs—call for closer scrutiny and contemplation to unravel their complexity. Such pictorial complication of the shape of the letter renders it more difficult to read, more opaque and mysterious, and also, as with any enigma, more powerful.

Over the course of several centuries, the makers of medieval manuscripts gradually separated drawing from writing, pictorial representation from lettering. Instead of depicting an initial letter *as* the body of its author (either a human body or a figurative form of divinity such as the vine-as-Christ), they turned to depicting an initial letter as enclosing or framing the body of its author, and eventually to depicting the body of the author outside the letter altogether, in a separately framed rectangle resting on or above an increasingly simplified and regular initial. What drawing manifested or represented (depending on the degree of the viewer's participation in the illusion of authorial presence) in all these instances was the relationship between the signifying subject and his written trace: he empowered it because he *was* it or inhabited its interior or supervised it.

The separation or elimination of drawing from writing, begun before the invention of the printing press, was institutionalized thereafter for technical and economic reasons. Likewise color, which had already been reduced to very light tints in the late fourteenth-century illuminating technique of *grisaille,* was eliminated by the printing process.[1] These changes are reflected in the representations of writing and the manuscript page in certain deluxe illuminated manuscripts and incunabula of the late fifteenth and sixteenth centuries, which we might have expected to be engaged, instead, in preventing the divorce between drawing or coloring and writing. What is perhaps most striking about the early Renaissance examples I have selected—as compared to medieval examples of colorfully designed and animated letters—is the way the different illuminators have used drawing to demystify handwritten letters by picturing and representing them as "dead" letters devoid of being and movement, black marks on a piece of parchment, an artificial representation different—and visually distanced (via linear perspective)—from the life depicted realistically (sometimes with trompe l'oeil effects) in the space surrounding or apparently subtending the inscription.[2] We have already seen one early—late fourteenth-century Lombard—example of this tendency in a manuscript of the secular, vernacular text of *Giron le courtois* (fig. 72), whose illuminator turned the text columns into representations of writing on unfurled flaps that hide part of an underlying scene in an imaginary space behind (symbolically prior to) the words representing that scene.

Almost exactly a century later, the elaborate monumental frontispiece to Alexander Cortesius's *Laudes bellicae* represents the opening verses of a contemporary Latin text as handwriting, devoid of any pictorial design, on a tattered ancient fragment of thick, hole-riddled parchment with mutilated margins (fig. 96). This antique-looking fragment of parchment appears tied (at its upper right) to the column of a Renaissance stone memorial and tacked (along its top) to a framed plaque on which is inscribed, in incised-looking capitals in a continuous classical script, the first two verses of the poem, minus the initial letter *I,* which appears as if engraved in relief on a small separate plaque to their left. Just above these, on another framed plaque that seems to form part of the stone monument, the title of the work appears engraved in Roman capitals. There is a wealth of fascinating detail here, but I would call attention to the way writing is being represented in this manuscript, which was written and illuminated after the introduction of printing.

By representing a Renaissance Latin text as handwritten on a tattered old parchment that has survived the centuries in a fragile, fragmentary state, the illuminator flatters the contemporary text with a classical pedigree. Yet not all of the text is represented as fragile; its title and opening lines are

FIG. 96. Frontispiece to the *Laudes bellicae* of Alexander Cortesius, illuminated by Bartolomeo Sanvito circa 1480–90. Wolfenbüttel, Herzog August Bibliothek, Cod. Guelf. 85.1.1. Aug.2, fol. 3r. Photo courtesy of the Herzog August Bibliothek.

apparently engraved on plaques fixed to the stone memorial (to which the handwritten parchment fragment is also fixed by ties and tacks). Even more impressive than the representation of writing's fragility here is the representation of its permanence (writing as epigraphy, letters incised in stone) or of the desire for its permanence (the tacking and tying in place of the manuscript). In this frontispiece to a book that is itself handwritten and designed, the representation of a handwritten inscription nailed to an engraved, monumentalized one may suggest the transformation of handwriting into print and the way pictorial representation helped to create a new mythology that would empower printed writing by likening it, or making us see it as, letters engraved in stone. Print could defend and "close" a text only by fixing its letters "permanently," that is, the same letters in the same places in every one of the edition's multiple copies. The lettering of the text of the *Laudes bellicae,* whether represented as handwriting or epigraphy, is depicted as devoid of figures, as a "dead" letter without any animating pictorial designs. Nevertheless, the depiction filling the "marginal" space surrounding and subtending the inscription still works to empower the writing here: by creating an illusion of writing's monumental permanence (which would compensate the loss of the earlier illusion of living presence in the trace evoked by the pictorial fetishizing of the letter itself). Even illuminated Renaissance manuscripts, whose project might seem archaic, register the contemporary abandonment of the handwritten trace in favor of printing and the accompanying necessity of inventing new mythologies to empower writing.

On a page from a Book of Hours made in Bruges around 1490, for example, the artist known as the Master of Mary of Burgundy represented the text as a piece of a manuscript held taut by ropes to a thin window frame through which we view scenes of Christ's Passion (fig. 97). Of this particular page, Otto Pächt has observed: "If early on in the Middle Ages we talked of a page of script that contained a picture, we can now say that the picture contains a page of script. The picture has triumphed over script."[3] Separated from writing in a clearly extratextual space, pictorial representation here competes with writing and effectively drains the letter of life (as opposed to animating it as in earlier medieval examples, where picture and letter were conflated).

FIG. 97. Text tied into a window frame over scenes of Christ's Passion. Book of Hours illuminated in Bruges by the Master of Mary of Burgundy circa 1490. Madrid, Biblioteca nacional MS Vitr. 25-5, fol. 14r. Photo courtesy of the Biblioteca nacional.

Had it been inscribed and illuminated a century earlier, what we might have expected to see on this page would be a text with a large historiated initial *D* (beginning the word *domine*) in the upper-left-hand corner; this framed initial would have contained a depiction of Christ bearing the cross, while depictions of chimerical figures and scenes from everyday life would be relegated to the largely blank margins surrounding the inscription. Were this historiated initial painted in an archaic manner, Christ's foot or another figure's limb would project over the initial letter in the direction of the viewer, for early historiated initials were depicted as matrices of revelation. The figures of or in early medieval letters always seemed to move forward toward the viewer. Yet on this particular page illuminated in the late fifteenth century, the inscribed letters appear fixed in the foreground, while the pictured figures recede behind them so that our eye seems to pierce through and behind the text to apprehend them. As represented by this illuminator, the opacity of the letter is not a consequence of the wealth of figures it spawns and reveals (as with the Kells chi) but rather of the fact that the letter and the written text are material objects that cannot be seen through. Here the very absence of writing—the apparent excision of a historiated initial—in the upper-left-hand corner of the foregrounded manuscript page is what allows us to see the action in the background of Christ bearing the cross.

By tying the text into a windowlike frame in this way and letting us see around and partially through it—much as did the illuminator of the Hours of Charles of France, who depicted the inscribed text, with its historiated initial, framed and dangling by a chain in a deeply recessed window (fig. 71)—the Master of Mary of Burgundy may be suggesting that the ideal text would be totally transparent, a window onto the represented, a signifier that could present the signified undistorted. Thus, although he demystifies writing in one way (showing it to be devoid of the living presence of any signifying subject, fragmentary and powerless—unlike earlier animate knotwork letters—to move or to bind), he may also be suggesting a new mythology that would empower writing by idealizing its transparency, its capacity to represent accurately, a new mythology that would attempt to close the gap and deny the difference between signifier and signified (rather than between signifier and signifying subject). There is, however, considerable ambivalence in this representation of writing as representation, for the pictured fragment of a manuscript page blocks our vision (and comprehension) with its opacity everywhere but in the upper-left-hand corner, where the transparency of the "virtual" historiated letter (which exists only in our imagination) allows us to see through the written text.[4]

In another late fifteenth-century Latin religious manuscript, the Italian illuminator relegated picture and letter to seemingly different spaces, separated drawing from writing, by depicting a ragged hole in the upper-left-hand corner of the manuscript page, where a historiated initial *C* should, conventionally, have been (fig. 98). This depicted hole in the vellum, with its torn edges, has the effect of seeming to turn a "real" manuscript page into the representation of one, "real" letters into represented ones. Through the depicted hole (where the historiated initial would have been, but now "is" only virtually, transparently), we see an Annunciation scene drawn according to linear perspective, which creates the impression of a deep space receding behind the foregrounded writing. The pictured scene and the letters forming words both represent the Annunciation, and we know that a drawing of the Virgin and Gabriel is actually no closer to being the Virgin and Gabriel than is a written text about them made up of ink marks representing words representing ideas of the Virgin and Gabriel. Nevertheless, the pictorial representation is much more powerful than the literal, verbal one. Such realistic depiction works a kind of image magic upon us so that, in spite of what we know to be true, we mentally confound the signifier (the drawing) with the signified (the original event of the Annunciation) and imagine a pictorial representation as a revelation. The letters, on the other hand, are here pictured as lifeless, fragile (for their vellum support is torn) and physically distant from the life they would represent (but partially conceal by their own opacity). Depiction undercuts the power of the writing on this page by showing it to be mere representation.

And yet this illuminator, like the Master of Mary of Burgundy, would also seem to be trying to suggest the ideal of a transparent writing that would function like realistic depiction and give us the illusion that there is no difference between signifier and signified. By replacing a conventional historiated initial with the hole where a historiated initial apparently once was, he leaves a sort of transparent initial in the viewer's mind, a "virtual" letter through which we perceive the scene of Annunciation represented by the drawing (and also by the adjacent written text). How paradoxical

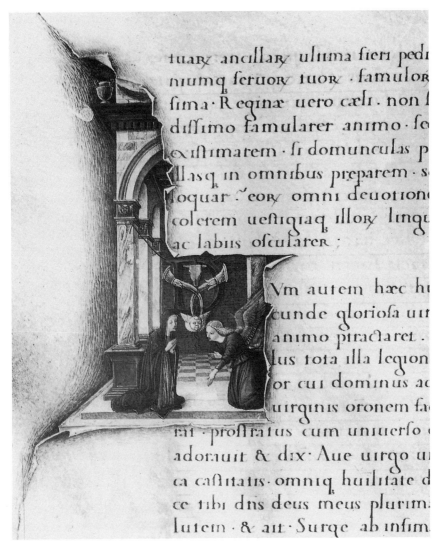

tuaҗ ancillaҗ ultima fieri pedi
niumq feruoҗ tuoҗ · famuloҗ
fima · Reginæ uero cæli · non l
diffimo famularer animo · fe
exiftimarem · fi domunculas p
llasq̃ in omnibus preparem · s
oquar ~ eoҗ omni deuotion
colerem ueftigiaq̃ illoҗ linqu
ac labiis ofcularer ;

Vm autem hæc hu
cunde gloriofa uir
animo piradaret ·
lus tota illa legion
or cui dominus ac
uirginis oronem fi
ni · proftratus cum uniuerfo
adorauit & dix · Aue uirgo u
ca caftitatis · omniq̃ huilitate d
ce tibi dns deus meus plurim.
lutem · & ait · Surge ab infim.

FIG. 98. Annunciation scene from a late fifteenth-century Venetian manuscript of *Columba.* Vienna, Österreichische Nationalbibliothek Cod. 1591, fol. 69v. Photo Österreichische Nationalbibliothek.

that the Annunciation—the moment of the Word's fleshly incarnation, which early medieval illuminators tended to represent (as in the Kells chi) as an incarnation of divinity in the "bodily" form of writing—should be the pictorial figure of a letter that is itself immaterial, not physically present. Yet, the longer one looks at this page, the more this virtual initial *C* (perhaps ever so slightly suggested by the curve of the depicted arch) seems to be realized in the pictured figures. Somewhat like a drawing by Escher in which figure and background are reversible, this Renaissance manuscript page is finely balanced between two orders: the old order of revelation, which used the image magic of pictorial design to animate letters (and thus to encourage the reader or viewer to imagine the signifier as signifying subject); and the new order of representation, which used the image magic of pictorial design in an illustrative way, to show what and how writing signified, to suggest that reading was like looking through a window (and thus to encourage the illusion of writing's transparency and of the identity of signifier and signified).

APPENDIX

# *The Jesting Borders of Chaucer's* Canterbury Tales *and of Late Medieval Manuscript Art*

In her 1969 essay "Medieval Poetry and the Visual Arts," Elizabeth Salter noted how important art historical studies have been to our understanding of the form and meaning of the *Canterbury Tales*—of their Gothic structure, as treated by Charles Muscatine in *Chaucer and the French Tradition* and by Robert Jordan in *Chaucer and the Shape of Creation,* of their symbolism or iconography as treated by D. W. Robertson in his *Preface to Chaucer* (and, we might now add, by V. A. Kolve in *Chaucer and the Imagery of Narrative*). After a warning about the necessarily inconclusive nature of comparing verbal and visual arts, Salter went on to suggest a further analogy: between the visual designs of the margins—or borders—of certain late medieval manuscript pages and the verbal "frame," as we usually call it, of the *Canterbury Tales,* that is, the general and individual prologues and "links" that contextualize the tales. Salter made the following astute comparisons between visual and verbal borders:

> [A]s fourteenth-century illuminators often found licence, in their border-work, to experiment fruitfully with new dramatic themes and forms, so Chaucer innovated, unchecked, in his "borders" to the *Tales*. . . . Like many illuminated pages of later medieval books, the *Canterbury Tales* does not properly adjust border materials to main subjects. The frame, like the wide, packed, and errant borders of many manuscripts, contains or fails to contain, an explosive life of its own, secular and dramatic; such a life advances upon the more static and conventional material of many of the *Tales*. . . . [I]n the whole relationship of border to main subject, frame

to *Tale,* Chaucer and the illuminators often give us the impression that the marginal zone is alive, and the scene in the center only a picture.[1]

That no Chaucer scholar, to my knowledge, has pursued Salter's insight may be, in part, because of the dearth of seemingly relevant art historical analyses of "marginal" art, which for a long time was dismissed in one of two ways: either from the outset, as frivolous nonsense unworthy of study, or as representation of sin that should be resisted—mentally censored or moralized—by the pious reader. In introducing her groundbreaking catalog of *Images in the Margins of Gothic Manuscripts,* published in 1966, Lilian Randall pointed out how frequently the art of the margins had gone undescribed in modern art historical analyses, which focused instead on the iconography of the more "central" images, that is, the miniatures framed by initial letters or in rectangles.[2] By the late sixties and early seventies, Randall was calling attention to the humorous, playful aspects of Gothic marginalia, whereas, in an article in 1957 entitled "Exempla as a Source of Gothic Marginal Illumination," she had tended to moralize it, treating it—by analogy to the verbal structure of sermons ending with moralized proverbs or popular stories—as a clever way of warning against sin.[3] Robertson, in his *Preface to Chaucer,* published in 1962, cited Randall's 1957 essay, the only one then available to him, and applied the same sort of iconographical reading to Chaucer's fabliaux, arguing that these were to be moralized after the manner of the sinful imagery in the margins of late medieval manuscripts. Many Chaucerians were skeptical, not so much of the notion that visual marginalia were meant to be moralized (for this would have amounted to attacking the conclusions of another discipline), but of the notion that Chaucer's fabliaux were meant to be moralized. This put a damper on further comparison of the *Canterbury Tales* with Gothic marginal art for over two decades.

In a precocious essay in 1983, "Game in Myn Hood," Sarah Stanbury used Gothic marginal imagery as well as Latin wordplay (on *cucullus* for hood or head and *cuculus* as cuckold or bastard) to explore the sense of proverbs using the word *hood* in the works of Chaucer and anonymous medieval writers. Just as the "margins" have replaced the center as the focus of attention in other fields of academic inquiry, so also in art history the formerly neglected "border" regions of the manuscript page are now being scrutinized and written about with gusto. To note but a few of these signs of attention, Michael Camille's *Image on the Edge: The Margins of Medieval Art,* published in 1992; Madeline Caviness's 1993 essay in *Speculum* offering a feminist reading of Jean Pucelle's marginal images in the Hours of Jeanne d'Evreux (images often suggestive of *dépucelage* [deflowering] with reference to fourteen-year-old Jeanne's marriage); and Lucy Freeman Sandler's 1996 essay, in a special issue dedicated to Lilian Randall, on the various types of word illustration in the margins of the Luttrell Psalter.[4] Conferences, too, are now being devoted to the sole subject of manuscript margins. In 1994, from Oregon to Oxford, there were conferences entitled "Peripheral Visions: Reading the Margins in the Middle Ages" and "Undefined Fields in the Medieval Book: Margins, Borders, Spaces."

Recent art historical scrutiny of marginal imagery has resulted in a more complex understanding of its possible meanings. In addition to representing folly or sin, or serving as a mnemonic device,[5] the marginal imagery may comment critically on, travesty, burlesque, or contest the authority of the text and images inscribed in the center of the page. Adding philology to his eclectic method of analyzing marginal images in *Image on the Edge,* Camille shows how certain marginal figures visually represent liberties taken with the sense of the text; such figures may be the rebuslike signs of deliberately debasing interpretations based on grossly materialistic literalism and bilingual puns (whereby a vernacular sense is attributed to a Latin word or syllable).[6] In 1988, in *The Game of Love: Troubadour Wordplay,* I argued that the figures in or extending into the borders of several troubadour songbooks represented deliberately "foolish" textual interpretation.[7]

Here I would like to make another contribution to the theory that certain kinds of Gothic marginalia are signs of play on the part of their designers. This by no means precludes their being understood otherwise—even moralized as signs of sinfulness—by other viewers and readers. Unlabeled pictures are notoriously open to interpretation. For example, a marginal image in the Hours of Jeanne d'Evreux such as tilting at the hole in a barrel (fig. 99) may evoke the marriage and deflowering of Jeanne d'Evreux, the young bride of the French king, who ordered the book made as a gift for her. Caviness has argued that Jeanne herself can hardly have found such imagery amusing. Yet others may well have. Such a marginal allusion to *dépucelage* may have served as a kind of visual "signature"—via a rebuslike pun—for the manuscript's chief illuminator, Jean "Pucelle." Furthermore, the burlesque tilt may be perceived as a low parody of the scene of Christ's betrayal depicted on the page above it.

The symbolic sense of marginal, "unruled" space as Other is fundamental to the liberation of the protean forms and what we might almost call the polymorphous perversity of Gothic margins. I believe, in addition, that the use of marginal space for all kinds of playful jesting was authorized by a pun or near pun in medieval English, Anglo-Norman, and northern French involving two words that could be spelled and pronounced alike, two words now distinguished in French as *bords* (borders) and *bourdes* (jests). Folk etymology assumes a common root or fundamental identity between two similar-sounding words, so that, in this case, borders would be the appropriate place for jests, *bordes* for *bordes* (or *bords* for *bourdes,* as we would say in French today).

FIG. 99. Christ's betrayal (*above*) and a burlesque tilt at the hole in a barrel (*below*). Hours of Jeanne d'Evreux. New York, The Metropolitan Museum of Art, Cloisters Collection, MS 54.1.2, fol. 15v. Photo Metropolitan Museum of Art.

The great variety of different kinds of Gothic marginal figures—monkey business, wonderfully incongruous creatures, jesters and minstrels, jousting and gaming, illustrations of fabliaux—represent the many possible kinds of jesting or *bourdes.* The *Middle English Dictionary* gives a wide range of meanings involving both actions and words for the French loan word *bourde* (also spelled and pronounced *borde* or *burde* or *b[o]urte*):

—an amusing story, anecdote, exemplum
—a boastful or bawdy story
—a joke, jest, witty remark
—game, sport, amusement, entertainment, fun
—joking, jesting, levity, frivolity
—prank, trick, amusing incident or adventure
—marvelous event or wonder[8]

That the earliest surviving example of full-fledged Gothic marginal illumination was done in England, in the mid-thirteenth-century Rutland Psalter, would hardly disprove the theory that a punning identification between the words for "borders" and "jests" helps to explain the nature of marginal art. The Rutland Psalter was made and illuminated for Edmund de Laci, that is, in and for a milieu almost certainly sufficiently bilingual to be able to play on the equivocal senses of French words and French loan words. The drolleries of late thirteenth- and fourteenth-century Gothic margins were elaborated for and appreciated mainly by French speakers in the north of France and the low countries and by bilingual people in Britain (the French- and English-speaking noble and bourgeois elites).[9]

For English and French speakers today, however, the pun on the medieval words for "borders" and "jests" is occulted in several ways: by the more distinctly differentiated pronunciation of these two words in modern French (*bords* and *bourdes*); by the loss of the very term *bourdes* (meaning jests) in modern English; by our tendency to think of and designate the nontextual space on the manuscript page as margins rather than as borders; and, perhaps most important, by our mental distance, as visually oriented readers, from what Bruno Roy has termed the medieval "culture of the equivocal," which was based on play with sounds.[10]

The word *margin* (from Latin) is attested in late fourteenth-century English usage. Chaucer used it to designate the border of a page in his *Treatise on the Astrolabe* ("The names of the sterres ben writen in the margyn of the riet there as thei sitte," 1.21.8); in this same text, Chaucer used the term *bordure* many times to designate the calibrated circumference of the astrolabe, so that another term was necessary to signify the outermost space on the page. In Continental French, however, the word *marge* is not attested until the end of the fifteenth century; the prevalent term was "border" (variously spelled as *bord, bort, bors,* and so on). For example, an inventory entry of 1387 records payment to "Huguelin de Champdivers, illuminator of books, living in Paris . . . for having illuminated along the borders ('par les bors') and bound a large Book of Hours for the Duke of Turenne."[11] Filled with figures, the border space might also be called a *bordëure* in medieval French or, in Middle English, *bordure* (the orthography in Chaucer), *border, bordour,* and *burdire.*

The conventions of word formation are interiorized unconsciously during the process of learning any language, even if one learns it late in life. Medieval speakers of the vernacular had to depend heavily on their notions—based on the logic of analogy—of how to form words, for they had no vernacular dictionaries to tell them whether a word form that would seem to be possible, because it fit conventional morphological patterns, had been authorized by previous use. In this respect, the medieval dictionaries of the vernaculars that we have at our disposal today are highly misleading: they present an image of the language very different from the aural one a medieval speaker would have interiorized. The very notion of an "authorized" vernacular lexicon is an anachronism in the Middle Ages. A word form that one could not remember hearing before, if it fit conventional patterns, was still within the realm of the possible as long as there was no dictionary to prove that it was "not a word."

With this enormous cultural difference in mind, let us engage now in a speculative exploration of the possible senses of the syllable *bord* and its variant forms in medieval French and English. Relying on the logic of analogy, we might suppose that the infinitive form for the act of designing a border would be *border* in French, and that the name for a border maker would be *bordeur* or possibly *borderesse.* A small border might be called a *bordel.* But, easy as they are to imagine, *border, bordeur, borderesse,* and *bordel* are not attested with these meanings in modern dictionaries of medieval French. We are told that *bordel* meant "brothel"; *borderesse,* "prostitute"; *border* or *behorder* meant "to joust" or to fight with or play at hitting a mark with a lance; a *bordeor* was a "maker of jests," not a maker of borders. The French words *borderie* and *bordelage,* which might seem to refer to what happens in borders, are attested with the following senses: *borderie* = trickery (*tromperie*), lies, foolishness; *bordelage* = public debauchery and impudicity.

The possibilities for wordplay were, if anything, even richer in England than in France, especially in bilingual circles, for the repertory of possible puns based on French words and French loan words was extended by means of native English ones. Certain words attested in modern dictionaries of the French written and spoken in England (Anglo-Norman) seem not to have been used on the Continent—for instance, the word *border* meaning "to make a border" and also "to tighten by pulling." The repertory of puns based on more recent French loan words was augmented by words perceived to be English (that is, French loan words long since naturalized). Thus, according to the *Middle English Dictionary,* the noun *bor* meant "boar"; *bore* meant "hole," sometimes even "anus"; and *bore* (also spelled *bour, bur*) meant "cottage." *Bord* in Middle English meant "border" (borrowed from French *bord*), but also "board" and all the senses that derived from it, such as "ship," "shield," "gaming or dining table," and "board." *Burde,* the Middle English word for "maiden" or "damsel," could sound very like English *borde* (a variant spelling of *bourde,* meaning jest) and also like *bord* (meaning border), for the weak final e of *burde* could be elided or dropped in certain contexts, provoking ambiguity.

Certain anglicized forms of French loan words evoked puns more readily than Continental cognates. *Border* as a Middle English noun (more often spelled *bordier* in French) meant a "cottager," a rustic tenant of the lowest class; but the noun *border* in Middle English (or *bourder* or *bourdour*) also meant "a storyteller, a mocker, a minstrel or jester." In Middle English the infinitive *borden* (also spelled *bourden,* from French and Anglo-Norman *border* or *bourder*) meant "to joke, mock, play games"; the infinitive *borden* (also spelled *bourden,* from French and Anglo-Norman *behorder* or *bohurder*) meant "to joust, to tilt at, or to charge a boar with a spear." Although unattested, the logical Middle English infinitive form for "to make borders" would also be *borden*. In French, a *bordon* (in Anglo-Norman, a *burdun*) was a bagpipe or, more specifically, its pipe or drone, or a droning sound. But the same orthography—*bordon*—also signified a grey mullet (a buzzing insect of the bee family) and a long staff (especially a pilgrim's staff with a knotted, gourd-shaped head for a handle). This list of French, Anglo-Norman, and English words containing the syllable *bord* and lending themselves to confusion and wordplay could go on and on and become more and more entangled, but my point, I trust, is already clear.

The kinds of jokes (*bourdes*) that we find represented in the manuscript borders of Gothic Psalters, Books of Hours, and even some vernacular romances such as *Lancelot,* are suggested by this list of *bord* words. Illuminators not only represented playful jesting going on in the margins—minstrelsy, jonglerie, various kinds of trumpeting, and monkey business—but they themselves played with the reader or viewer by inventing verbal and visual puns in the margins. Sometimes it is difficult to distinguish between representation of play and playful representation. Horn blowing or "trumpeting" may represent play, but it may also pun on *tromperie* (trickery), one kind of *bourde.* Some puns are purely visual, such as burlesque imitations or grotesque deformations of the sacred or serious figures occupying the central space on the page; other puns work more like rebuses in that words and ideas are represented by visual figures. For example, the idea of the border and of its making may be suggested by a drawing of a boat (*bord*),[12] a dinner or chess table (*bord*),[13] a bagpipe, a buzzing insect, or a gourd-headed staff (*bordon*),[14] a brothel (*bordel*),[15] a jester or jongleur (*border* or *bourder*),[16] a rustic engaged in rustic activities (a *border*),[17] a joust or a tilt at the quintain (*borde* or *bourde*), and so forth.[18] Fourteenth-century Psalters, Books of Hours, and romances offer a host of border *bourdes,* that is, jesting representations of the border.

Because this sort of marginal play was fashionable in the late fourteenth century both in England and in northern France and the low countries, Chaucer must have seen examples of it. Indeed, I would suggest that Gothic marginalia may have provided an important model for the aesthetic structure of Chaucer's *Canterbury Tales,* a collection of texts he "borders" with *bourdes* in much the same way. The connective passages we have called "links"—which modern readers have enjoyed for their "realism" or "naturalism," their dramatic interaction, and also for what Muscatine called their "noise and horseplay"[19]—may be Chaucer's attempt to supplement his collection of tales with the verbal equivalent of Gothic marginal illumination. Even certain passages that we have not usually called links but that are not part of the tales proper, such as prologues and epilogues, have a "bordering" function. I like to think of the envoy to the Clerk's tale of patient Griselda in this way. So much seriousness and *sentence* in the tale provoke a facetious reaction couched in grotesque, semibestial imagery reminiscent of the incongruous hybrids of Gothic margins and the ludicrous battles between the sexes figured there: suddenly Chichevache, the patient wife-eating cow, appears on the scene, and women are imagined strong as camels, fierce as tigers, loud as mills, pursuing and piercing their quailing husbands with "arrows of crabbed eloquence" (4.1177–1212).

We might even think of the relationship of some Canterbury tales to others in Chaucer's compilation as "bordering." In the first fragment or series of linked tales, the didactic romance of the Knight is "bordered" by the *bourdes* of the following fabliaux (of the Miller, Reeve, and Cook), which coarsely mock its idealism in various ways. These fabliaux are the verbal equivalent of Gothic marginalia. Indeed, comic scenes from medieval fabliaux are among the many kinds of *bourdes* figuring in the borders of the page. For example, the scene from the fabliau of *Barat et Haimet* in which one thief steals another's britches as he climbs a tree, thus baring his bottom, is represented in the border of a fourteenth-century Flemish Psalter (Bodleian, Douce 6, fol. 135).[20] As V. A. Kolve has pointed out, it is in the margins of Gothic manuscripts that we must look to find imagery such as that the Miller describes verbally in his tale—the bum-baring, ass-kissing imagery of the fabliaux.

Burlesque *behordes* or tilts at the target of the naked human buttocks or anus appear frequently in Gothic margins and put one in mind of the burlesque joust in the Miller's tale, with Absalon driving a red-hot coulter at Nicholas's bared bottom. In the Rutland Psalter (London, B.L. 62925, fols. 66v and 67r), for example, the illuminator placed his burlesque *behorde* (Middle English *borde* or *bourde*) at the bottom of two consecutive pages facing each other, a verso and a recto, so that the reader could turn the page to help the point of the lance held by the ostrich-riding ape on the verso reach its target, the exposed buttocks of a naked man bending over in front of him on the recto. (Whether the ape moves forward to impale the man or the man moves backward to impale himself depends on the direction in which the reader turns the pages.)[21] This burlesque tilt is a visual jest as well as an instance of punning, rebuslike play (involving similar-sounding words for tilting, jesting, and bordering).

Chaucer may have been working in his *Canterbury Tales* toward what might be called concentric groupings of texts so that—sometimes on the smaller scale of the tale and its links or appurtenances, sometimes on the larger scale of a whole series of tales—*sentence* would be encircled or bordered with *solaas* in the manner of the pages of certain Gothic Psalters, Books of Hours, and vernacular romances. As Elizabeth Salter warned, analogies between visual and verbal art are interesting, but rarely entirely convincing. We will probably never know for sure exactly what motivated Chaucer to give his collection of stories what we have long called, by analogy to visual art, a "frame." It would be better if we ceased to use this term, for it suggests a kind of containment or delimitation that was foreign to Chaucer's aesthetics. The manuscript pages of fourteenth-century Books of Hours and other pious texts, like the idealizing or pious stories of Chaucer's *Canterbury Tales,* did not have frames, properly speaking, but instead borders. And these Gothic borders were not so much delimiting boundaries as open spaces, areas open to multiple senses and interpretations. In the hands of secular illuminators making manuscripts for secular patrons, as in the hands of Geoffrey Chaucer, borders became places for *bourdes,* for contest and mockery, for interpretation in a more vulgar or a different register than that required by the center, for the opening up and out of meaning, not for limiting or shutting it in.

# NOTES

The following abbreviations appear in the notes and the bibliography:

CCL   *Corpus christianorum, series latina.* Turnhout, Belgium: Brepols.
CCM   *Corpus christianorum, continuatio medievalis.* Turnhout, Belgium: Brepols.
PG    *Patrologia cursus completus, series graeca.* Paris: J. P. Migne, 1857–66.
PL    *Patrologia cursus completus, series latina.* Paris: J. P. Migne, 1841–64.
SC    *Sources chrétiennes.* Paris: Cerf.

For source citations, Arabic numbers separated by periods will refer to book, chapter, and section or part. In the case of nonbiblical texts, Arabic numbers separated by a colon will refer to volume and page (or column for the *Patrologia* series). In the case of biblical texts, Arabic numbers separated by a colon will refer to chapter and verse. Exceptions, such as volumes published in separately bound parts, will be spelled out in words. All citations from the Greek fathers will be to the facing Latin translations of the *Patrologia graeca* or to the French ones of the *Sources chrétiennes* series.

English translations of the Vulgate Bible will be taken from the Douay-Rheims version. The names of biblical writers will be cited in their current English spellings: Ezekiel, Ezra, Isaiah (rather than Ezechiel, Esdras, Isaias). Latin citations of the Vulgate will be from the Weber edition. I will add punctuation, rather than presenting Vulgate citations *per cola et commata.* Vulgate numberings will be used in references to the psalms.

Unless otherwise stated, all translations will be my own.

## Introduction

1. Lanham, *Electronic Word,* p. 134.

2. Lanham, ibid., p. 128, makes the following predictions about ways that electronic writing will soon be animated to form a new kind of writing that he calls "dynamic alphabetic expression": "Prose as we know it, printed prose, is based on an aesthetic of black and white linear renunciation. We use 'figures of speech' but we never let the figures realize themselves in their native iconic form. . . . Now, they can explicate themselves in animations selected by the reader. The text will move, in three dimensions. . . . [W]e will add the dimension of color. . . . [W]e can add sound to our reading as well. Word, image, and sound will be inextricably intertwined in a dynamic and continually shifting mixture." As I will demonstrate in chapter 3, there is in fact a very important, although little understood, tradition in medieval manuscript illumination of realizing certain figures of speech—especially Christ's—in letters designed so as to incorporate pictures.

3. Nor is this desire to animate writing restricted to the West. Grabar, *Mediation of Ornament,* p. 58, quotes a contemporary Chinese writer: "The essence of beauty in [Chinese] writing is not found in the written word, but lies in response to unlimited change; line after line should have a way of giving life, character after character should seek for life movement." Likewise, in Egyptian hieroglyphic writing of high quality, scribes made an effort to enliven graphic signs by varying them, as Hornung notes in "Hieroglyphs," p. 278: "In the same text the same word can be written in several ways, and even the same sign can vary in its exact form. In an inscription of high artistic quality, no hare or falcon is identical to the others. . . . Life is not repetition but variation. This was imperative for an Egyptian artist, including the scribes, sculptors, and painters of hieroglyphic inscriptions."

4. Van Moé, *Lettre ornée,* p. 8. Van Moé's volume is, nevertheless, a pale reflection of the splendor of the hand-painted, engraved reproductions of ornamented letters, pictorial motifs, and full-page illustrations in the eleven completed oversize folio volumes (financed generously by the French Ministries of the Interior and of Public Instruction) of Bastard's *Peintures et ornements des manuscrits.*

5. The virulence and longevity of the reaction against subjective appreciation in art historical study can be measured by Garnier's admonitions in his pathbreaking and enormously useful classificatory study of the visual language, or iconography, of gesture (*Langage de l'image,* p. 29): "The qualifiers whereby one expresses a personal emotion menace iconographic analysis in multiple ways. For the objectivity of the given they risk substituting the subjectivity of the felt; the richness or the poverty of the costume, the aesthetic quality of the forms engender judgments about the realities they cover. This literature, if it renders an analysis more agreeable in appearance, weighs it down, leads to confusion, dilutes the essential instead

of emphasizing it. The difference between the descriptive epithet and the appreciative one can be slender. Only sobriety in description permits relations to be understood in their essentiality." Garnier's is a positivistic scientific attempt to discover the rules of a "universal language" of medieval images that will permit us to read their sense "correctly," in effect, to read straight "through" them: "In order to establish, with probability, then with certitude, the signification of the elements and the relations that constitute iconographic language, the research must be based on numerous documents permitting the establishment of scientifically valuable series whose interpretation gives a sufficient guarantee of objectivity" ("Lecture de l'image," p. 109).

Although perhaps necessary to establishing the desired taxonomy of gesture, there is something troubling about an objectivity obtained by suppressing emotional responses to the object under consideration, and even, in this case, by suppressing from conscious perception a part of the object itself, which is sometimes a designed letter. The simplified black-on-white line drawings Garnier uses to illustrate his analyses of the semiotics of gesture and position in medieval illuminations serve the purpose not only of producing a more economical edition by avoiding photographs but also of eliminating everything about the manuscript page's design (including the colors) that Garnier considers inessential, as he explains by analogy to architectural structure (an analogy that bespeaks a modernist, antiornamental aesthetics): "In order to disengage the major architectural lines, one must pass over the fantasies of ornament, without ignoring them, but situating them in their place, that is, maintaining their 'accidental' character with respect to the signification" ("Lecture de l'image," p. 109). Garnier's line drawings have the effect of divorcing pictorial representations of human gestures and movement—animation—from letters, drawing from writing. For example, to illustrate the idea of disequilibrium, Garnier provides a line drawing of a prostrate rider being crushed under his fleeing horse's hooves (p. 123); if we turn to the plate section at the back of *Langage de l'image,* we see that the prostrate rider on this particular manuscript page of Gregory's *Moralia in Job* (Garnier's fig. 30) forms the tail of an initial *Q*. In most cases, such a restorative comparison is not possible, because the plate section provides photographs of only a few of the manuscript pages from which the line drawings are abstracted.

6. Footnote references to color plates in this widely available edition will be given whenever possible.

7. The most extreme example of this modernist, antiornamental aesthetic is Loos's 1908 essay, "Ornament and Crime," wherein the architect associates ornament with primitive amorality and eroticism and judges it a sign of backwardness or degeneracy when resorted to by individuals in modern cultures. Loos states his position baldly: "The evolution of culture is synonymous with the removal of

ornament from objects of daily use" (p. 100). "The lack of ornament is a sign of intellectual power" (p. 103). On modernist antipathy to ornament, see also Steiner, "Postmodernism and the Ornament," pp. 60–63.

8. Suggestive on ornamentation as transformation is Coomaraswamy, *Christian and Oriental Philosophy of Art,* p. 18: "We are often told, and not quite incorrectly, that primitive ornament had a magical value; it would be truer to say a metaphysical value, since it is generally by means of what we now call its decoration that a thing is ritually transformed and made to function spiritually as well as physically."

9. This is not to deny the enormous utility to the study of designed letters of a fundamental collection of paleographical facsimiles such as Lowe's *Codices latini antiquiores.* A historical outline of the changes in basic script styles can be found in Bishop, *Latin Palaeography.*

10. Toubert, "Lettre ornée," p. 379.

11. Paris and Pannier, *Vie de Saint Alexis.* In this edition, which purports to be "an attempt at total restoration" (p. vii) of a preexisting eleventh-century poem, Gaston Paris devotes only one sentence (p. 2) to description of the content and illustration of the base manuscript, neglecting even to mention that the *Alexis* precedes a Psalter. On the Paris and Pannier edition, see also Kendrick, "1123?," and Camille, "Philological Iconoclasm." For black-and-white photographic reproductions from the manuscript, see Pächt, Dodwell, and Wormald, *St. Albans Psalter.*

12. In "Editing Old French Texts," p. 30, Speer notes a very early instance of the use of lithography: in 1836, in the first edition of the *Voyage de Charlemagne,* Francisque Michel included a color plate of the first folio of the previously unknown manuscript (which he had discovered in the British Museum in the course of his state-appointed mission to explore for French national treasures there). In this exceptional instance, the color reproduction of the first page attested to the existence of the newly discovered artifact. Only recently, in Christine Marchello-Nizia's 1984 edition of the *Roman de la poire,* in what Speer signals as a "welcome innovation for the SATF series" (p. 32), has the Société des anciens textes français (founded by Gaston Paris) begun to publish extensive photographs of manuscript illuminations, other than supposed "author portraits." The Early English Text Society, on the other hand, published facsimile editions of some important manuscripts, which, in effect, served to caution the iconoclasm of critical editions of texts found in these manuscripts. For example, in 1923 Israel Gollancz published an EETS facsimile edition of the illuminated manuscript containing the sole surviving copy of *Sir Gawain and the Green Knight* (London, British Library, MS Cotton Nero A.x.Art.3). In 1940, when Gollancz published his EETS critical edition

of this text, he included one photograph of the opening page of writing, with its pen-flourished initial, and none of the illustrative illuminations.

13. Carruthers, *Book of Memory,* p. 256. In stressing manuscript art's exemplary function of suggesting "how to" form memory images, Carruthers refines the thesis of Yates, *Art of Memory,* p. 81, who posits that some images in manuscripts may have served as memory images or originated in them:

> though one must be extremely careful to distinguish between art proper and the art of memory, which is an invisible art, yet their frontiers must surely have overlapped. For when people were being taught to practise the formation of images for remembering, it is difficult to suppose that such inner images might not sometimes have found their way into outer expression. Or, conversely, when the "things" which they were to remember through inner images were of the same kind as the "things" which Christian didactic art taught through images, that the places and images of that art might themselves have been reflected in memory, and so have become "artificial memory."

14. Alexander, *Decorated Letter,* color plate 1.

15. Carruthers, *Book of Memory,* p. 257.

16. Ibid.

17. Freedberg, *Power of Images,* p. 32.

18. The English translation of Gregory's letter is by Chazelle, "Pictures, Books, and the Illiterate," p. 139. See also, on Gregory's statements, Duggan, "Was Art Really the 'Book of the Illiterate'?" The notes to these two essays refer to the major scholarly analyses of the Byzantine controversy over iconoclasm and its Carolingian repercussions in the *Libri carolini.*

19. Grabar, *Mediation of Ornament,* p. 61, remarks on this transfer of power from the painted or sculpted image to the image of writing in the Islamic world: "The concomitant result of the rejection [of mimetic representation] was the elevation of writing into the main vehicle for signs of belief, power, legitimacy, and any one of the functions for which images were used elsewhere. The best-known early examples of these 'images of the word,' as they have been called, are the coins of late seventh-century caliphs." Compare Kessler, "On the State of Medieval Art History," p. 173: "Because it recorded God's word, the book was elevated in Christianity to the position once occupied by the cult statue. Embellished, it was to have the visual effect befitting its spiritual content."

20. Lerer, *Literacy and Power in Anglo-Saxon Literature,* pp. 16–17.

21. I will use the term *Insular* to designate manuscripts made in what are today Ireland and Great Britain.

22. Note, for example, the angular, runic-looking lettering on the opening

pages of two Gospel texts, which I have reproduced from the Lindisfarne Gospels (fig. 31) and the Book of Kells (fig. 59). Higgitt, "The Display Script of the Book of Kells," comments (p. 215), "Whether or not the Kells scribes borrowed specific runic forms, familiarity with runes no doubt contributed in a more general way to the taste for rectilinearity and angularity in insular decorative capitals."

23. Nordenfalk, *Celtic and Anglo-Saxon Painting,* p. 8, notes the "almost talismanic" effect of incorporating earlier types of pictorial designs into writing: "The very process of writing changed from a simple means of communication to something almost talismanic, by being combined with ornament—a totally new and persuasive concept of the book which was to prove fruitful all through the early Medieval centuries."

24. Grabar, *Mediation of Ornament,* p. 109: "Within the mass of perceptible categories available, the contemporary eye excerpts writing immediately after figural representations. It is as though, in the development of one's discourse of perception and thought about an object, writing is the next layer to be identified after mimetic themes."

## Chapter 1

1. *Newsweek,* European edition, 18 April 1994, p. 5, concerning "Oregon poet Donal Eugene Russell, whose will stipulated that skin from his corpse be used to cover a volume of his works."

2. David Ganz, "'Mind in Character,'" cites examples from the classical and late classical periods of authors who added postscripts in their own handwriting to letters dictated by and otherwise written by their secretaries. Jerome's comment on Saint Paul's practice is particularly remarkable for his suggestion of how the original readers of Paul's letters would imaginatively project upon his handwriting Paul's *person* testifying to the veracity of the document: "So that he [Paul] should remove all [of] the letter which he sent from the suspicion of forgery he subscribed it in his hand at the end, saying 'The greeting of Paul in my hand which is the sign in every letter: thus I write, the grace of Lord Jesus Christ be with all of you.' . . . [H]e subscribed his letter with his own hand . . . so that when they recognized the strokes of the letters they thought they could see him who had written them" (trans. Ganz, p. 284). "Et ut totam epistolam quam mittebat, suspicione erueret falsitatis, manu sua in fine subscripsit, dicens: Salutatio mea manu Pauli, quod est signum in omni epistola: ita scribo: Gratia Domini nostri Jesu Christi cum omnibus vobis. . . . epistolam manu propria subscribebat . . . ut dum litterarum apices recognoscunt, ipsum se putarent videre, qui scripserat" (*PL* 26:434).

3. A similar effect has been noted by Dynes, "Imago Leonis," p. 40, concerning a famous page of the Echternach Gospels: "Unlike the lion and the frame, the final element, the parchment support, usually goes unmentioned in discussions of the miniature. Yet it plays more than a passive role. . . . The painted elements may thus be regarded as a kind of tatooing [*sic*], enhancing a skin whose organic origins are still readily apparent, and drawing attention to the membraneous and permeable nature of the skin, which admits the color into its pores and tautly connects the uncolored areas."

4. For example, the 1411 inventory of the royal library in the Louvre describes the Breviary of Jean de Bourbon thus:

> Item—another Breviary covered in satin lined with blue taffeta, embroidered with the arms of the queen, with two clasps, each with four pearls, and at the end of each of the aforementioned clasps a silk lace with a pearled button and a strip of gold metal with two pearls, with the central stone missing, historiated and illuminated in a formal Latin script in two columns, beginning on the second folio of the Psalter with the words *mini qui* and ending *tion et les trois.*

This description from Paris, B.N.F., MS fr. 2700, fol. 97v, no. 581, is cited by Avril and Lafaurie in *Librairie de Charles V,* p. 98.

5. Ginzburg, *Myths, Emblems, Clues,* p. 107.

6. Michael Camille's personal testimony in *Master of Death* is another exception (p. viii): "I still remember the morning in the magnificent manuscript room at the Bibliothèque Nationale in Paris when I first opened MS fr. 823, which records what I shall argue was his name—Remiet. I can recall being struck by how much it felt like an encounter with more than just another 'hand,' or even a name, that I had somehow come face to face with a person who was somewhere in the paint. Yet how could that be? How can an individual be transmitted by a few marks and colours on a parchment surface? How can a series of images in a few dozen old books suggest something of the flesh and blood of the individual body?"

7. Derrida, *Of Grammatology,* pp. 12–13, for example: "[P]honocentrism merges with the historical determination of the meaning of being in general as *presence.* . . . The epoch of the logos thus debases writing considered as mediation of mediation and as a fall into the exteriority of meaning."

8. Derrida, *Ecriture et la différence,* p. 339, from the author's gloss on his lecture "Freud and the Scene of Writing."

9. Hust, *Signatures célèbres,* pp. 7–8. To emphasize the inevitability of the signature as a natural image of the person, Hust couples the profiled shadows (the silhouettes) of famous men with their signatures.

10. Pulver, *Symbolisme de l'écriture,* pp. 15 and 20. For further commentary on the development in the nineteenth century of a "science" of divining character from handwriting, see Fraenkel, *Signature,* pp. 211–22.

11. This cartoon by Jennifer Bevill illustrated an essay by Jodi Daynard, "Floppy Disks Are Only Knowledge, But Manuscripts Are Wisdom," *New York Times Book Review,* 28 March 1993, p. 27. Daynard asks, "How is it, after all, that I can thumb through the brittle [manuscript] pages of John Cheever's 'Falconer' and, by dint of smell, feel the author's presence as surely as the blind feel a wall before they touch it?"

12. For example, the fabled inventor of Chinese writing is supposed to have been inspired by the natural trace of bird tracks. The earliest Chinese pictograms were thus copies of the outlines or imprints of the body of a living thing or a part of its passing body. See Kristeva, *Langage cet inconnu,* p. 83.

13. The fingerprint as an individual "signature" predates nineteenth-century detective science. Gandilhon ("Dactyloscopie et les sceaux," pp. 98–100) remarks that the Chinese and Japanese seem to have used fingerprints as signatures from at least the seventh century. In twelfth-century France, the imprints of one or two fingers on waxen seals seem to have served as counterseals to guarantee the authenticity of engraved seals. Gandilhon points to one case in which an inscription contemporary with the document describes its only seal as a fingerprint in wax: "sealed in red wax, where the first joint of one of his fingers was the only imprint, without any other signet" (Paris, Archives Nationales, JJ 170, no. 108).

14. Here and elsewhere in this book, I use the pronouns "he" and "him" inclusively to avoid the awkwardness of repeating "he and she" and "him and her." Although the great majority were male, there were female scribes and illuminators throughout the Middle Ages, in early medieval monastic settings as well as in later medieval secular ones. See, for example, Robinson, "A Twelfth-Century *Scriptrix*" for evidence of nuns as scribes in England and on the Continent in the early Middle Ages, and for images of women writing up to 1400, Smith, *"Scriba Femina."*

15. Lanham, *Electronic Word,* p. 9, calls "black and white, continuous printed prose" an "act of extraordinary stylization, of remarkable, expressive self-denial," which we were taught to accept as "the norm of conceptual utterance." In "Graphic Design," p. 116, McCoy defines the conventions of the "classical text tradition" from the reader's, rather than the writer's, point of view: "The reader accepts the conventions of the printed page and agrees to disregard the visual character of the letterforms, rendering traditional typography nearly invisible. Book typography is . . . without expressiveness."

16. McCoy, "Graphic Design," p. 117, goes on to note twentieth-century challenges to the notions, fostered in "classical book design," of "typography as neutral form" and of "the traditional compositional separation of type and image": the

first challenges came from visual artists (cubists, futurists, constructivists, dadaists) and poets experimenting with "visual" poetry; the next, from the new profession of graphic design in advertising, which "developed as a new form of functional graphic communications separate from the tradition of book design."

17. Beeren and Schoon, *Graffiti,* p. 20.

18. Ibid., pp. 38–39.

19. Ibid., p. 26.

20. Ibid., p. 56.

21. Derrida, *Of Grammatology,* pp. 122–23.

22. In Greek, the word *graphein* signified writing, drawing, and painting (Vernant, "Présentification de l'invisible," p. 25). Likewise, according to Bosworth and Toller's *Anglo-Saxon Dictionary,* the Old English word *wrítan* (along with its Germanic cognates) could mean both "to form letters, to write" and "to draw a figure" (such as a cross). *Wrítan* was apparently used in this double sense in the late tenth-century colophon ascribing to Eadfrith of Lindisfarne the designed writing of the Lindisfarne Gospels, which will be discussed later.

23. On Erté's letters designed as women, see Barthes, *Obvie,* pp. 99–121. Barthes himself connects the designs of such modern letters with medieval ones (p. 110): "Before Erté (but it is a new epoch, so completely has it been forgotten), the Middle Ages deposited a treasure of experiences, of dreams, of meanings, in the labor of its uncials; and graphic art—if we could throw off the empiricist yoke of our society, which reduces language to a simple instrument for communication—ought to be the major art surpassing the futile opposition between the figurative and the abstract: because the letter at the same time means and means nothing, does not imitate yet symbolizes, simultaneously dismisses the alibi of realism and that of aestheticism."

24. Even so, some readers manage to individualize printed books in their imaginations, as Manguel testifies in *A History of Reading,* p. 16: "Printing has given us the illusion that all readers of *Don Quixote* are reading the same book. For me, even today, it is as if the invention of printing had never taken place, and each copy of a book remains as singular as the phoenix."

25. Tory, *Champ fleury,* p. 43. The full title of Tory's work, printed by himself in Paris in 1529, was *Champ fleury, Au quel est contenu lart & Science de la deue & vraye Proportion des Lettres Attiques, quon dit autrement Lettres Antiques, & vulgairement Lettres Romaines proportionees selon le Corps & Visage humain.* See also Lafont, *Anthropologie de l'écriture,* pp. 207–8, on Tory's assimilation of the human form to that of the letter.

26. Tory, *Champ fleury,* p. 47.

27. The tradition of animating the letter with human shapes was verbal as well as visual. For example, in the thirteenth century in his *Abéces par ekivoche,* Huon

le Roi de Cambrai characterized letters by their shapes as well as by the words they initiated. For example, the letter *k*, because it had two "stomachs" (like a very fat man in profile), was for Huon a figure of the greedy prelate (pp. 5–6).

By the late Middle Ages, shop design books for commercial manuscript production presented models for letters of the alphabet formed by human figures. To form the shapes of different letters, human figures performed acrobatic contortions, used tools or instruments that prolonged their silhouettes, or were accompanied and extended by animals or grotesques. See Scott, *Later Gothic Manuscripts,* fig. 350, for a reproduction of the letters *K* through *P* from the early fifteenth-century figure alphabet of London, British Library, MS Sloane 1448A, fol. 25v.

28. Fraenkel, *Signature,* p. 10. Using the example of the fingerprint, she states that in the Middle Ages, as in Mesopotamia, "the sign had the value of a symbolic sign and not a simple trace. Over the course of time, the sign was naturalized" (p. 191). Fraenkel's conviction that medieval people did not mythologize signs as natural traces seems to be based partly on the oversimplified notion that the Council of Nicea laid all sorts of beliefs in image magic to rest among Christians everywhere, who thereafter believed in the merely representative status of images: "Following the Council of Nicaea, the controversy over images ceased and the conceptual apparatus elaborated over several centuries was no longer used or even transmitted. The problematic of icon/imprint no longer had any reason for being and disappeared in favor of the more traditional one of representation" (p. 208).

29. Dumezil, "Tradition druidique," pp. 328–29.

30. Ibid., p. 327.

31. Ibid., p. 326, citing Plutarch's *Life of Numa,* 22.2.

32. Hamilton and Cairns, *Collected Dialogues of Plato,* p. 521.

33. Ibid., p. 522.

34. Havelock, *Preface to Plato,* p. 199.

35. In the second half of the fifth century B.C. (out of a didactic intent or to remedy dissatisfaction with writing's disembodiment?), the Ionian alphabet was dramatized, with twenty-four women playing the parts of letters, in a text entitled *Spectacle of the Alphabet (Grammatike theoría).* On this strange play, see Svenbro, "Grèce archaïque," pp. 74–77.

36. Just how much articulatory punctuation there was in classical Latin scripts is not entirely clear. Saenger ("Silent Reading," p. 377) argues that word separation was an early medieval, largely Insular, invention, while Wingo (*Latin Punctuation in the Classical Age,* pp. 14–15, 132) points out that classical Latin was punctuated with a medial point to separate words, clauses, and sentences (as opposed to contemporary Greek, which was written in a continuous script that would be widely imitated in Latin only in the postclassical era). See also Parkes, *Pause and Effect,* pp. 9–13.

37. Riché, "Rôle de la mémoire," p. 134.

38. Camille, *Image on the Edge,* pp. 63–64, notes that letters are sometimes depicted as vines being taken into the mouths of people and suggests that we should understand these as images of monastic "rumination": "The monk was meant to feed not on the flesh of animals but on the Word of God in a muscular mastication—a *ruminatio,* so-called, that released the full flavour or meaning of the text." Hugh of Saint Victor gives advice on monastic rumination of the Word (*Didascalicon,* p. 94): "One must often turn [these things] over in the mind and regurgitate them from the stomach of one's memory to taste them, lest by long inattention they disappear."

39. Jousse, *Manducation de la parole,* p. 48.

40. Jousse, *Anthropologie de la geste,* pp. 229–38.

41. Meyer, "Notes on the Art and Ornament," p. 27.

42. Kris and Kurz, *Legend, Myth, and Magic,* note that, just as a person's shadow was considered by earlier peoples to be a part or extension of the person, so also a shadow "captured" by tracing it was considered to contain the presence of the person. (And a captured image might open to magical manipulation the person from whom it emanated.) As long as the picture was believed to remain connected to the person who produced it (that is, the person from whom the image naturally emanated, not the tracer of the image), the signifier (the person's image) was merely an extension of the signifying subject (the person); it was a Signifier. Kris argues, further, that not until this belief in "the identity of picture and depicted" declined did "a new bond [make] its appearance to link the two—namely, [a much closer visual] similarity or likeness" (pp. 75–77).

43. Diringer, *Writing,* p. 38.

44. Kristeva, *Langage cet inconnu,* p. 74.

45. On early *achiropiites,* see Kitzinger, "The Cult of Images," pp. 104–5, 113–15; and Grabar, *L'iconoclasme byzantin,* pp. 19–40.

46. Gerald of Wales, *Topographia hibernica,* pp. 123–24.

47. Ibid.

48. Schmitt, *Raison des gestes,* p. 100:

All the ancient civilizations, in particular those—Hebraic, Greco-Roman, Germanic—whose heritage has weighed most heavily on medieval culture, recognized the importance of the hand. In Roman law, the word *manus* has the sense of "power," and its derivatives designate either legal gestures having the function of transmitting, taking back or recognizing a power, or else this power itself: thus the gesture of the father who, in order to recognize his child, takes it and lifts it above the ground; or the authority of the husband over his wife, held *in manu mancipioque* by her husband; or again the *manumissio,* the freeing of the slave out of the *manus* of his master; or the *mancipatio,* the legal transfer of a possession.

Schmitt's valuable discussion of the languages of gesture in the Middle Ages relies to a considerable extent on pictorial representations thereof—such as the hand of God appearing in the miniatures of the Utrecht and Stuttgart Psalters—but only in full-page depictions, framed miniatures, or illustrations otherwise physically separate from the forms of alphabetic inscription. He is not interested in gesture incorporated into the letter nor in ways that pictorial depictions of gesture as part of or surrounding the letter may empower it.

49. In *From Song to Book,* Huot emphasizes the performative (as well as the illustrative) function of many late medieval miniatures: "The presence of the miniatures [in a manuscript of Guillaume de Machaut's poetry] adds an important theatrical dimension to the written text; in the absence of the performer, they provide a visual representation of the voice speaking each piece" (p. 260).

## Chapter 2

1. Gombrich, *Sense of Order,* pp. 19–20. In a functionalist rhetoric, there is little place for sheer display or ornament. Unless the ornaments of style serve to clarify or illustrate ideas, they are not truly ornaments but flaws. Indeed, Quintilian in *Institutio oratoria* (8.3.11) insists that "true beauty cannot be separated from utility" ("Numquam vera species ab utilitate dividitur").

2. Jerome, "Ad Laetam," *PL* 22:876; trans. Wright, pp. 364–65. Jerome also criticized "what the common people call uncials," a term that may refer, in this first surviving use of it, to the enlarged size of these letters and possibly also to the weight of gold used in their design. On Jerome's critique of fancy manuscripts, see Nordenfalk, *Spätantiken Zierbuchstaben,* pp. 89–96.

3. On these early purple-and-gold Gospels, see McGurk, "Oldest Manuscripts," pp. 11–12.

4. See Marrou, *Histoire de l'éducation,* 1:234, for the Greek method of teaching the *ductus* of the letter (by holding and directing the child's hand while retracing a lightly inscribed model letter), and 2:70 for Roman methods (guiding the hand, but also engraving into a wax-covered tablet letters that the child retraced by following the grooves).

5. Augustine, *Christian Doctrine* 2.4, trans. Robertson, p. 36.

6. In *Tractatus* 24.2 of his commentary *In Johannis evangelium* (*CCL* 36:244–45), Augustine briefly refers to the outward appearance of letters in order to contrast our response to pictures with our response to letters: "For a picture is seen in one way, letters are seen in another. When you see a picture there is nothing else to do but to see and to praise; when you see letters this is not everything, since you also feel the urge to read." (Aliter enim videtur pictura, aliter videntur litterae. Picturam cum videris, hoc est totum vidisse laudasse; litteras cum videris, non hoc

est totum, quoniam commoneris et legere.) To stop at admiration of the exterior beauty of letters—which he explicitly equates here with their evenness and regularity—is an entirely inadequate response, for we must go on to read and understand them, which he likens to examination "in depth" or to a search for "profundity" (in short, what I have called "reading through"). For more on this passage, as well as an English translation of it, see Chazelle, "Pictures, Books, and the Illiterate," pp. 146–47.

7. Kitzinger, "Cult of Images," p. 149.

8. Augustine, *De moribus ecclesiae catholicae* (PL 32:1342), discussed by Kitzinger, "Cult of Images," p. 92: "It is from St. Augustine that we first hear in unambiguous terms of Christians worshiping images. Among those who had introduced superstitious practices in the Church, he mentions *sepulcrorum et picturarum adoratores,* thus linking the cult of images to the cult of tombs."

9. See Duggan, "Was Art Really the 'Book of the Illiterate'?," p. 235, for this translation from the *Doctrinale* of the English Carmelite Thomas Waldensis, also known as Thomas Netter, the "hammer of the Lollards." Netter defends images against Wycliffite iconoclasm in this passage (which follows immediately upon his quotation of Pope Gregory's famous defense of pictures): "Qui ergo picturarum vetat imagines laicis, proximum est ut clericis scripturas inhibeat. Nam ipsa scriptura quid est nisi pictura quaedam, et verbi mentis, vel vocis imago?" (3:916–17, 925–27).

10. Gregory the Great, *Epistolae* 9.209, CCL 140A:768. English translation from Chazelle, "Pictures, Books, and the Illiterate," p. 139.

11. This is the subject explored both by Chazelle, in "Pictures, Books, and the Illiterate" (where she argues that Gregory did not believe illiterate people could learn something they did not already know by studying pictures), and by Duggan (who argues the contrary and that Gregory was wrong) in "Was Art Really the 'Book of the Illiterate'?"

12. Later interpreters of Gregory's famous letters pointed out even more clearly than he had done the indirect nature of religious depiction; what a religious image was supposed to represent was not the direct experience of Christ on the cross, for example, but rather the Gospel *story* of Christ's crucifixion. Religious depictions were supposed to be understood as signs of words (illustrations), and not as direct imitations of life. This is how Abbot Gilbert Crispin defined the relation of pictures to writing in the early twelfth century: "Just as letters are shapes and symbols of spoken words, pictures exist as representations and symbols of writing" (translation from Duggan, "Was Art Really the 'Book of the Illiterate'?," p. 231). See also Carruthers, *Book of Memory,* p. 222: "Gregory says that the picture is for learning a story, 'historia.' It is not, in our sense, a picture of some thing but rather the means for memorizing and recollecting the same matter or story that written let-

ters also record." There were, of course, exceptions to this tendency to subordinate event to text, as for example Durandus of Mende in his thirteenth-century *Rationale divinorum officiorum* 1.3.65 (*CCM* 140:36): "Per picturam quidem res gesta ante oculos ponitur quasi in presenti generi videatur" (For deeds are placed before the eyes in paintings, and so appear to be actually carrying on; translation from Kessler, "Diction in the 'Bibles of the Illiterate,'" p. 300). Nevertheless, in a religion of the book, authority is made to seem to reside in the written text of Scripture—even more than in the deeds and events Scripture records.

13. Bede, *De templo* (*CCL* 119A:212–13). The English translation is from Meyvaert, "Bede and the Church Paintings," pp. 68–69.

14. Meyvaert, "Bede and the Church Paintings," pp. 69–70.

15. One "ascended" from the material to the abstract, from pictures to words, and hence to true knowledge of God, for "pictures, relics, miracles, and saints could all augment religion, but the mysteries were sealed in words," as Kessler remarks in "Pictorial Narrative and Church Mission," p. 88.

16. Chazelle, "Matter, Spirit, and Image," p. 166.

17. For the Latin texts and English translations of these passages from Theodulf, see Chazelle, "Matter, Spirit, and Image," pp. 169, 181.

18. Translation from Kessler, "Diction in the 'Bibles of the Illiterate,'" p. 299.

19. Feminist scholars have recently begun to call this the Psalter of Christina of Markyate, from the name of the woman who owned, rather than the abbey that produced, the manuscript. For discussion of the implications of this new designation, see Caviness, "Anchoress, Abbess, and Queen," pp. 107–13.

20. For reproductions of these pages, see Pächt, Dodwell, and Wormald, *St. Albans Psalter*. Gregory's Latin text beginning "Alius est picturam adorare" and a French translation of it both appear on p. 68 of the Psalter.

21. Art historians have argued that the Psalter itself preexisted the present compilation and was not originally produced for presentation to Christina of Markyate; sometime after its completion, this Psalter was chosen—perhaps because of its abundant historiated initials—for inclusion in a compilation intended for a holy woman. On the compilation of the Saint Albans Psalter manuscript for Christina of Markyate, see Pächt, Dodwell, and Wormald, *St. Albans Psalter,* pp. 162–63, and Kendrick, "1123?," pp. 25–30. The issue of medieval women's literacy is treated, for example, by Grundmann, "Frauen und die Literatur," pp. 129–61.

22. Troyes, Bibliothèque Municipale, MS 458, vols. 1 and 2. For a reproduction of one such initial—an *A* formed by the body of a winged dragon and monster heads—from vol. 2, fol. 59v, of Saint Bernard's Bible, see Cahn, *Romanesque Bible Illumination,* fig. 196. Nevertheless, as Alexander suggests in "Scribes as Artists," p. 106, Saint Bernard's ire may have motivated a Cistercian statute of 1131 requiring that initial letters in manuscripts be painted in only one color and without de-

piction ("litterae unius coloris fiant et non depictae")—a statute that was apparently not rigorously applied.

23. Translation cited from Rudolph, "Bernard of Clairvaux's *Apologia,*" p. 127.

24. For example, Riegl resorted to hypotheses about lost originals of extant copies in order to offer a photograph of a manuscript page from an eleventh-century Armenian Bible in which the letters are formed by birds and fish as evidence of an oriental "source" for seventh- and eighth-century Western European bird and fish initials (*Altorientalische Teppiche,* pp. 166–67, fig. 33). Less than two decades later, Zimmerman (*Vorkarolingische Miniaturen,* pp. 5–6) easily and rapidly refuted the theses of Eastern origins argued by Riegel and Strzygowski (*Der Dom zu Aachen,* pp. 53–54).

25. Lafont, *Anthropologie de l'écriture,* p. 115.

26. Wirth, *Image médiévale,* p. 122.

27. On the basis of ninth-century allegorizing exegesis of the Book of Revelations by Alcuin and Haimo of Auxerre, Kessler (*Illustrated Bibles from Tours,* pp. 75–76) suggested that, in the upper register, "the book of the seven seals is the Old and New Testaments united," with the seven seals representing "seven modes of expression used in the Scriptures," which are clarified only through Christ. In the lower register, the veil being lifted by the human figure is the veil of "the obscurity of the Old Testament which is lifted by Christ."

More recently, Dutton and Kessler, in *Poetry and Paintings,* have argued that the very similar Apocalypse miniature of the First Bible of Charles the Bald uses the image of an enthroned man unveiling his face in the lower register to personify "all the authors of the Bible who had enunciated God's message . . . emphasized by the 'tuba' of prophecy raised to his face" (p. 65). They go on to suggest that "the enthroned man is thus the embodiment of the written document being opened above" and call to witness Beatus of Liébana's eighth-century statement, in *Adversus Elipandum,* 1.99 (*CCM* 59:76), that "the face of the Bible had been veiled from Moses until Christ and was revealed at the end of the Bible to John" ("Velata fuit Moysi usque ad Christum bibliotecae facies, et in fine huius bibliotecae revelata est. Et inde sic incipitur revelatio Ihesu Christi"). According to Beatus of Liébana, the whole compilation of books of the Bible (or "biblioteca") is to be understood as one book ("tota biblioteca unus liber est"), and as one man ("totus sic est intellegendus tamquam unus homo"). If one book equals one man, this man must be Christ, whom Beatus of Liébana treats here as the revelation—through human embodiment—of Holy Scripture.

28. This is not to suggest that there is only one way of understanding Christ's gesture of displaying an open codex, nor that interpretations should be mutually exclusive. For example, as one press reader pointed out, Christ may display Scripture in painting and sculpture in his role as teacher. In Romanesque apse painting,

such as the fresco from San Clemente de Tahull now in the Museum of Catalan Art in Barcelona, just over a slit window facing east, a mandorla-encircled Christ flanked by the letters alpha and omega holds up a codex inscribed with the legible words *Ego sum lux mundi* ("I am the light of the world"), which echo Christ's words according to the Gospel of John 12:46 ("Ego lux in mundum veni") as well as other self-definitions beginning with "Ego sum" (e.g., "I am the living bread"; "I am the way, the truth and the life"; "I am the alpha and omega"). This type of painting represents Christ's role as teacher or "illuminator" of divine truths. But even here it is Christ's "alter ego"—the codex—that speaks by displaying the Word to enlighten us. The open codex may be taken as a mere support for an identifying rubric, but it may also be understood as an embodiment of Christ. Christ's presence may be represented by the painting of the enthroned human figure, but it is also represented by the open codex proclaiming "Ego sum"—and it may be materialized, as well, by the morning light pouring through the slit window. For a color plate of this fresco, see Duby, *Moyen âge,* p. 197.

29. For reproductions of these letters, see Nordenfalk, *Vergilius Augusteus.*

30. Nordenfalk, "Before the Book of Durrow," p. 165. In his *Spätantiken Zierbuchstaben,* Nordenfalk pointed out how anticlassical decorated letters were (pp. 22–23), and he noted that ornamental initials appear in manuscripts owned by the Western church before that of the Eastern, for it was only in the late seventh century that they appeared in Eastern manuscripts (p. 18).

31. Nordenfalk, *Vergilius Augusteus,* p. 30. See also Ermini, *Centone di Proba.* On fourth-century Christian interpretation of Vergil's fourth eclogue as a prophecy of Christ, see chapter 7 of Comparetti, *Vergil in the Middle Ages,* and Courcelle, "Exégèses chrétiennes," pp. 294–319.

32. Facsimiles of both these manuscripts have been published: Vatican lat. 3225, *Vergilius Vaticanus,* with a commentary volume by Wright; Vatican lat. 3867, *Vergilius Romanus,* with a commentary volume edited by Lana.

33. Weitzmann, *Illustrations in Roll and Codex,* p. 46, has argued for the existence of illustrated Homer rolls against Bethe (*Buch und Bild im Altertum*), who concluded that Greek literary texts were never illustrated. Surviving examples of illustration on papyrus rolls are of medical and scientific texts, and these illustrations are unframed and lacking any illusionistic devices of setting such as landscapes (Weitzmann, *Illustrations in Roll and Codex,* p. 52). They are not narrative illustrations but demonstrative ones, showing what a constellation looks like, for example.

34. Nordenfalk, *Vergilius Augusteus,* p. 28 and figure. A lithographic reproduction of an epitaph signed "Furius Dionysius Filocalus scribsit," with the incised letters painted in red, as they originally were, can be found in Rossi, *Roma sotterranea cristiana,* vol. 2, table 3. Other examples of similarly hooked letters are scat-

tered throughout the volumes of this edition and those of the *Inscriptiones christianae urbis romae* series begun by Rossi in 1861.

35. Nordenfalk, *Vergilius Augusteus*, p. 26.

36. Ibid., p. 30.

37. According to Porfyrius's preface, the copy he presented to Constantine (no longer extant) was, at least for the first poem, written in gold and silver on purple. The critical edition of Porfyrius's *Carmina* is edited by Polara.

38. In the ninth century Rhabanus Maurus would elaborate on this method of creating supraliteral senses through pictorial figures of letters, figures that transgress the rules of classical reading and inscription evoked (or revived) by the "ground" of a continuous script. In manuscripts such as Paris, B.N.F., MS lat. 2421, Rhabanus's Holy Cross poems (*De laudibus sanctis crucis*) are presented as a kind of renovation of Porfyrius's figural poems collected at the back of the codex. Rhabanus's poems, as opposed to Porfyrius's, all center on the figure of the cross (*PL* 107:133–262). For a black-and-white facsimile edition that cannot recapture the splendor of the gold on purple and different-colored grounds of Vatican, MS reg. lat. 124, see *Hrabanus Maurus*, edited by Müller. Further analysis of Rhabanus's Holy Cross poems can be found in Sears, "Word and Image." Sears points out, pp. 341–42, that even though Rhabanus used pictorial figures to redirect our reading of letters and thus to reveal further senses of the text ("pictorial forms singled out certain letters in the matrix which, read a second time, formed verses in their own right"), he did not take for granted that pictorial figures, especially those constructed with abstract geometrical forms, were sufficient to clarify the sense of his poems; to this purpose, he added lengthy prose commentaries called "*declaratio figurae*."

39. Photographs of Christian epitaphs with the *T* greatly enlarged to evoke a cross can be found in Wilpert, "Croce sui monumenti della catacombe," table 7.

40. Lengthy illustrated essays synthesizing previous research on each of these symbols are presented in the volumes edited by Cabrol and Leclercq, *Dictionnaire d'archéologie chrétienne*. See, for example, the essay by J. P. Kirsch under *ancre*, vol. 1, pt. 2, cols. 1999–2031; the essay on the dove (*colombe*) notes that on two funerary monuments the dove bears a tiny cross on its head and that, in other cases, the dove perches atop a cross (vol. 3, pt. 2, cols. 2211, 2213). Both of these configurations will later appear in designed letters.

41. Clement of Alexandria, *Paedagogum*, 3.11 (*PG* 8:634B; *SC* 158:125). On pictorial symbols in the catacombs see Brunn, "Symboles, signes et monogrammes," pp. 73–166.

42. Rossi, *Roma sotterranea cristiana*, vol. 1, table 26, fig. 1.

43. Ibid., vol. 1, table 23, fig. 4.

44. Ibid., vol. 2, table 57, fig. 32.

45. Wilpert, "Drei altchristliche Epitaphfragmente," pp. 375–76, argues that this instrument must be a candle illuminating the monogram, and not a brush being wielded by the dove to paint or rubricate the monogram, because the artist would have shown the wrapping of the bristles on a brush. How Wilpert can know how this artist would have designed a paintbrush is unclear.

46. On these different types of cross monograms, see Nordenfalk, *Spätantiken Zierbuchstaben,* p. 63.

47. For these elaborations, see under *hameçon* (hook) in the *Dictionnaire d'archéologie chrétienne,* edited by Cabrol and Leclercq, vol. 6, pt. 2., col. 2035. As early as the second century, Tertullian had explained the fish as a figure of the baptized Christian and of Christ: "[W]e being little fishes, as Jesus Christ is our great fish, begin our life in water, and only while we abide in the water are we safe and sound" (*De baptismo* 1.3) (*PL* 1:1198–99; *CCL* 1:277).

48. Dölger, *Fischsymbol,* p. 153. See also Origen, *Commentaria in evangelium secundum Matthaeum* 13.10 (*PG* 13:1119–20). In a well-known passage from *The City of God* (18.21), Augustine continues this tradition, calling the Greek word for fish (ιχθυς) a "mystical name" for Christ.

49. For images of Christ flanked by alpha and omega from the catacombs of Piero and Marcellino and of Comodilla, see, for example, Grabar, *Premier art chrétien,* figs. 234 and 237. The earliest dated inscription of a cross with alpha and omega just under the crossbar appears in an epitaph from the year 382. A photographic reproduction of this appears in Wilpert, "Croce sui monumenti della catacombe," table 7, no. 2.

50. The idea that Christ was incarnated in the letters of Scripture (the Old Testament) before his incarnation in the flesh, so that the text itself of Holy Scripture may be understood as the body of Christ, seems to go back to the opening of Origen's homilies on Leviticus (*In Leviticum*), where he explicitly compares the covering of the Word of God with a veil of flesh through Christ's incarnation with its covering by the veil of the letter in the texts of the lawgivers and prophets (that is, the Old Testament). Repetitions and variations on the theme that the "letter" of Scripture is the "body" of Christ may be found in Jerome, Ambrose, Augustine, John the Scot, Claudius of Turin, and Rupert of Deutz, among many others. This subject will be treated more fully at the beginning of chapter 3.

51. A chi-rho monogram flanked by alpha and omega appears in a colophon ending a work by Lactantius in a manuscript dated to the second half of the fifth century. See Nordenfalk, *Spätantiken Zierbuchstaben,* table 14, no. 2, for a reproduction of this colophon. If the purpose of this design is to indicate the Christianity of the writing, placement at the beginning of the text (as in the slightly later example from the Gospel of John) might be more effective. On the enclosure of

Paris, B.N.F., MS lat. 10439 in a reliquary, see Lowe, *Codices latini antiquiores,* vol. 5, no. 600; and McGurk, "Oldest Manuscripts," p. 21.

52. Nordenfalk's table 62 of *Spätantiken Zierbuchstaben* offers further examples of fish alphas from this particular Orosius manuscript. The column was understood by early commentators as a figure of Christ's divinity and his humanity (among other things), according to Rhabanus Maurus's *Allegoriae in sacram scripturam* (*PL* 112:899, under the word *columna*).

53. For photographic reproductions of some of these figural letters, see Nordenfalk, *Spätantiken Zierbuchstaben,* tables 26–31, or the first plate volume of the color facsimile edition of Dioscurides, *Codex Vindobonensis Med. Gr. 1,* edited by Gerstinger.

54. Nordenfalk, *Spätantiken Zierbuchstaben,* p. 65.

55. One of the most famous statements to this effect is Gregory the Great's apology for his lack of eloquence in the dedicatory letter prefacing his *Moralia in Job* (*PL* 75:516): "I do not avoid the confusion of barbarism, I disdain to observe the order of words, the modes of verbs, the cases of prepositions, because I consider it supremely inappropriate to subject the words of the heavenly oracle to the rules of Donatus."

## Chapter 3

1. Origen, *In Leviticum* 1.1 (*PG* 12:405; *SC* 286:66):

Sicut in novissimis diebus Verbum Dei ex Maria carne vestitum processit in hunc mundum et aliud quidem erat, quod videbatur in eo, aliud, quod intelligebatur— carnis namque adspectus in eo patebat omnibus, paucis vero et electis dabatur divinitatis agnitio—, ita et cum per prophetas vel legislatorem Verbum Dei profertur ad homines, non absque competentibus profertur indumentis. Nam sicut ibi carnis, ita hic litterae velamine tegitur, ut littera quidem adspiciatur tamquam caro, latens vero intrinsecus spiritalis sensus tamquam divinitas sentiatur. Tale ergo est quod et nunc invenimus librum Levitici revolventes. . . . Sed beati sunt illi oculi, qui velamine litterae obtectum intrinsecus divinum Spiritum vident.

I have cited in my text the English translation of Smalley, *Study of the Bible,* p. 1.

2. Quoted by Lubac, *Exégèse médiévale,* vol. 1, pt. 1, p. 193.

3. Gregory the Great, *In librum I regum,* 4.123 (*PL* 79:268; *CCL* 144:359): "Nam scriptum est: *Littera occidit, spiritus vivificat.* Hoc quidem facit omnis divina littera. Nam littera corpus est; huius vero corporis vita, spiritus." (For it is written: *The letter kills; the spirit gives life.* Every divine letter does this. For the letter is a body whose life is, in truth, the spirit.)

4. Maximus the Confessor, *Capita theologiae et oeconomiae* 2.60 (*PG* 90:1150–51): "[Verbum] ubi ad homines venit . . . , ex iis disserens quae illis consueta exque usu essent, historiarum aenigmatumque et parabolarum obscuriorumque sermonum varietate compositum, caro efficitur." See also Lubac, *Histoire et esprit,* p. 344.

5. John the Scot, *Commentarius in evangelium Iohannis* 1.1 (on John 1:27) (*PL* 122:307B; *SC* 180:156): "Duobus quippe modis divinae legis expositores incarnationem dei verbi insinuant. Quorum unus est, qui eius incarnationem ex virgine . . . edocet. Alter est, qui ipsum verbum quasi incarnatum, hoc est, incrassatum litteris rerumque visibilium formis et ordinibus asserit." (It is in a dual way, indeed, that the exegetes of the divine law explain the incarnation of the Word: one of which teaches that he took flesh from the Virgin . . . ; the other is that this same Word is as if incarnated, that is, embodied in the letter of Scripture on the one hand and, on the other, in the ordered shapes of visible things.)

6. *Glossa ordinaria,* on the Book of Leviticus, preface (*PL* 113:298): "Origenes quoque ait: . . . sic verbum Dei per prophetas profertur ad homines, ibi carnis, hic litterae velamine tectum. Littera tanquam caro aspicitur: spiritualis sensus tanquam divinitas sentitur." (Also, Origen says, ". . . thus the word of God is proffered through prophets to men—there covered in flesh, here by the veil of the letter. The letter, as flesh, may be seen; the spiritual meaning, as divinity, may be felt.")

7. Jerome, *Tractatus in psalmos,* on Psalm 145 (*PL* 26:1250–51; *CCL* 78:326): "Panis Xpisti et caro eius sermo divinus est et doctrina caelestis" (The bread of Christ, and his flesh, is the divine discourse and the heavenly doctrine). On Jerome's interpretation of scriptural doctrine as the body of Christ, see Morin, *Etudes, textes, découvertes,* p. 243.

8. Morin, *Etudes, textes, découvertes,* p. 243, citing from Jerome's commentaries on Psalm 131 and on Mark 8:1–9.

9. Augustine, *Enarrationes in psalmos* 4.1, on Psalm 103 (*PL* 37:1378; *CCL* 40:1521): "nec mirandum nobis sit, quia propter infirmitatem nostram descendit ad particulas sonorum nostrorum, cum descenderit ad suscipiendam infirmitatem corporis nostri."

10. With respect to early Insular letters, Neuman de Vegvar puts this succinctly in *Northumbrian Renaissance,* p. 87: "Writing was essentially foreign to pre-Christian Celtic culture. Christianity presented not only the new concept of the written word, but also the understanding of these words as the Word. The great Insular initials can be understood as a tribute to the Word itself, manifested mystically in the written words of Scripture." Some of the most surprising visual representations of this idea of the materialization of the Word in Scripture before assuming a human body occur relatively late. They make explicit what was previ-

ously implicit. In a thirteenth-century *Bible moralisée* in French (Vienna, Öster-reichische Nationalbibliothek, cod. 2554, fols. 16r–16v), the illuminator several times pictures the infant Christ literally sandwiched between the covers of a large codex that serves as a kind of cradle for him. These images are reproduced and commented on by Camille, "Visual Signs of the Sacred Page," pp. 114–15, figs. 3 and 4. In a nativity scene from the Rohan Hours (Paris, Musée Jacquemart-André, MS 2, fol. 73v), the infant Christ is again shown cradled in a clasped codex of Scripture. Lesley Smith in *"Scriba Femina"* reproduces this image (fig. 2) and re-marks how it illustrates "the identity of the eternal Word with the Word made flesh" (p. 22). The "eternal" Word here is shown in two physical forms. As Smith points out, the Word couched in ink on the animal skins of a codex is also "made flesh." Two phases of the Word's incarnation are suggested in many later medieval Annunciation scenes of Mary reading Scripture at the moment of conceiving Christ. Smith calls attention to one exceptionally explicit manuscript illumination (Ferrara, Statuti MS 47, unnumbered): "a book flies into the room in place of the dove" and travels down on rays aimed at Mary's womb (p. 22 and fig. 8).

11. The conventional shapes of medieval handwritten letters of the alphabet depended upon the period and place, with different scriptural styles being devel-oped and used in different monastic, and later secular, milieux. For a general intro-duction to different scripts, see Bishop, *Latin Palaeography*.

12. Aethelwulf, *De abbatibus*, pp. 18–20. In "Ultan the Scribe," pp. 104–5, Law-rence Nees argues—I think unconvincingly—against the use of the example of Ultan to support the current scholarly consensus that "the decoration of books with figures, colour, and ornament, was very highly regarded in the early Insular monasteries and won fame for its practitioners." Nees argues that the only thing clear from Aethelwulf's praise of Ultan is that Ultan was a scribe, because the key phrase "ornamented books with fair marking" ("notis ornare libellos") may sim-ply mean that he wrote a nice script, and in that way made books beautiful.

13. Tradition attributes the writing and designed letters of the Cathach of Saint Columba to the saint, as well as the writing and design of the Book of Durrow, which has a colophon requesting prayers for the scribe Columba. According to Neuman de Vegvar, *Northumbrian Renaissance,* p. 83, this colophon, which shows signs of erasure and rewriting, suggests that "the manuscript may be either a copy of a work by the saint, or a pious forgery." Even if the Book of Durrow is a "pious forgery," the colophon attribution to Columba helps to sacralize this magnifi-cently designed text of the Gospels and to give it the status of a relic by supporting the implicit testimony of the awesome designs themselves with an explicit testi-mony to their origin in communication with the divine, that is, in the sainthood of their copyist. According to Werner, "Cross-Carpet Page," p. 221 n. 238, the true

writer of the Book of Durrow may have been Adomnan, Abbot of Iona, author of the *Life of Saint Columba,* who was reputed for his scribal ability, as were earlier abbots of Iona.

Although the Lindisfarne Gospels, written to honor Saint Cuthbert and placed in contact with Cuthbert's shrine, came to be considered part of Cuthbert's relics, a colophon attributes the writing of the book (and this probably includes its pictorial design) to Eadfrith, Bishop of Lindisfarne Abbey. This monastery may have had a tradition in the eighth century of acknowledging the authority of exquisite scribe-illuminators by promoting them to positions of power. The Barbarini Gospels are signed by one Huigbald, probably the same man who was abbot of Lindisfarne from 760 to 803, and there is some evidence in the extant Book of Cerne for a lost "Book of Aethelwald"—Aethelwald was bishop of Lindisfarne from Eadfrith's death in 721 until 740. For these attributions, and further evidence that scribes were also designers and painters, see Henry's introduction to *Book of Kells,* pp. 211–14, and Dodwell, *Anglo-Saxon Art,* pp. 55–56.

14. Rupert of Deutz, *De Trinitate: In Ezechielem* 2.12 (*PL* 167:1473; *CCM* 23:1707): "super vilem litteraturam spiritualis intelligentiae conspicit ornamentum, quisquis oculos habet ad videndum." Furthermore, Rupert implicitly equates the letter of Scripture with the body of Christ in his explanation of the vision that motivated (and authorized) his exegetical writings (*Super Mattheum* 12) (*PL* 168:1593–1602; *CCM* 29:372–83). Because Rupert had, in his vision, embraced and kissed the living body of Christ on a crucifix, and because Christ had opened his mouth "to let the kiss be deep, . . . [he] became certain . . . that he had been chosen to penetrate into Christ's mysteries and would be privileged to understand doctrine 'considerably better than the Fathers.' Thus he began to write" (Lerner, "Ecstatic Dissent," p. 37).

15. Quoted without attribution by Lubac, *Exégèse médiévale,* vol. 1, pt. 1, p. 103: "vero scrutans mens hominis altitudinem prophetiae velut hamo piscem Dominum Christum de profundo Scripturarum levaret."

16. Rupert of Deutz, *Super Mattheum* 7 (*PL* 168:1456B; *CCM* 29:200): "si petieritis piscem, id est si legentes volueritis cognoscere Christum, cuius sacramentum quodammodo ita latet in Scriptura legali atque prophetica, sicut piscis in aqua . . ." ([I]f you would seek the fish, that is, if in reading you would like to recognize Christ, whose mystery lies hid in Scripture—the Law as well as the Prophets—even as a fish in water . . .)

17. Ambrose, *Hexaemeron* 5.7.17 (*PL* 14:213): "Evangelium est mare, in quo piscantur apostoli."

18. Drewer, "Fisherman and Fish Pond," p. 542.

19. The Gospels as "living water" are also figured as a fountain (the Fountain of Life) and as the four rivers (sometimes depicted with fishing birds beside them)

that emanate from Paradise. For examples of this iconography, see Underwood, "Fountain of Life," figs. 26 and 58. The earliest reference to such iconography comes from the inscription (*titulus*) Paulinus of Nola invented to explain a mosaic in the early fifth-century basilica of Saint Felix: "He [Christ] himself, the rock of the Church, stands upon the rock, / From which flow four sonorous springs, / The Evangelists, living streams of Christ" (Underwood, "Fountain of Life," p. 73).

20. See Augustine, *De doctrina christiana,* 3.5–9, on spiritual understanding as "Christian liberty" (*PL* 34:68–70; *CCL* 32:82–85); Bede, *In Marci evangelium,* 4.14.15, and *In Lucae evangelium,* 6.22.12, on the "narrowness of the letter" (*PL* 92:270D, 594D; *CCL* 120:376, 609); Bernard, *In epiphania domini,* 2.2, on the "liberty of spiritual understanding" as opposed to "servitude to the carnal letter" (*PL* 183:148B). For more on this theme, see Lubac, *Exégèse médiévale,* vol. 1, pt. 1, p. 354, and *Histoire et esprit,* p. 169.

21. Richard of Saint Victor, *Expositio in cantica canticorum* 15 (*PL* 196:450B): "Oculi ergo devotae animae sunt columbarum, quia sensus eius per Spiritum sanctum sunt illuminati." (Therefore, the eyes of a devout soul are doves' eyes, for their perceptions are enlightened by the Holy Spirit.)

22. For reproductions of these dove-*a*s see Nordenfalk, *Spätantiken Zierbuchstaben,* table 45, figs. e and f (from Split, Kapitelbibliothek, unnumbered MS, fols. 160 and 196).

23. Cassiodorus, *De institutione divinarum litterarum* 4 (*PL* 70:1115): "Est enim multiplex et infinitus divinorum eloquiorum intellectus. Siquidem in penna pavonis una eademque mirabilis ac pulchra innumerabilium colorum varietas conspicitur in uno eodemque loco eiusdem pennae portiunculae." (Indeed, the intelligence of divine eloquence is multiplex and infinite, if it is true that, in the plume of the peacock, the very same marvelous and beautiful variety of numberless colors may be seen in one and the same spot of a very tiny portion of the plume.) Cassiodorus seems to be playing here on double meanings of plume (as feather and as pen), spot (the eye of the peacock's tail and the textual *locus* as a passage or a topos of rhetorical invention), and colors (natural pigmentations and figurative expressions). See also John the Scot, *De divisione naturae* 4.5 (*PL* 122:749C). The eternal life symbolized by the peacock in early Christian art may help to explain the depiction of initial letters of Holy Scripture as peacocks.

24. Jean-Claude Bonne makes this point suggestively in "Rituel de la couleur," p. 135: "Figures and colors submit forcibly or lithely to the letter, but they toy with [dominate] it as well, as if, in giving it a living body, it were a matter of realizing in writing a potential force, of bringing out an energy inscribed as a spilling over of painting in writing."

25. Alexander, *Decorated Letter,* color plate 23.

26. Basil, *In psalmos* 9, on Psalm 44 (*PG* 29:407C): "Therefore, the queen, that

is, the soul which is joined with the Word, its Bridegroom, not subjected by sin but sharing the kingdom of Christ, stands on the right hand of the Savior in gilded clothing, that is to say, adorning herself charmingly and religiously with spiritual doctrines, interwoven and varied. Since, however, the teachings are not simple, but varied and manifold, and embrace words, moral and natural and the so-called esoteric, therefore, the Scripture says that the clothing of the bride is varied" (trans. Way, *Saint Basil,* p. 291).

27. John Chrysostom, *In epistolam ad Hebraeos* 17.5 (*PG* 63:130); trans. Gardiner, *Homilies,* p. 48. Cited in Kessler, "Medieval Art as Argument," p. 60.

28. Kessler, "Medieval Art as Argument," p. 65.

29. John of Damascus, *Orationes pro sacris imaginibus* (*PG* 94:1361). Cited by Kessler, "Medieval Art as Argument," p. 62.

30. This paraphrase from Methodius's *Life of Euthymius of Sardis* comes from a manuscript source, Cod. CP. Chalc. mon. 88, fol. 247v, as cited by Gouillard, "Le synodikon de l'orthodoxie," p. 173.

31. Kessler, "Medieval Art as Argument," p. 69.

32. As Osborne points out in "Use of Painted Initials," pp. 76–77, it is not until the ninth century that figurative initials appear in a manuscript from Constantinople (Paris, B.N.F., MS gr. 510), and these initials are imitations of Western examples, for "the substitution of the actual strokes of the letter by fish is a western phenomenon, characteristic of Italian and Merovingian manuscripts from the sixth through the eighth centuries." The marine creatures precociously juxtaposed to letters in the early sixth-century Vienna Dioscurides manuscript produced in Constantinople are never incorporated into the body of letters to replace parts of letters. (In this respect, they are like the Christian hieroglyphs of doves, fish, and the like juxtaposed to letters in Roman catacomb inscriptions.)

33. Hugh of Saint Victor, *De arca Noe mystica* 7 (*PL* 176:695B): "Nos ad significandam historiam viridem colorem posuimus, ad tropologiam croceum, ad allegoriam caeruleum." (We have used the color green to signify history, saffron for tropology, azurite [deep blue] for allegory.)

34. Alexander, *Decorated Letter,* color plate 3.

35. Augustine, *Sermones ad populum* 300.3 (*PL* 38:1377D): "Clavis Testamenti veteris, crux."

36. Lubac, *Exégèse médiévale,* vol. 2, pt. 1, p. 146.

37. Attributed to Bede, *Hexameron* 2 (*PL* 91:81C): "*T* vero littera crucis figuram tenet; et si apicem solum qui deest in medio suscepisset, non iam figura crucis sed ipsum crucis esset signum manifesta specie depictum." (Truly the letter *T* has the form of the cross; and if only it had received an apex missing in the middle, then it would no longer be just a figure of the cross, but this same depicted sign would be a manifest aspect of the cross.)

38. Suntrup includes a list of manuscripts containing such initials in "*Te Igitur-*Initialen," pp. 278–382; see also the discussion of *Te* and *Vere dignum* monograms and of depictions of an initial *T* as the crucifixion in Pächt's *Book Illumination,* pp. 38–44.

39. For examples of transfigured letters from the catacombs, see Brunn, "Symboles, signes et monogrammes," p. 123.

40. A cross inscribed in the circular loop of the letter may evoke Christ's body. In early tomb inscriptions a circle engraved with a cross (sometimes in the form of a chi [X] superposed on an iota [I] to form a six-pointed figure) signified the Eucharistic host. For a reproduction of one such figure (above a chalice representing Christ's blood) on a sixth-century tombstone from Vienne, see Karkov, "The Chalice and Cross," fig. 29.1.

41. Nordenfalk, *Spätantiken Zierbuchstaben,* table 62 (from Florence, Laurentian Library, MS Plut. LXV.1).

42. Alexander, *Decorated Letter,* color plate 1.

43. Ibid., color plate 4.

44. In her essay on the illumination of manuscripts of the *Canterbury Tales,* pp. 562–63, Margaret Rickert noted marginal instructions to early fifteenth-century illuminators using the terms "hole venett" (full page vine border or "vignette") and "demi vinet" (partial vine border).

45. Ambrose, *Enarrationes in psalmos* 41, on Psalm 1 (*PL* 14:943D): "In mysticis fructus est, in moralibus folium contemplatione mysteriorum coelestium. Nam virtutes sine fide, folia sunt." (In the mystical sense is the fruit; the leaf, in the contemplation of heavenly mysteries for their moral lessons. For virtues without faith are leaves.)

46. Gregory, *Moralia in Job* 6.1.2 (*PL* 75:730C; *CCL* 143:285). Isidore of Seville took up this same idea in *De ecclesiasticis officiis,* 1.11.2 (*PL* 83:745C; *CCL* 113:9): "Illa lex vetus velut radix est, haec nova velut fructus ex radice. Ex lege enim venitur ad evangelium" (That old law is like the root; this new law is like the fruit that comes from the root. For we come from the Law to the Gospels). Later medieval exegetes such as Philip of Harveng, *Epistolae* 1, to Wederic (*PL* 203:12D), modified the plant metaphor to contrast the superficial foliage of words (leaves = literal sense) with their truthful fruits (of spiritual sense): "non solum verbis frondosa, sed et veritate fructuosa litterae superficies invenitur" (the literal surface is discovered to be not only leafy with words but fruitful in truth). On these tropes, see Lubac, *Exégèse médiévale,* vol. 1, pt. 2, pp. 436, 465.

47. Innocent III's remarks on the significance of the *T* of "Te igitur" are cited by Gutbrod, *Die Initiale,* pp. 18–20.

48. Another version of the figure of Christ-the-vine begins to appear in the late twelfth century within initial letters such as the *B* beginning the first phrase of

the Psalter, "Beatus vir" ("Blessed the man"). Rather than emanating from and enveloping the letter, the vine usually springs up from the body of a sleeping (dreaming) Jesse depicted within the bottom loop of the *B*, and it branches and leafs upward through Christ's human lineage, including David and Mary, to "flower" at the top into Christ and realize visually the prophecy of Isaiah 11:1: "And there shall come forth a rod out of the root of Jesse, and a flower shall rise up out of his root." The allegorical flower or "fruit" of the letter (that is, the Christological sense of the psalms) is depicted inside the frame of the letter *B*, although not incorporated into the limbs or body of the letter proper. The reader who began reading the Book of Psalms with such a designed initial might look "inside" the letter to discover its spiritual sense; Christ is depicted within the letter both figuratively, under the general aspect of a vine, and literally (mimetically or "realistically"), as the small human figure in which the vine culminates or flowers. Psalter manuscripts featuring a tree of Jesse in the illustration of the first psalm are listed in the tables of Haseloff's *Die Psalterillustration.*

49. In 692, the Eastern church, in an official canon, actually prescribed the replacement of symbolic representations of Christ as lamb with representations of his human form "so that we may perceive through it the depth of the humiliation of God the Word and be led to the remembrance of His life in the flesh." On this canon see Kitzinger, "Cult of Images," p. 121.

50. On the iconoclast controversy, see Sahas, *Icon and Logos.* The ecclesiastical and imperial politics behind this battle over images are very complicated, but the two basic theoretical positions were, on the one hand, that pictures were conventional signs, divorced from the real essence of what they represented, and, on the other, that the picture could capture the essence of, and have the same powers as, the prototype. In spite of their argument that mere men were incapable of making icons and that the only true icon was the bread and wine of the Eucharist, Western iconoclasts nevertheless feared the power of realistic depiction, for they recognized that people believed—superstitiously, idolatrously—in the *identity* of picture and prototype. Western defenders of images, on the other hand, argued that people were not such dupes but that they understood pictures as useful, manmade means of *representing* prototypes. People were undoubtedly capable (and still are) of holding simultaneously these contradictory beliefs about the relationship between picture and prototype.

51. Paul's expression deliberately recollects Psalm 104:4: "See ye the Lord, and be strengthened: seek his face evermore."

52. On the letter chi as cross (identified as the *crux decussata*) in exegetical writings, see the rich essay by Lewis, "Sacred Calligraphy," pp. 142–44. In place of the human head and abstract shoulders of the chi on the chi-rho page of the Book of Kells, we see, on the chi-rho page of the earlier Book of Durrow (Dublin, Trinity

College, MS 57, fol. 23v), a small cross, which may serve to identify the lithe-limbed Durrow chi as Christ. (For a reproduction of this page, see the facsimile edition by Luce, Meyer, Simmons, and Bieler, *Evangeliorum quattuor codex Dura-machensis,* or Werner, "Cross-Carpet Page," fig. 21.) Christ's incarnation in the letters of the Gospel text is made more obvious by giving the letters a human face, a pictorial device that may have been suggested by both pagan and Christian figural conventions: on the one hand, by the human head terminals on bridle mounts and other artifacts of Celtic metalwork (see Youngs, *Work of Angels,* figs. 116 and 117b, for example); on the other hand, by imagining the chi as a (tilted) cross and treating it in a manner similar to the Golgotha cross, which was sometimes topped by a bust of Christ. Early examples of crosses topped with busts of Christ survive in the Valerianus Codex, where a haloed man's head and shoulders surmount a gem-studded cross (my fig. 87), as well as on early flasks of pilgrims to the Holy Land. For the images depicted on these *ampullae,* see Grabar, *Ampoules de Terre Sainte,* plates 11, 16, and 18; and Weitzmann, "Loca Sancta," pp. 31–55. For the bust of Christ depicted atop a Golgotha cross in a seventh-century Roman mosaic, see Belting, *Likeness and Presence,* p. 107 and fig. 56.

53. Although she does not discuss the frontal human bust above the great chi, Lewis does identify the head at the junction of the rho and iota with Christ ("Sacred Calligraphy," p. 144): "The curving terminal of the Rho ends in a startling human head which may also signify the *nomen sacrum.* . . . This remarkable visage signals the intersection with the Iota, to which the Alexandrian Fathers extended their speculations on the *nomen sacrum* to stress that Christ [*I*esus, beginning with iota] is the Logos." Lewis understands the great chi as an image of the Logos incarnate, based on the exegesis of early Greek fathers such as Justin, who in his *Apologia* (1.60) "asserted that the Son of God was formed like a Chi and praised the Chi-cross as the greatest symbol of the power of the Logos Incarnate" (p. 143). On the chi-rho page of the Book of Kells, we witness the process of incarnation, as the Logos takes on the material form of the letter(s) of the Gospel text, as well as the beginnings of a human body in the spread-eagled, leaping "limbs" suggested by the chi-cross and the fully realized faces of Christ atop the first three letters of his Greek name.

54. See also Nordenfalk, *Spätantiken Zierbuchstaben,* table 4 (from Munich, Bayerische Staatsbibliothek, MS lat. 6234).

55. For reproductions of some initial letters supported by angels, patrons, scribes, and authors, see Gutbrod, *Die Initiale,* pp. 148–55.

56. Origen, *Selecta in psalmos,* on Psalm 1, pt. 4 (*PG* 12:1082D): "solvant quos ipsis nodos exhibuimus" (we showed by loosening those very knots).

57. Gregory the Great, *Moralia in Job* 11.17.26 (*PL* 75:966B; *CCL* 143A:601): "Cum enim mysticos allegoriarum nodos per explanationem solvimus, in lumine

dicimus quod in tenebris audivimus" (For when we loosen the mystical knots of allegories through explanation, we say in the light what we have heard in the dark); *Homiliae in Hiezechihelem prophetam*, 1.9 (*PL* 76:870A; *CCL* 142:123): "Initium libri in Hiezechihel propheta magnis obscuritatibus clausum et quibusdam mysteriorum nodis ligatum ... discussimus." (We have examined the beginning of the book of the prophet Ezekiel, closed by great obscurities and bound by the knots of mysteries.)

58. Gregory the Great, *Quadraginta homiliarum in evangelia* 1.20.4 (*PL* 76:1162B): "sed etiam corrigiam calceamenti eius solvere, id est incarnationis eius mysterium perscrutari non se dignum esse perhibuit" (but he did not claim himself worthy even to untie the lace of His shoe, that is, to see into the mystery of His incarnation); Bede, *In Lucae evangelium* 1.3.16 (*PL* 92:356A; *CCL* 120:80): "Corrigia ergo calciamenti est ligatura mysterii. Iohannes itaque solvere corrigiam calciamenti eius non valet quia incarnationis mysterium nec ipse investigare sufficit." (Therefore, the lace of His shoe is the knot of mystery. And so John is not able to untie His shoelace, because he himself is not adequate to investigate the mystery of the incarnation.)

59. John the Scot, *In Iohannis evangelium* 1, on John 1:27 (*PL* 122:306D–307A; *SC* 180:153–54): "Si itaque calciamentum verbi caro verbi est, non incongrue corrigiam calciamenti eius subtilitatem et investigabilem perplexionem mysteriorum incarnationis intellige. Cuius mysterii altitudinem solvere indignum se praecursor iudicat."

60. John the Scot, *De divisione naturae* 5 (*PL* 122:1010AB): "Non enim alio modo sanctorum prophetarum multiplex in divinis intellectibus contextus potest discerni, nisi per frequentissimos non solum per periodos, verum etiam per cola et commata transitus ex diversis sensibus in diversos, et ab eisdam iterum in eosdem per occultissimas crebrissimasque reversiones" (For in no other way may the complicated text of the holy prophets, in their divine intelligence, be explicated— except by very frequent transition from various senses to others, not only from one sentence to the next, but truly even from one clause or part of a phrase to the next, and back again from these to those by the most secret and repetitive returns). John goes on to call Scripture a "concatenated" text, intricately woven by the Spirit with "Daedalus-like twists and turns" intended to exercise our intelligence. Such metaphors implicitly liken following the sense of Scripture to following the trace of a very wily animal.

61. For pictures of animal interlace incised in metal objects such as the early eighth-century Tara brooch, the Monymusk reliquary, and the Sutton Hoo buckle, see Henderson, *From Durrow to Kells*, figs. 31, 87, 154, and 158. See also Youngs, *Work of Angels*, for further reproductions of brooches, buckles, and

mounts featuring metalwork or filigree patterns of animal interlace. In "Le 'dieu lieur,'" pp. 147–48, Eliade notes the importance in all magico-religious practices of the orientation of the force thought to reside in the knot or in the action of tying a knot: "[T]he orientation may be positive or negative, whether one takes this opposition in the sense of 'beneficial' or 'baleful' or else in the sense of 'defense' or 'attack.'"

62. On knotted strands as calendars and records, and on other primarily tactile mnemonic devices (such as the Catholic rosary), see Day, *Quipus and Witches' Knots.*

63. The same may be true of the pagan spiral or "pelta" motifs, which the scribal exegetes of certain Insular Gospels so successfully reused and reinterpreted, thereby redirecting their whirling energy into a revelatory expression of the divinity incarnate in the very letters of the Gospel text. Seeming to spin out of the limbs of the great chi on the chi-rho page of the Book of Kells, for example (color plate 1), are circles filled with circles containing whirling spirals, which may recollect Ezekiel's vision of a "wheel within a wheel" as explained by exegetes such as Ambrose, *Expositio in psalmum 118* 4.28 (*PL* 15:1250B), and Gregory, *Homiliae in Hiezechihelem prophetam* 1.6.12–15 (*PL* 76:834–35; *CCL* 142:73–75), who saw the wheel within a wheel as a figure of the New Testament in—and moving or motivating—the Old: "Rota intra rotam est Testamentum Novum, sicut diximus, intra Testamentum Vetus" (A wheel inside a wheel is the New Testament, as we say, inside the Old Testament). With the energy of so many spiraling wheels, the Kells illuminator depicts the first letter of Matthew's Gospel as a powerfully motivated and motivating force.

64. Gregory the Great, *Homiliae in Hiezechihelem prophetam* 1.4.1–3 (*PL* 76:815–16; *CCL* 142:47–49).

65. Bede, *In Lucae evangelium,* prefacing letter to Bishop Acca (*PL* 92:304D; *CCL* 120:7). Cf. Irenaeus's description of the Gospels (*Adversus haereses* 3.11): "The Word ... has given us the Tetramorphic Gospel, governed by one only Spirit." Translation from Henry, *Irish Art in the Early Christian Period,* p. 181.

66. Dynes, "Imago Leonis," p. 36.

67. Henry, *Book of Kells,* p. 194, interprets this figure, along with two others, as an image of the Godhead:

On f. 12r a figure with two boughs shows his head and feet behind the large M in the beginning of the *Argumentum* of Matthew: on f. 291v a figure appears behind the frame of St. John's portrait, and on f. 202r another one peers over the tailpiece of the genealogy. This last is surely 'The Lord' mentioned just above and a similar explanation for the other figures is likely, the figure behind the frame of St. John's portrait being fairly obviously the Word. They have in common the fact that they are not fully revealed to the eye; they appear under a frame or a letter, more suggested than described, the painter trying to convey by this device the unknowable character of God.

Whether the man behind the *M* on folio 12r is understood as an image of the Godhead, or of the Spirit in the form of a man inspiring Matthew and assuming the form of the letter, the effect is the same: to authorize, quite powerfully, the Gospel text.

68. Meyer, "Notes on the Art and Ornament," p. 41, has noted the commingling of bodies in these "evangelist symbols" under the canon table arches: "All four on 1r have human arms; on 5r the eagle has one hand. On 2v and 3v the lion of St. Mark has the thin legs of the bull and it has hooves, while the lion on 290v has a bird's body. On 1v and 2v the bull has a bird's body; on 5r the bull and the lion in the tympanum have birds' bodies, but their own natural forelegs. The meaning of the emblem is always seen in the head." Surely, however, the meaning lies in the mixture, in a multiple unity, and not in a reductive interpretation.

69. Meyer, "Notes on the Art and Ornament," p. 38, calls these creatures "snake dragons" having a "long, broad muzzle, not unlike a duck's bill, [and] . . . circular eyes . . . surrounded by ovals running to a point behind which, as a rule, a ribbon interlacing issues." Usually, however, ribbons are elongations of physical features that extrude more than do the whites of the eyes, features such as tails, limbs, tongues, hair, crests, manes, horns, and so on.

70. Art historians have suggested recently that highly ornate early Insular Gospel books containing evangelist pages may have been displayed during the rites of induction of catechumens into the church in the early Middle Ages, because one such ceremony (described, for example, in the Sacramentary of Gellone, *CCL* 159:65–73) involved exegesis of the nature of the evangelists and their animal symbols, explanation intended to "open the ears" of the catechumens to the spiritual significance of the Gospels. See, for example, the chapter entitled "Gospel Manuscripts and Early Medieval Liturgies" in Farr, *Book of Kells* (pp. 41–50). If this theory is correct, certain illuminated Gospels may have served to open the eyes, as well as the ears, to spiritual sense (so that the new converts might see traces of the Spirit or the outline of the Cross instead of a tangle of snake dragons, for instance).

## Chapter 4

1. In "Texts, Scribes and Power," p. 100, Goodman suggests that the origin of Jewish "reverence for physical texts" may lie in this biblical incident.

2. Goodman, "Sacred Scripture," p. 105.

3. Ibid., translating from a Hebrew manuscript (t Yad. 2:12). Religious texts were also used as phylacteries or amulets. Rather than defiling whoever touched them with naked hands, the power enshrined in these texts (written very small and usually encased in leather) protected those who wore or owned them (Goodman, "Texts, Scribes and Power," p. 100). Early Christians sometimes used miniature texts of the Gospels in much the same way. According to John Chrysostom, women and children in late fourth-century Antioch wore a small codex of a Gospel text around their necks as amulets (cited by Fox, "Literacy and Power," p. 140). The miniature size of three of the earliest surviving codices containing all or parts of the Gospel of John (the Chartres, Stonyhurst, and Stowe Gospels) has led to speculation that they too were worn about the persons of their owners as amulets. For example, on the Chartres Gospel of John (my fig. 18, actual size), see McGurk, "The Oldest Manuscripts," p. 8: "The smallest Latin Bible manuscript, indeed early Latin codex, is the uncial Gospel of St John in Paris (BN, lat. 10439; *CLA* V, 600) dating from the turn of the fifth and sixth centuries, which measures 71 × 51 mm, with eleven lines per page confined to a written space of 45 × 34 mm. It may have been worn as an amulet before it was deposited inside the eleventh-century reliquary of the Virgin's shirt at Chartres where it was found in 1712."

4. Goodman, "Sacred Scripture," p. 103.

5. Ibid.

6. Goodman notes that in Jewish culture "religious power was enshrined within the physical object on which the divine teachings were inscribed" ("Texts, Scribes and Power," p. 100).

7. For a description of early Roman liturgical ceremonies involving the kissing of the Gospels with naked lips yet their handling with covered hands, and their unsealing and resealing in a book shrine, see O'Carragáin, *"Traditio evangeliorum,"* pp. 414–16.

8. Cahn, *Romanesque Bible Illumination,* p. 20.

9. Wirth, *Image médiévale,* p. 156, cites this preface to Anastasius the Librarian's Latin translation of the acts of the Second Council of Nicea, which is included and countered in the argument of the *Libri carolini* (PL 98:956): "aiunt namque quod non sit quodlibit opus manuum hominum adorandum; quasi non sit codex Evangeliorum opus manuum hominum, quem quotidie osculantes adorant, venerabilior canis, quem non esse opus manuum hominum, procul dubio non negabunt."

10. Centuries later, critics of medieval English Lollard iconoclasm pointed out that the Lollards committed idolatry themselves in adoring the codex of Holy Scripture. See Aston, *Lollards and Reformers,* p. 110: "The divine attributes of the Bible assumed heightened power in Wycliffe's thought, and Wycliffites, who had so many reservations about worshipping the lifeless matter of dead images, seem

to have been less than inhibited about revering the text of holy scripture. Kissing the holy book, as the priest kissed the gospel after reading it at mass, seemed to them a legitimate gesture of worship. But, as was pointed out by their opponents, there was a certain inconsistency among the heretics for thus 'venerating, kissing and saluting the Gospel, revering the very manuscript', while simultaneously claiming that living trees were more worshipful than carved images."

11. This illustration preceding the Book of Proverbs in Paris, B.N.F. Syriac, MS 341, fol. 118r, is reproduced in Cahn, *Romanesque Bible Illumination,* fig. 11. In other media, veiling of the hands appears even earlier, as in a fifth-century wall mosaic in the archbishop's chapel in Ravenna, where Christ holds a codex in covered hands, as Bearman points out in "Origins and Significance," p. 181, note 49.

12. The translation of this Old English colophon is from Alexander, *Insular Manuscripts,* p. 39.

13. Bruce-Mitford has argued that this enigmatic figure is supposed to be Christ, for the gold inscription on the initial page (f. 27r), "IHS XPS Mattheus homo," suggests as much by identifying Christ as the image of man who inspired Matthew. A much later gloss (f. 259r) seems to make the same identification: "Matheus ex ore Christi scripsit" (Matthew wrote [words] from Christ's mouth). For a summary of these arguments, see Alexander, *Insular Manuscripts,* pp. 37–38.

14. Reproductions of these canon table arches can be found in Alexander, *Insular Manuscripts,* figs. 97–107. The early ninth-century book of private devotion known as the Book of Cerne (Cambridge University Library, MS Ll.I.10) reverses the usual order quite curiously by placing under the arch on "ground" level the animal emblem of spiritual inspiration, holding a Gospel book with naked hooves, while in a roundel at the top of the arch appears a bust of the evangelist, who uses his cloak to cover the hand with which he holds up the Holy Word. For color reproductions of these frontispieces and discussion of their unusual iconography, see Brown, *Book of Cerne,* p. 74 and plates 1–4.

15. See the Last Judgment page from Saint Gall, Stiftsbibliotek, MS Ed. 51, p. 267, reproduced as fig. 206 in Alexander, *Insular Manuscripts.* In this image from an Irish Gospel book made in the second half of the eighth century, Christ, in the center of the upper register and flanked by two horn-blowing angels, holds up a codex in his robe-covered left hand, while holding a cross against his body with his right arm and making a gesture of benediction with his right hand.

16. In *Poetry and Paintings,* Dutton and Kessler have recently made a convincing argument that this Bible should be called the First Bible of Charles the Bald, and not the Vivian Bible, "particularly since Charles was the certain recipient of the Bible and the evidence indicates that the monastery, and not Vivian, was its true donor" (p. 34). Count Vivian may be represented in the presentation scene (my fig.

57) simply because he was the newly appointed lay abbot at the time of the Bible's presentation (and not because, as formerly supposed, he instigated the making and gift of it).

17. These figures are identified in the Latin poem explaining this presentation scene, translated by Dutton and Kessler, *Poetry and Paintings*, p. 118: "This painting actually shows how the noble warrior / Vivian with the company now presents this book / in which the most eminent [brothers] are before [and] after the father: / beloved Tesmundus, just Sigualdus, supreme Aregarius. / . . . Behold, these humble ones are bestowing the book upon you alone, lord; / on behalf of blessed Martin and the brethren."

18. Whereas we tend to think of ocular vision as a way of knowing or apprehending that *substitutes* for physical contact, medieval people tended to imagine vision as a *kind* of physical contact. Hence the power of the "evil eye."

19. Gombrich, *Sense of Order*, pp. 263–64.

20. Nees, "Fifth-Century Book Cover," p. 5.

21. Gutbrod, *Die Initiale*, p. 145.

22. On the apotropaic power of the cross, the Evangelists, and interlace (Nees, "Fifth-Century Book Cover," pp. 5–6):

[T]hat a magical potency was credited to the Evangelists in Great Britain at least as early as the tenth century is quite evident from several sources. Most extraordinary of these, in which the power of the Evangelists is dramatically linked with that of the cross, is an elaborate ritual prescription for the fertilization of bewitched fields from a tenth-century medicinal book, in which four crosses, each inscribed with the names of the Evangelists at the ends of the four arms, were to be buried in the corners of the barren field amid prayers, libations and other ceremonies. The apotropaic power of the cross, still alive today in magic and (if only semi-consciously) in popular religious practice, is repeatedly attested throughout the Christian world from the earliest period. . . . Even the interlace decoration of the cross in the Book of Durrow miniatures may have served such a purpose, and the combination of Evangelist symbols, cross and interlace in a single image adds up to a source of considerable apotropaic potency.

23. On the earliest surviving book shrine, found in 1986, see Kelly, "Lough Kenale Book Shrine," pp. 280–81.

24. Nordenfalk, *Celtic and Anglo-Saxon Painting*, p. 19, remarks on the talismanic power of the cross on a codex of the Gospels, as wielded by Adomnan of Iona: "An Irish legend makes Adamnán of Iona perform a miracle from a great distance in favor of another abbot, exclaiming: 'Wonder not that the sign of the Cross by the power of the Gospel traverses quicker than a wink of the eye all the

elements up to heaven.' In saying so, he is reported to have raised in his hand a Gospel Book, the cover of which, like that of the Lindau Gospels in the Morgan Library, might have featured as its decoration a large cross."

25. Numerous examples of such initials from different Insular manuscripts can be found reproduced in Alexander, *Insular Manuscripts;* Temple, *Anglo-Saxon Manuscripts;* Kauffmann, *Romanesque Manuscripts;* and Dodwell, *Canterbury School of Illumination.*

26. Cassiodorus, *Institutione divinarum litterarum* 30 (*PL* 70:1145): "Tot enim vulnera Satanas accipit quot antiquarius Domini verba describit." Translation by Jones, *Introduction to Divine and Human Readings,* p. 133.

27. Although she does not comment on the instrumentality of the book, several of these representations of Christ holding up an open codex while treading on the beasts are reproduced by Openshaw in "Weapons in the Daily Battle": fig. 6 (Stuttgart Psalter), fig. 10 (Odbert Psalter), fig. 11 (Winchcombe Psalter), fig. 12 (Crowland Psalter), fig. 28 (Tiberius Psalter). See also Temple, *Anglo-Saxon Manuscripts,* fig. 259, from the Crowland Psalter, Bodleian Douce 296, fol. 40. Exegetes typically understood Christ to be the true treader of the dangerous beasts of Psalm 90:13 ("super aspidem et basiliscum ambulabis et conculcabis leonem et draconem"). When the pages lie open with the recto on the right, the full-page Crowland Psalter image of Christ treading lion and dragon on folio 40 recto both prefaces and overlays Psalm 51, which is written "underneath" it, on folio 40 verso. The initial of Psalm 51, beginning "Quid gloriaris in malitia" (Why dost thou glory in malice) shows a human warrior with shield and sword following Christ's example to attack a leafy-tailed dragon, which forms the tail of the letter *Q*. See also Openshaw, "Battle between Christ and Satan," on the image of Christ trampling the beasts in the Tiberius Psalter.

28. These charms are collected and discussed in Storms, *Anglo-Saxon Magic,* and Cockayne, *Leechdoms, Wortcunning, and Starcraft.* For the "holy drink against tricks of elves and against every temptation of the fiend," see Storms, no. 18, and Cockayne, vol. 3, p. 11, no. 11. In both written and spoken forms, John's Gospel and certain psalms were thought to be powerful instruments for curing typhoid fever. In this case, the leech (physician—who must sometimes have been a village priest) was supposed to write on the sacramental paten a series of crosses flanking the Greek letters alpha and omega and the first words of John's Gospel, which he would also sing: "In principio erat verbum et deus erat verbum. Hoc erat in principio apud deum. Omnia per ipsum facta sunt." (In the beginning was the Word, and the Word was God and was with God in the beginning. All things were made by him.) This writing was to be washed off the paten with holy water into a drink prepared of specially concocted herbs, over which the leech would then sing the Credo, Paternoster, and several psalms considered to be charms: the twenty-two

stanzas of Psalm 118, beginning "Beati Immaculati" (Blessed are the immaculate), and the twelve prayer psalms. Eventually, both the leech and the sick man would sip the drink three times (Storms, no. 27; Cockayne, vol. 2, no. 62, pts. 2–3). On the continuation into the sixteenth century of such uses of psalms, parts of the Gospels, and other religious texts, see Duffy, *Stripping of the Altars,* pp. 209–16, 266–87.

29. Translated by Openshaw, "Weapons in the Daily Battle," p. 24 (*PG* 87:3018–19): "Credite mihi, filioli, nihil ita perturbat, et concitat, et irritat, et vulnerat, et perdit, atque contristat, et contra nos commovet daemones, ipsumque perditionis auctorem Satanam, sicut perpetua psalmorum meditatio. Nam omnis quidem divina Scriptura utilis nobis est contristatque non mediocriter daemones, non tamen ita sicut psalterium."

30. *PG* 87:3019: "Nam cum psalmos meditamur, partim quidem nobis ipsis Deum laudando oramus, partim vero maledicti insequimur daemones.... Et iterum: Lacum aperuit, et effodit eum, et incidit in foveam quam fecit. Convertatur dolor eius in caput eius, et in verticem ipsius iniquitas eius descendet."

31. Trans. Openshaw, p. 33 n. 104, with slight corrections from Bruyne, *Préfaces de la Bible latine,* pp. 77–78: "Canticum psalmorum ... effugat daemones, expellit tenebras, efficit sanctitatem.... [D]ominum ostendit, diabolum offendit, voluntatem inlicitam extinguit.... [O]mne mallum occidit ... ab omnibus vitiis sollicitudo est, certamen bonum cotidie est, radices malorum omnium expellit, sicut lorica induit, sicut galea defendit.... Qui diligit canticum psalmorum assidue, non potest peccatum agere." Openshaw suggests that a homily of Saint Basil on the first psalm may have been the source, although much transformed, of this text.

32. On the prophylactic power ascribed to this psalm from Cassian on, see Sims-Williams, *Religion and Literature,* pp. 277–78.

33. *Collationes* 10.10, trans. Chadwick, *Western Asceticism,* pp. 240, 242. Cited by Sims-Williams, *Religion and Literature,* p. 278.

34. Finlayson, *Celtic Psalter,* p. vi.

35. Whether they appear as parts of, within, or outside initial letters, Helsinger in "Images on the *Beatus* Page" explains images of combat (between David and Goliath, or between David and the lion or bear, or between jousting knights) as well as images of pursuit (especially the stag hunted by men and by hounds) as figurative representations of the Christian soul's struggle. These recollect the psalmist's frequent pleas to God for aid against his enemies, which may be understood as the Christian soul's pleas for help in conquering or escaping the diabolical forces that threaten his salvation: "Set at the head of the psalms, this image of the Christian soul persecuted through life by the forces of evil would have served as a preface to the whole, perhaps recalling the psalmist's recurring cry, 'Salvum me fac'" (p. 165).

36. "Vivus est enim Dei sermo et efficax et penetrabilior omni gladio ancipiti"

(Epistle to the Hebrews 4:12). Paul's trenchant metaphor for Scripture is depicted in twelfth- and thirteenth-century manuscripts of his Epistles, which feature images of Paul, often inside the loop of the initial *P* beginning his texts, bearing both an upraised sword and a codex or scroll, a codex impaled on a sword, or simply an upraised sword. For reproductions of these initials, see Eleen, *Illustration of the Pauline Epistles;* fig. 70 reproduces a kind of presentation scene in which Paul hands the bishop Timothy a codex impaled on a sword (representing his own divinely inspired Epistles addressed to Timothy).

37. Jerome, *Breviarum in psalmos* (*PL* 26:824): "[P]er titulum intelligitur, in cuius persona cantatur, aut in persona Christi, aut in persona Ecclesiae, aut in persona prophetae" ([B]y the rubric [of the psalm] may be understood the role in which it is sung, whether in the role of Christ, or of the Church, or of a prophet).

38. Salmon, *'Tituli psalmorum'*, p. 15.

39. Ibid., p. 9.

40. Likewise, in scenes of the harrowing of hell, Christ's victory over the devil and his salvation of souls was depicted as a forced regurgitation. On resurrection as regurgitation, see Bynum, *Resurrection of the Body,* p. 149, plates 13 and 14.

41. Translation from Robertson, *On Christian Doctrine,* pp. 83–84. *De doctrina christiana* 3.5.9 (*PL* 34:69; *CCL* 32:82–83): "Cum enim figurate dictum sic accipitur, tamquam proprie dictum sit, carnaliter sapitur. Neque ulla mors animae congruentius appellatur, quam cum id etiam, quod in ea bestiis antecellit, hoc est, intellegentia carni subicitur sequendo litteram."

42. A more reassuring and authoritative image of the "good fight" is that on the opening page of Augustine's *Tractatus psalmorum* in a manuscript written before 1060 at the monastery of Mont Saint-Michel. There are two arched niches at the top of the page, the one on the right containing the figure of Augustine writing his spiritualizing interpretation of the psalms under angelic inspiration, and the one at the left containing Saint Michael treading on and spearing the dragon. In an unframed space on the bare page directly below Saint Michael, King David sits playing his harp and singing his psalms. The image of Saint Michael slaying the dragon not only identifies the particular monastic provenance of this manuscript, but it also demonstrates the effect of Augustine's spiritual understanding of the Davidic psalms—or of any interpreter's. To arrive at a spiritual understanding of the psalms is to fight the good fight and to do successful battle with the devil. But the battle is never completely won. Reading the Old Testament is a continuous struggle against the "letter." In eleventh- and twelfth-century initials from religious manuscripts written in this same monastery, combat is constantly renewed, and it takes place within or against the coils of the letter, which often form part of a ferocious or monstrous adversary that a human "warrior" struggles against, sometimes armed with shield and uplifted sword, sometimes in the nude (to sug-

gest a human soul and the spiritual nature of the battle). For reproductions of these images, see Dosdat, *L'enluminure romane au Mont Saint-Michel,* figs. 4 (color) and 10; and Alexander, *Norman Illumination at Mont St. Michel.*

43. That illuminators sometimes deliberately represented the tentacular tendrils of the letter as impediments to be struggled against may provide a better explanation for the phenomenon observed by Alexander in *Norman Illumination at Mont St. Michel* (p. 186, plate 54e) and explained by him, with respect to one such Beatus initial (Bordeaux, MS I, fol. 261), as a somewhat inept distortion owing to lack of space within the letter for both vines and scenes with battling figures: "[T]he scene of David fighting the lion takes place in the midst of an entangled scroll. This leaves little room for the protagonists who are squeezed away at the bottom of the letter. Moreover, it has even dictated the composition of the scene in a way which distorts the story. *For David grasps not the lion but the plant scroll, as if it, not David, was the attacker*" (my emphasis).

44. Modern readers may be misled by the distinction in the spelling, and presumably also the pronunciation, of the main dictionary entries for these words in modern dictionaries of medieval French and Anglo-Norman. To the extent that early medieval spelling was phonetic, the spellings that follow the main entry for these words indicate a fairly wide variety of pronunciations. For example, according to the *Anglo-Norman Dictionary,* the noun for "leaf" could be spelled, and presumably pronounced, in a great variety of ways: *fuille, feille, foille, feile, folie, foillie, fullie.* In some of these cases, the *l* seems to have been pronounced as a dental; hence the spelling *folie,* which is the same as that for the noun meaning "folly" or "madness," which was spelled *folie* or *foli.* A similar situation existed for the verbal forms of the word. According to Godefroy's *Dictionnaire de l'ancienne langue française,* the verb meaning "to commit folly" or "to mock or befool someone" was spelled and pronounced *folier,* but also *follier, foliier, foloier, foloyer, foleier, folaier, feloier.* The earliest example given, from the Norman Wace's twelfth-century *Roman de Rou,* is spelled *foleier* (or in the same manuscript, *foliier*). The verb for "to sprout leaves" (or "to leaf through a book" [modern French *feuilleter*]) was also spelled variously: *fueillier, fueller, fuillier, foillier, foilier, follier, foeulier, feuillier.* In comparing these two lists, we find that the two different verbs are spelled, and presumably pronounced, in exactly the same way in one case: *follier.* In early Norman and Anglo-Norman French, the *l* of both words may have been dentalized (rather than palatalized, as it would be in later Parisian French, as for example in modern French *feuille*). A dental pronunciation of the *l* in the two words would make them very nearly homonyms, and it could stimulate wordplay that was visually expressed by the shape-shifting leafy follies of the letter.

45. As Dodwell pointed out in *Canterbury School,* p. 10, the "favorite construction for the Beatus initial of Anglo-Saxon illumination" was the "biting head"

initial, which is the name he gives to the monstrous mask or head through which pass, and are thus joined, the upper and lower loops of the initial *B*.

46. Origen, *In canticum canticorum* 3.12.8 (*PG* 13:171A; *SC* 376:616). "Venatores Domini" (hunters of the Lord) was Ambrose's name for exegetes in his *Expositio in psalmum 118* 6.10, explaining Psalm 118 (*PL* 15:1271A). On the trope of scriptural interpretation as hunting, see Lubac, *Exégèse médiévale,* vol. 1, pt. 2, p. 593.

47. Scripture is described as a labyrinth, for example, by Jerome at the beginning of the fifth century in his *Commentaria in Ezechielem* 14 (*PL* 25:448D; *CCL* 75:677): "Ita est ego, sanctarum scripturarum ingressus oceanum et mysteriorum Dei ut sic loquar labyrinthum" (The entrance to the ocean of sacred Scriptures and of the mysteries of God is such that I may call it a labyrinth). The comparison was still being made in the twelfth century by Rudolph of Saint Trond, *Vita sancti Lietberti* 3 (*PL* 146:1451AB): "[M]irantibus magistris penetrat labyrinthos Scripturarum, et . . . complicata disserat" ([T]o the teachers' amazement, he penetrates the labyrinths of Scriptures and . . . explains complications). For the metaphor of Scripture as forest in exegetical writings, see Jerome, *Epistles* 64.20, "Ad Fabiolam" (*PL* 22:619): "infinitam sensuum sylvam" (the endless forest of meanings); Gregory the Great, *Homiliae in Hiezechihelem prophetam* 1.5.1 (*PL* 76:821B; *CCL* 142:57); Manegold of Lautenbach, *In librum psalmorum,* on Psalm 28 (*PL* 93:624D); Paulinus of Nola, *Libellus sacrosyllabus contra Elipandum* 7 (*PL* 99:158A); Jonas of Orleans, *De institutione laicali,* preface (*PL* 106:124A); Rhabanus Maurus, *Allegoriae in sacram scripturam,* under the word *silva* (*PL* 112:1054B); Peter Damien, *Antilogus contra Judaeos* (*PL* 145:42C); and, for further examples, Lubac, *Exégèse médiévale,* vol. 1, pt. 1, p. 119.

48. A common metaphor for spiritualizing interpretation of Scripture was ascent, the discovery of a "higher" meaning. For Origen, the historical sense of Scripture, its "letter," was to be used as a "ladder" to ascend to the spiritual sense: "historia tanquam scala utentes" (using history [the literal sense] like a ladder) (*Commentaria in evangelium secundum Joannem* 20.3, *PG* 14:575C). In the twelfth century, in *De Trinitate: In exodum* 3.24–25, Rupert of Deutz likened the work of the exegete to scaling Mount Sinai (*PL* 167:673D–674AB; *CCM* 22:716–17).

49. Alexander, *Decorated Letter,* color plate 14.

50. When clambering initials appear in texts by Priscian, as they do (see, for example, Dodwell, *Canterbury School,* plates 11c and 15b), the sense of the struggle upward, or the struggle against beasts in the thickets of the letter, can hardly be specifically Christian, but it may suggest "overcoming" the letter in the more basic sense of mastering it. In effect, reading or the achievement of literacy is depicted as a struggle, a combat, which has the effect of valorizing the reader's efforts to

decipher words, their relations to one another, and eventually meanings. Merely because a particular pictorial design was copied in new contexts does not necessarily mean that it has no sense and becomes "purely decorative" in the new context; new senses can be invented in the process of translating the design to its new context. Likewise, when a clambering initial with a beast-hunting scene or struggle with a dragon appears in a manuscript collection of medical treatises, it does not have to be understood as pure decoration, even though, as part of a medical text, it cannot represent psalmody or the reading of Scripture as spiritual battle. Medieval medicine drove out the evil that caused illness so that, for example, the hunter who has hold of a dragon's tail, while the dragon has hold of the man's foot, in the "clambering" initial *I* of one medical treatise (British Library, MS Royal 12 Exx, 124v; Dodwell, *Canterbury School,* plate 14c), may well suggest the reader's attempt to conquer illness (and evil) by struggling to understand this medical text.

51. Otto Pächt, in *St. Albans Psalter,* p. 148, points out that this novel marginalization of a combat scene was not done from lack of space within the letter but was deliberate, for a "Norman or Anglo-Norman illuminator would easily have found space within the framework of the initial even for a secondary scene ... [and] have interwoven the little pair of fighting knights into the coils of the acanthus filling the loops of the B." Indeed, 150 years later, in the Huth Psalter, made after 1280 in Lincoln or York, a highly eclectic English illuminator was capable of interweaving through the leafy interior coils of a Beatus *B* two knights on horseback charging at each other, as well as David aiming his slingshot at Goliath, *and* a tree of Jesse. (For a reproduction of this initial, see Morgan, *Early Gothic Manuscripts, 1250–1285,* no. 332.)

52. A full transcription of this Latin gloss is given by Pächt, *St. Albans Psalter,* pp. 163–64.

53. For a consideration of the image of fighting knights on the Beatus page of the Saint Albans Psalter in the larger context of pictorial images of struggle and representations of the "good fight" (physical combat as a figure for spiritual battle), see Alexander, "Ideological Representation of Military Combat."

54. For an example, from the last decade of the twelfth century, of marginalized scenes of hunting and struggle that would earlier have been featured inside the letter, see Morgan, *Early Gothic Manuscripts, 1190–1250,* fig. 49, from the Leiden Psalter (Leiden, Bibliotheek der Rijksuniversiteit, MS lat. 76A). On this Beatus page opening the Psalter, in a rectangular frame surrounding the initial *B* rather than in the interior of the initial, naked men struggle with each other, with beasts, and with the coils of the vine.

55. As Leroquais pointed out in *Livres d'heures manuscrits,* vol. 1, p. vi, Books of Hours were collections of liturgical offices and prayers for the use of the faithful—

in effect, breviaries for laypeople. These developed from abbreviated and re-arranged private Psalters and, by the fifteenth century, had become widespread and extremely various in their contents.

56. Likewise, in a Book of Hours made for a Frenchwoman named Marie around 1270–80, sixteen of twenty-one historiated initials feature a lone lay-woman in a posture of devotion or prayer, whereas the margins are replete with images of secular distractions or amusements such as hunting, jousting, music-making, and hybrid creatures that attract the wandering eye. As opposed to such distractions, reading the central text block of this Book of Hours is a relatively unproblematic act of piety, and the images of private devotion in the historiated initials reinforce this idea. For reproductions from this manuscript on loan to the Cloisters Museum (New York, Metropolitan Museum of Art, MS L.1990.38), see Bennett, "Hours for Marie."

57. A descriptive anatomy of such incongruous creatures can be found in Sandler, "Reflections on the Construction of Hybrids," pp. 51–65.

58. Randall, *Images in the Margins*, in a note concerning her fig. 383.

59. Alexander, *Decorated Letter*, color plate 29.

60. The Salvin Hours is by no means the first Insular manuscript to push strug-gle out of the enclosure of a letter into its excrescences. See, for example, the glossed Psalter from around 1200 in which the Beatus initial contains a tree of Jesse, and the two coiled extenders of the *B* are interwoven with doggish-looking beasts (Liverpool City Library, MS f.09I.PSA, fol. 1; Morgan, *Early Gothic Manu-scripts, 1190–1250*, no. 104); or the Glazier Psalter from around 1220–30, in which huntsmen, hounds, stags, and nude men struggle through the tight, concentric coils of the two extenders of the Beatus *B* (New York, Pierpont Morgan, MS Gla-zier 25, fol. 5v; Morgan, *Early Gothic Manuscripts, 1190–1250*, no. 160).

61. Grabar and Nordenfalk, *Romanesque Painting*, p. 182.

62. Toubert, "Formes et fonctions de l'enluminure," pp. 95–96.

63. Baltrušaitis, *Réveils et prodiges*, pp. 154, 182, 199.

64. A similar point is made by Caviness in her analysis of the effects of the mar-ginal images of the Hours of Jean d'Evreux in "Patron or Matron?," p. 348: "The sexual innuendo and cumulative impact on the viewer of the grotesques have been underestimated, since the color, size, and centrality of the sacred subjects demand attention; these others are marginal, yet I find them as insistent as a hoard [*sic*] of small children tugging at my skirts and sleeves. They seem to struggle against the ordered lines of the written word (which constitute the prayers), powerful distrac-tions to be resisted by the reader intent upon her devotions. Indeed, most were sufficiently repellent as to direct the eye back into the words, and thus they control the reader."

65. For further examples and reproductions, see Hamburger, *Rothschild Canticles.*

66. On the beaver's self-castration, as related and allegorized in the *Physiologus,* see McCulloch, *Medieval Latin and French Bestiaries,* p. 95: "It is stated in the allegory that those who wish to live chastely should sever themselves from sin and throw it in the face of the devil, who will depart when he sees that nothing belongs to him."

67. The history of this story of the tiger's diversion or seduction by mirrors is analyzed by McCulloch in "Tigre au miroir," pp. 149–60. Before 1218, the Picard writer Pierre de Beauvais wrote a French *Bestiaire* including the story of the tiger, which he moralized as follows: "Let us take warning not to be like the tiger. . . . Amon the prophet says that this world is exemplified by the forest in which tigers live and that it is essential that each of us be attentive about protecting his young— that is, his soul." He went on to explain that the hunter's throwing mirrors in the tiger's way, to divert her as the hunter flees with her cubs, exemplifies the devil's throwing in our way "the great foods, the great pleasures of the world, the clothing, the horses, the beautiful women, and all the other precious things we desire." See McCulloch, "Tigre au miroir," pp. 152–53, for the Old French citation.

68. Playful uses of pictorial figures in the borders of medieval manuscripts are treated in an earlier essay wherein I discussed, in connection with the structure of Chaucer's *Canterbury Tales,* the late medieval concept of "borders" (Old French *bordes*) as the proper place for *bourdes* (Old French *bordes*), that is, visual and verbal jokes. This essay, originally published in French in the *Bulletin des anglicistes médiévistes,* is appended to this book.

69. Caviness, "Patron or Matron?," pp. 357–62.

70. In the fifteenth century, reading one's Book of Hours assiduously "put the devil behind one," as is illustrated in a manuscript made for a secular patron, probably in London, around 1415–20 (Brussels, Bibliothèque Royale, MS IV.1095, fol. 27v). To the side of the text proper, the male patron stands and reads his Hours, while his guardian angel, holding a shield, flogs an ugly devil behind him. The "combat" of monastic psalmody has been tamed down for lay readers: if they concentrate on their reading, they need not worry about the devil. This image is reproduced by Scott, *Later Gothic Manuscripts,* vol. 1, fig. 199.

## Chapter 5

1. On methods of closing and fixing the texts of such contracts, see Fraenkel, *Signature,* p. 33, and for the Middle Ages, Clanchy, *From Memory to Written Record,* pp. 308–17.

2. In medieval charters the power of knots to close and fix was brought to bear both literally and figuratively; some southwestern French charters state that the legal action described was validated by the tying of knots by the acting parties or their witnesses, called *nodatores*. See Fraenkel, *Signature,* p. 68, and Giry, *Manuel de diplomatique,* p. 656.

3. This Latin admonition appears in Dijon, Bibliothèque Municipale, MS 13, fol. 150v. Oursel, *Miniatures cisterciennes,* provides both the Latin text (Annex, p. 26) and a French translation of it (p. 27), as well as reproductions of pages from this Bible.

4. For reproductions of these initials from Dijon, Bibliothèque Municipale, MS 14, fols. 122v and 158r, see Oursel, *Miniatures cisterciennes,* plates 8 and 10.

5. Cahn (*Romanesque Bible Illumination,* p. 142) argues that this particular initial is not an image of John's divine inspiration, presumably because of the monastic tonsure of the figure in the grip of the eagle. However, many earlier examples could be cited of tonsured evangelists. The anachronistic coiffure helps to conflate the medieval scribe with the inspired evangelist, and thus to sanctify the medieval copy. Oursel describes the figure thus (*Miniatures cisterciennes,* p. 27): "The Eagle symbolic of the evangelist John presses its talons into the sensory organs of the Evangelist figured as a Cistercian monk."

6. Lewis, "Enigma of Fr. 403," p. 33, notes John's gesture but explains it otherwise: "To compensate for the removal of John's desk from the model, the Paris designer ingeniously shifts the seer's writing of the text to the manuscript itself, where he now begins to pen the letter 'p' of 'Apocalipsis,' a device that occurs again in one of the last miniatures in Morgan 524." Had he wanted to make space for a writing desk, this illuminator could have done so. John's gesture of writing the rubric of the manuscript before our eyes is not a compensation but a clever invention that serves to present a copy of a translation as the inspired, original transcription of the Book of Revelations.

7. McGurk, "Oldest Manuscripts," pp. 19–20.

8. Geary has argued that, because the physical matter of a relic has no special significance on its own, "something essentially extraneous to the relic must be provided: a reliquary with an inscription or iconographic representation of the saint, a document attesting to its authenticity, or a tradition, oral or written, which identified this particular object with a specific individual or at least with a specific type of individual (a saint)." By contrast, Geary argues, "a manuscript will always have some potential significance to anyone capable of reading it" (*Furta Sacra,* pp. 5–6). Although this is true in the sense that a bone cannot testify to its belonging to a powerful saint in the way a text can testify to its being inspired by God or written by a particular saint, yet there was in the early Middle Ages a need to distinguish

divine and saintly writing from ordinary human writing by means of pictorial, as well as verbal, testimonies—among them, enriching, awesome pictorial designs. In *Iconoclasme byzantin,* p. 37, André Grabar speculated that the cult of images arose out of the cult of relics and the need to identify them: "From the fifth century, at the latest, that is, from the beginning of the cult of relics, these reliquary containers were decorated with religious images." By direct contact with the relics whose presence they proclaimed, images were imbued with supernatural powers, becoming relics themselves.

9. Brosses, *Du culte des dieux fétiches,* p. 15.

10. Clerc, *Théories relatives au culte des images,* p. 29.

11. For the citation from Gregory see the footnotes to my chapter 3.

12. On images of the Virgin and of Christ unpainted by human hands, see Belting, *Likeness and Presence,* pp. 49–56.

13. Dodwell, *Anglo-Saxon Art,* pp. 46–47, notes that their artistic talents aided some monks to preferment and gives many examples of abbots and even abbesses reputed for their calligraphic or artistic skills. Until the eleventh century, abbots and bishops apparently continued to practice scribal and artisanal crafts. But, according to Dodwell, we should not give much credence to observations in monastic chronicles and saints' lives of a saint's skill at making sacred texts and other religious objects: "[S]tatements that works were made by saints need to be treated with special caution. These claims advanced the merits of the objects concerned as objects of devotion [in effect, relics], and such attributions might owe more to pious hope than historic fact" (p. 49). Particularly in the case of an elaborately designed text or religious object, attribution to a saintly maker might be a way of accounting for the exceptional, awesome visual quality of the object; as a relic, it testified to the saint's supernatural powers and its own. Dodwell goes on to suggest that the artistic talents of abbots, bishops, and especially saints became a kind of incidental topos of religious chroniclers and hagiographers. Had these men not achieved recognition as leaders, he argues, their artistic abilities would have gone unremarked:

> [I]t was not as artists, but as abbots, or bishops, or particularly saints, that monks were most likely to commend themselves to the attention of the chroniclers who might then, incidentally, remark on their intellectual or artistic talents. It is only in the context of those who achieved high office or great sanctity that chroniclers give us information that is at all helpful [about early medieval craftsmanship]. . . . Dunstan was in turn a monk, an abbot and an archbishop, he was at the same time a saint. His positions of authority and his qualities of holiness attracted the attention of writers, who then give other information about him, such as the fact that . . . he was a musician, a scribe, and a painter. (pp. 52–53)

Dodwell may be wrong here. The praise of artistic accomplishments is not necessarily "incidental"; nor need we suppose that these talents were probably no greater than ordinary and that they were noted in saintly and authoritative religious figures only because they were already powerful. On the contrary, the frequency of occurrence of such a hagiographic topos may suggest its importance as a sign. Exceptional artistic ability was considered to be a divine gift, a mark of divine favor and aid—in short, an important manifestation of saintliness and of divine authority.

14. On Columba's visitations by the Holy Spirit, who inspired him with understanding of the Scriptures, see Adomnan's *Life of Saint Columba* (3.19), pp. 123–24.

15. The identification of Eadfrith as scribe comes from a colophon added to the Lindisfarne Gospels in the tenth century by the glossator Aldred, who apparently recorded local tradition concerning the manuscript's production. A transcription and translation of this colophon appears in Millar's introduction to *Lindisfarne Gospels*. For further examples of early monastic scribes as illuminators, as well as for a basic survey of and bibliography on manuscript production, see Alexander, *Medieval Illuminators*.

16. In "Lindisfarne Scriptorium," p. 156, Brown remarks, "[The Lindisfarne scriptorium seems to have] adopted a practice in the manufacture of manuscripts *de luxe* whereby one master was responsible for the body of the work, perhaps implying a desire for homogeneity or that the work was seen as one person's *opus Dei*, embodying their own act of devotion. There are no signs here of a master allowing a trainee to take a hand in the work." An ambitious scribal exegete might, by the virtuosity of his designs, "prove" that he was inspired by the Spirit in inscribing a religious text. To parcel out the work to others in a workshop would undermine any such demonstration of the divine working through and sanctifying a particular individual.

17. *Lives of Saints from the Book of Lismore*, p. 176: "Many, then were the churches he [Saint Columba or 'Colomb Cille'] marked out, and the books he wrote, to wit, three hundred churches and three hundred books. Though the book that his hand would write were ever so long under water, not even a single letter therein would be washed out [literally, 'drowned']." That the letters of books written by saints were impervious to water seems to have been a topos of the Irish saint's legend. The life of Saint Ciarán in the Book of Lismore, for example, relates how the saint's Gospel book, accidentally dropped into the lake by a careless monastic brother, was finally fetched to shore when the strap got caught around the foot of a cow bathing in the lake in summer. Despite its long immersion, and through Ciarán's grace, "when the gospel was opened thus it was a bright white, dry, without destruction of a letter" (p. 275). Drogin, *Biblioclasm*, pp. 99–100, cites

cases of holy texts owned or written by early Irish and English saints also proving—miraculously—impervious to fire.

18. Simeon of Durham, *Historia ecclesiae dunhelmensis,* pp. 67–68; translation by Millar, *Lindisfarne Gospels,* p. 6.

19. Grabar, *Iconoclasme byzantin,* pp. 37–38, notes that the *achiropiites* of Christ appeared suddenly at the end of the sixth century for use in military campaigns against the Persians. Along with an autograph letter addressed to King Abgar of Edessa, Christ supposedly sent his own image imprinted on a sort of banner to assure Christian victory. The display of this supernatural image of Christ was believed by contemporary chroniclers to have a terrible, undermining effect on the enemy, for it demonstrated in advance which side God was on.

20. The early ninth-century Book of Armagh (Dublin, Trinity College, MS 52) was exhibited in battle this way and recovered from the corpse of its guardian in 1177 after "participating" in the Battle of Down. On this episode, see Pierre Riché and Guy Lobrichon, *Moyen âge et la Bible,* p. 29.

21. Likewise, Armenian illuminated Gospels imagined as relics or incarnations of Christ were given special names such as "Savior of All" or "Resurrector of the Dead" and carried into battle to ensure victory. See Nersessian, *Armenian Illuminated Gospel Books,* p. 11.

22. "The great Gospel of Colum Cille [The Book of Kells], the chief treasure of the western world on account of its secular (*doendai,* literally 'human') cover, was stolen by night." This entry from the Annals of Ulster for 1006 is quoted and translated in Alton's historical introduction to the Book of Kells, *Evangeliorum quattor codex cenannensis,* vol. 3, p. 14. On the meanings of *doendai* and *cumdach,* see Ryan, "The Book of Kells and Metalwork," pp. 273–74.

23. Greek, Etruscan, and Roman oracles and prophecies initially took the form of nonverbal, nonalphabetic, "natural" inscriptions requiring interpretation: traces of avian flight in the sky, marks on the organs of sacrificed animals, and so forth. Even such "natural writing" was not for the interpretation of everyman, but had its caste of exegetes whose power depended on various techniques of controlling (and producing while claiming to merely receive) the "divine" signs and their meanings. Probably because an oracle was easier for the exegetes to control when written than when circulated by word of mouth, verbal oracles had to be "fixed" by alphabetic inscription. For example, when a person presented a question (usually in writing) to the oracle of Apollo at Delphi, the semiarticulate phrases and cries spoken in the first person by the ecstatic Pythia, as if Apollo were responding through her, were "transcribed" by priest-interpreters into enigmatic written verses, which the questioner then took to professional interpreters for explanation. All seekers thus carried away "official transcriptions" of the oracular responses to their questions. The Roman Sibylline books were compilations of

oracles "taken out of circulation to prevent private exegesis" by writing them down on linen cloth and shutting them up in a temple. These books, believed to hold the key to the future, were consulted by priests with respectfully cloth-covered hands, but only in times of crisis, at the order of the Roman senate. See Bouché-Leclercq, *Histoire de la divination,* vol. 3, pp. 96–101, on Apollo's oracle, and vol. 4, pp. 289–308, on the Sibylline books.

24. The Hebrew prophets were imagined to have inscribed divine dictation in their Old Testament books, which thus became the object of exegetical interpretation or divination. Both the Old and New Testaments were used, well into the Middle Ages, for the divinatory practice called *sortes sanctorum* (randomly letting the codex fall open and letting one's glance fall on a verse that, although not always clearly, would give God's answer to the question posed). In the early Christian period, this method was often used by the church to confirm elections to high ecclesiastical office. Gregory of Tours in his *Historia Francorum* (5.14) told the story of a son of Chilperic I who took the precaution of consulting the Psalter, the Book of Kings, and the Gospels on what would happen to him and whether he might obtain the kingship—and got an equally discouraging response from all three. Repeated ecclesiastical condemnation of the practice of *sortes sanctorum* over the centuries suggests its persistence. In the early eleventh century, for example, Bishop Burchard of Worms attempted to discourage it by meting out in his *Decretorum* 10.9 (*PL* 140:831) a year and a half of penance to laypeople and three years to clerics for the infraction. For further discussion of the medieval practice of *sortes sanctorum,* see Poulin, "Entre magie et religion," pp. 130–36.

25. For discussion of the visions of Hermas, a series of early Christian writings authenticated and empowered by verbal attestations to their divine inspiration, see Fox, "Literacy and Power," p. 132: "In his first vision (Hermas, *Vis.* 1.2), Hermas writes how he had seen an aged lady, sitting with a book which she was reading with an awesome expression, while telling him to pay attention. On his way to Cumae, he sees her again: she tells him to take the little book and copy it, which he does, 'letter by letter' because he could not 'distinguish the syllables' (2.1), and then the original is snatched away. Fifteen days later, after fasting, the text's meaning is revealed." After copying—mechanically, letter by letter, without understanding—at the bidding of the elderly, oracular woman, who turns out to represent the Christian church, Hermas serves as secretary to an angel to copy several other texts. Fox comments on the preservative effect of such verbal testimony affirming supernatural authorship: "On the highest authority, Hermas can assure us that his text is not his own invention and that his motives are not questionable. . . . The success of Hermas' heavenly dictation is shown in the high respect and breadth of circulation accorded to it by later centuries" (pp. 132–33).

26. Augustine, *De catechizandis rudibus* 9.13 (*PL* 40:320B; *CCL* 46:135).

27. Brown, "Lindisfarne Scriptorium," p. 157, notes that the Lindisfarne Gospels are "the first extant Insular manuscript to choose to represent the evangelists as scribes, rather than the terrestrial animal symbols of [the Book of] Durrow, although these zoomorphic symbols are still used as identifiers."

28. For color reproductions of all these evangelist pages, see the facsimile edition of the Lindisfarne Gospels, *Evangeliorum quattuor codex Lindisfarnensis*.

29. The supernatural origin of the evangelist's ink will become a motif in later representations of evangelical inspiration. For example, in a late twelfth-century Gospel lectionary from the Abbey of Saint-Amand (Antwerp, Mayer Van den Bergh Museum, MS Inv. 619, cat. I 297, fol. 67v), a seated Mark holds a closed codex and inkhorn while looking up over his shoulder at the Spirit in the form of a winged bull, who proffers him the divine letter in liquid form, not inscribed on a codex or scroll but as a full inkhorn. (For a reproduction, see Nieuwdorp, *Musée Mayer van den Bergh*, p. 49.) An earlier and more ingenious suggestion of supernatural ink can be found in the Carolingian Ebo Gospels. The page prefacing Matthew's Gospel shows, in the upper-right corner, a tiny angel (the Spirit as man) who unfurls an inscribed scroll in the direction of the scribe. The divine exemplar of this tiny scroll tapers until it seems to turn into a line of ink flowing into the evangelist's inkhorn. As Matthew catches the divine letter in its fluid form, he writes on the page of a bound codex while gazing intently, not straight down at the text he is inscribing, but diagonally in a direction that points to the text on the facing recto. The absence of visible lettering on the codex Matthew inscribes, along with the direction of his gaze, elides one codex with another to suggest that the elaborate knotwork initials and shiny, gold-lettered text of the incipit page of Matthew in the Ebo Gospels itself is the text written under divine inspiration. Reproductions of these two pages, fol. 18v and 19r, can be found in Mütherich and Gaehde, *Carolingian Painting*, plates 14 and 15.

30. Wormald, *Miniatures in the Gospels of Saint Augustine*, p. 1, does not discountenance the tradition that has associated this sixth-century Italian manuscript, once owned by Saint Augustine's of Canterbury, with Saint Augustine, the early missionary Gregory the Great sent to England and to whom, as Bede related, Gregory sent many books. Gregory upheld the usefulness of pictures in teaching those unable to read Latin in his famous letter to Serenus, bishop of Marseille (discussed in my chapter 2).

31. Irenaeus, *Adversus haereses* 3.21 (*PG* 7:949A; *SC* 211:404–6); Clement of Alexandria, *Stromates* 1.22 (*PG* 8:894A). This attribution of divine inspiration seems to stem from statements in the Book of Ezra that he behaved "according to the good hand of his God upon him" (1 Ezra 7:9).

32. In his consideration of the Book of Ezra's title to canonicity, Augustine did not, surprisingly, repeat this story of Ezra's divine inspiration in retrieving the

correct text of the Scriptures but instead reported that Ezra had been considered to be a historian rather than a prophet, unless perhaps a certain statement he made might be considered prophetic of the Incarnation (*City of God* 18.36). Even one prophetic passage could "save" a work of human erudition and make it worthy of canonization. Two chapters later, Augustine expressed the view that "even those men to whom the Holy Spirit certainly revealed matters that properly fell within the scope of religious authority may have written sometimes as men, thanks to historical research, and sometimes as prophets, by divine inspiration, and the two kinds were so different that one kind, such was the verdict, must be credited, as it were, to themselves, the other to God speaking through them" (*City of God* 18.38).

33. The nine large volumes on the shelves behind the scribe may recollect the nine volumes of Cassiodorus's famous sixth-century Bible (cf. Henderson, "Cassiodorus and Eadfrith Once Again"), which would tend to conflate Ezra with later scribes (not only Cassiodorus, but also the scribes of the Codex Amiatinus) who participated in the transmission of Holy Writ.

34. Friend, "Portraits of the Evangelists ... Part 1," p. 141, suggests that the veiled figure may represent *Sophia,* or "Holy Wisdom," yet he argues that "what is important is not so much whom the copyist of the *Rossanensis* thought the lady to be, but who, originally, she was," that is, a classical muse. See also Loerke's discussion of this figure of inspiration in the most recent facsimile edition, *Codex purpureus rossanensis,* vol. 2, pp. 153–62. Concerning Mark's visual expression, Loerke remarks: "The gaze of Mark, not directed at his pen or at the figure in front of him, suggests that the weightless image of *Sophia* is a thought in his mind" (p. 162). Loerke also notes that Mark's pose is not that of a classical author, "never shown in the act of writing," but rather that of a scribe, a mere instrument (p. 153).

35. Early exegetes such as Irenaeus, *Adversus haereses* 3.11.8 (*PG* 7:885B; *SC* 211:160–62), had "explained" the necessity of the number of the four Gospels by identifying them with the four columns upholding the church (as well as the four creatures of the prophetic books of Ezekiel and Revelations, the four parts of the world, and the four winds). For reproductions from early manuscripts in which the canon tables of the Gospels are depicted as temples or architectural structures, see Nordenfalk, *Spätantiken Kanontafeln.* In the Gospels, architectural canon tables conventionally appear on separate pages before (that is, at the entrance to) the holy texts, but in the ninth-century Drogo Sacramentary, temple-like architectural designs frame the actual words of the prefaces for the Easter week masses. Calkins compares this enshrinement of words to the "tabernacle-like structures ... used to house the bread and wine, the body and blood of Christ, on the high altar" ("Liturgical Sequence," p. 21).

36. The *Diatessaron,* only a fragment of which has survived, is discussed by Metzger, *Early Versions of the New Testament,* pp. 10–13.

37. That the other evangelists were perceived to have a less direct contact with the divine than John had is suggested by many manuscripts' distinctive visual treatment of John's inspiration (such as seizure of his head in the eagle's talons). Indeed, as Neuman de Vegvar points out in *Northumbrian Renaissance,* p. 183, the other evangelists "were instructed either by the incarnate Christ or by mortal men."

38. *City of God* (18.43), p. 35: "[W]here anything that is in the Septuagint is not in the Hebrew text, the same Spirit must have preferred to say it through the former rather than through the prophets, thus showing that these [seventy translators] as well as those were prophets. . . . [O]ne kind led the way in prophesying and the other came after with a prophetic translation of their words." On patristic views of the authority of the Septuagint, see Benoit, "Inspiration des septante," pp. 179–80, 184–85.

39. *City of God,* p. 31:

But although the Jews bear witness that his [Jerome's] very learned work is faithful, and assert that the Septuagint translators have gone wrong in many places, nevertheless the churches of Christ have passed judgment that no man is to be set above the authority of such a number, who were chosen for this great task by Eleazor, who was then high priest. For even supposing that there had not appeared among them one Spirit that was beyond doubt divine, and that the seventy learned men had like ordinary men compared the words of their translation so that what proved acceptable to all should stand approved, even so no one translator should be preferred to them. But since so great a sign of divinity was manifested in their case [that seventy isolated translators produced exactly the same text], it is certain that any other faithful translator of these Scriptures from the Hebrew into any other language either agrees with the Septuagint translators, or else, if he is seen not to agree with them, we must believe that the greater prophetic depth is found in the other version.

For a similar judgment, see *On Christian Doctrine* 2.15.

40. Jerome's prefaces to the Gospels and other books of the Bible, as they appear in different medieval manuscript versions, are edited in Bruyne's *Préfaces de la Bible latine,* pp. 153–55 for "Novum opus," and pp. 155–56 for "Plures fuisse" (Jerome's prologue to the Gospels). Prefaces by many other exegetes are also collected in this volume—for example, Eusebius's letter explaining the canon tables (p. 157).

41. On the greater survival rate of "reliquary" texts, see Gribomont, "Plus anciennes traductions," p. 43: "Often antique fragments have survived the centuries as relics, because people wanted to believe that they came from the hand of a venerated patron. Thus the most ancient Irish Psalter, passed down from generation to generation, served to cure cows—luckily, it was always the same leaf they plunged into the bucket to obtain the magic potion. Often enough, also, devotion found its

support in the exceptional luxury of a copy; thus, without intending to do so, the conserved documentation risks selecting a certain kind of edition, not always the most representative."

In the same volume, in "Plus anciens manuscrits de la Bible latine," p. 116, Petitmengin points out that ancient inscription per se did not garner any special respect, because a quarter of the remaining corpus of ancient biblical texts are palimpsests, that is, texts written on recycled parchment, after even older texts have been effaced. For an ancient manuscript to be protected and venerated as a relic (as was a manuscript attributed to Eusebius at Vercelli, to Columbanus at Bobbio, to Marcellinus at Ancona), it had to be believed, for one reason or another, to conserve in its trace some of the divine powers of its saintly writer. The marvelous distinction of richly designed writing, as I have already suggested, was taken as evidence of the scribe's divine inspiration and thus had the effect of hallowing the man as well as the manuscript.

42. The Insular scribal exegetes' depictions of the Spirit conflated with or showing through the image of the scribe is in keeping with Gregory the Great's insistence, in the preface to his *Moralia in Job* (1.2), that the Spirit authored the text of the prophet. To the question of why the Book of Job, if written by Job, speaks of Job in the third person, Gregory replies that Job is indeed the writer in the sense of scribe, but that it is "a waste of time to try to identify the writer, for we know by faith that the Holy Spirit is the author of the book. Because the author is he who dictated what to write, he who, by the mediation of the writer, gave us this story . . ." (*PL* 75:517AB; *CCL* 143:8).

43. Quoted and translated from the writings of Aldhelm by Sims-Williams, *Religion and Literature,* p. 180.

44. Even hagiographic texts, legends of local saints, were treated this way, as Heffernan has explained in *Sacred Biography,* p. 36:

[I]n the emergence of a written text as the official text of choice—in order to ensure the text's continued dominance—the authority on which the text is based must be spiritualized. A concomitant of the process of legitimation, this spiritualizing of the text takes one of two methods. First, we may find a steady disassociation of the text from its unique historical author. Such a process shrouds the document's origins in mystery and gives to the document an ahistorical, quasi-transcendental character; further, this process helps, paradoxically, to augment the document's status as an inspired text. . . . The second method is simply to declare from the outset that the document is the product of a divinely inspired minister of God.

45. As Alexander points out in *Norman Illumination at Mont St. Michel,* p. 173, Gregory is conventionally depicted with the Holy Spirit in the form of a dove at his ear, and this iconography is inspired by Paulus Diaconus's eighth-century ac-

count of an incident in Gregory's life: "During a long silence in St. Gregory's dictation, a scribe peeped through a curtain which divided him from the Saint and saw
the Holy Spirit as a dove sitting on his shoulder and speaking into his ear."

46. Reproduced in Temple, *Anglo-Saxon Manuscripts,* fig. 316.

47. See Alexander, *Norman Illumination at Mont St. Michel,* plate 20 and fig. 29a,
for examples of Augustine's inspiring angel from Avranches, MS 76, fol. A verso,
and MS 75, fol. C verso.

48. Book of Kells, *Evangeliorum quattor codex cenannensis,* edited by Alton and
Meyer, vol. 3, supplies transcriptions of seven Irish charters concerning properties
near Kells that were copied for safekeeping onto blank pages in the Book of Kells
in the latter part of the twelfth century. How better to preserve these records of
gifts than by ensuring their divine protection by inscribing them alongside the
trace of divinity (or, more commonly, though less permanently, laying charters between the leaves of the sacred book)? On the safekeeping of secular charters in
liturgical books (or close to the relics of a saint), see Clanchy, *From Memory to Written Record,* pp. 155–56, and Wormald, "Sherborne 'Chartulary,' " pp. 106–9. Wormald's explanation of why secular charters were copied into a liturgical book is
especially evocative: "[T]he Gospel books had something of the significance of a
reliquary, and relics were sometimes placed in their bindings; and, of course, some
Gospel books have been long associated with certain saints. What is of even
greater interest is that there are instances of documents being kept with relics. . . .
If, therefore, a document was copied into a Gospel book it presumably received
the same kind of protection as if it was preserved in a reliquary, in contact with the
remains or possessions of a holy person. Penalties for mutilation would be equal
to those for sacrilege" (p. 107).

49. On the implications of this dispute, see Clanchy, *From Memory to Written
Record,* p. 261, citing and translating Eadmer, *Historia novorum in anglia,* p. 138.

## Chapter 6

1. Foucault, *Ordre du discours,* pp. 29–30, 66: "[W]e ask that the author account
for the unity of the texts that we place under his name; we ask that he reveal, or at
least claim, the hidden sense that runs through them; we ask that he articulate
these in terms of his personal life and experiences, in terms of the real history that
saw them born. It is the author that gives to the troubling language of fiction its
unities, its coherent nexuses, its insertion in the real. . . . I think that—at least after
a certain period—the individual who set out to write a text upon the horizon of
which lurked a possible 'work' took upon himself the author function." See also
Foucault's "What Is an Author?," especially pp. 150–51, 158–59.

2. From the tentative beginnings of the "single author codex" (devoted to the

vernacular works of one person) compiled in the thirteenth century by people other than the poet, through the extensive late fourteenth-century compilations of poets such as Guillaume de Machaut and Jean Froissart, who supervised the production of codices containing their own *oeuvres complètes,* Sylvia Huot, in *From Song to Book,* effectively traces the institution and internalization of the "author function" with respect to French vernacular texts. See also my "The Monument and the Margin."

3. Minnis, *Medieval Theory of Authorship,* p. 10. For passages using these different spellings, see also Chenu, "Auctor, actor, autor," pp. 81–86.

4. Minnis, *Medieval Theory of Authorship,* p. 220 n. 7.

5. Chenu, "Auctor, actor, autor," p. 86, citing Evrard's grammar manual, *Grecismus.*

6. Cassin, "Sceau," p. 743. On the impressed bite of the donor and on fingerprints deliberately impressed on the backs of medieval waxen seals to serve as authenticating counterseals, see Gandilhon, "Dactyloscopie et les sceaux," pp. 98–102; and Fraenkel, *Signature,* p. 231. Clanchy, *From Memory to Written Record,* p. 316, points out that medieval charters often contain phrases, such as the following, that explain the reinforcing power of the seal: "And so that this gift and grant of mine and confirmation of my charter may last in perpetuity, I have reinforced the present writing with the impress of my seal."

7. Balogh, "Voces paginarum," p. 203.

8. For speculative reconstruction of early author portraits on papyrus rolls, none of which have survived (although verbal references to them have), see Weitzmann, *Manuscrits gréco-romains et paléochrétiens,* pp. 9–11.

9. In *Ancient Book Illumination,* p. 117, Weitzmann notes that, at the end of the first century A.D., in one of the earliest codices, a portrait of Vergil's countenance appeared on the first page of a volume of his works, for Martial refers to it in the second line of an epigram: "ipsa vultus prima tabella gerit." In the sixth-century Vergilius Romanus codex (Vatican, MS lat. 3867), the framed portrait of the seated author holding a scroll appears, not on a separate page prefacing the codex of his work as a whole, but within the text columns, above the beginnings of the second, fourth, and sixth eclogues (as if copied from the beginnings of separate papyrus rolls containing different sections of this text).

10. Folios 9v (seated evangelists) and 10r (standing ones) from the Rabula Gospels (Florence, Laurentian Library, MS Plut. I, Cod. 56) are reproduced by Friend, "Portraits of the Evangelists . . . Part 2."

11. In fact, some of the biblical figures represented, whom we regard as mere characters, may have been regarded otherwise by the manuscript's designers. For example, in the preface to his *Moralia in Job* (PL 75:517), Gregory proposed that

Job be considered the narrator of the book about his life, for he judged it useless to split straws over who the human narrator of a biblical text was, when the true author was divine and the human narrator a mere instrument.

12. See Friend, "Portraits of the Evangelists ... Part 1," figs. 45–61, for reproductions of these biblical author portraits from Paris, B.N.F., MS Syriac 341.

13. In *Illustrated Bibles from Tours,* Kessler points out that the "Majestas domini" frontispieces to Carolingian Bibles (two of which he reproduces in figs. 49 and 50) are "harmony pictures, testifying to the divine concord of the holy writings" and that they effectively illustrate Jerome's preface to the Gospels (beginning "Plures fuisse") wherein "the theophanic visions of Ezekiel and St. John are cited as the primary evidence of the authenticity and unity of the four Gospels" (p. 41).

14. Translated by Minnis, *Medieval Theory of Authorship,* p. 37, from Gregory, *Moralia in Job* (*PL* 75:517AB):

> Sed quis haec scripserit, valde supervacue quaeritur, cum tamen auctor libri Spiritus sanctus fideliter credatur. Ipse igitur haec scripsit, qui scribenda dictavit. Ipse scripsit, qui et in illius opere inspirator exstitit, et per scribentis vocem imitanda ad nos ejus facta transmisit. Si magni cujusdam viri susceptis epistolis legeremus verba, sed quo calamo fuissent scripta quaereremus, ridiculum profecto esset epistolarum auctorem scire sensumque cognoscere, sed quali calamo earum verba impressa fuerint indagare. Cum ergo rem cognoscimus, ejusque rei Spiritum sanctum auctorem tenemus, quia scriptorem quaerimus, quid aliud agimus, nisi legentes litteras, de calamo percontamur.

15. See, for example, the two vignettes of John holding up and staring at his pen in two different fourteenth-century Apocalypse manuscripts reproduced by Lewis, "Apocalypse of Isabella of France," figs. 38 and 40.

16. In *Die Initiale,* pp. 74–96, Gutbrod reproduces, mainly from twelfth-century religious manuscripts, a series of initial *I*s formed by the bodies of authors who are either haloed saints or prophets (some of the latter, such as David or Esther, being also kings or queens depicted with crowns, swords, scepters, and other signs of power).

17. Eleen, *Illustration of the Pauline Epistles,* p. 3, identifies this as an image of Paul and notes that the same fragmentary manuscript of Paul's Epistles has a frontal head of the author in another initial *P.* The innovative Christian scribe has placed within the circular loop of the letter a typical sort of classical author portrait—the head in a medallion, such as we see in the Carolingian Terence manuscript (my fig. 79).

18. Nordenfalk, *Spätantiken Zierbuchstaben,* p. 165, notes that human figures first appeared in Latin texts as parts of letters shortly before 800 all over Europe—

in religious texts written in Rome, in Charlemagne's realm, and in Britain and Ireland. It is possible that the Council of Nicea's anti-iconoclastic decisions in 787 may have stimulated such depictions.

19. A similar effect is achieved five centuries later, in a thirteenth-century lectionary from Monte Cassino (reproduced by Gutbrod, *Die Initiale,* p. 89, fig. 42): to the left of a text column, the standing prophet Isaiah's lifted arm culminates in his upraised index finger, which serves as an initial *I* and also points, as does the prophet's upward gaze, to the divine author of the text the prophet embodies (and inscribes).

20. This initial from Naples, Biblioteca Nazionale Vittorio Emanuele III, Cod. Vienna 58, fol. 44v, is reproduced by Weitzmann, *Ancient Book Illumination,* fig. 128.

21. On the effigy of the imperial seal as a permanent presence guaranteeing the signature, see Grabar, *Iconoclasme byzantin,* p. 70.

22. Other members of the French royal line in the late fourteenth century, and even King Richard II of England, embodied the initials beginning their legal documents in order to empower them. For a reproduction of the marriage contract of 1389 between Duke Jean de Berry and Jeanne de Boulogne, wherein the initial is formed by the Duke taking the hand of Jeanne (thus enacting the marriage), see Meiss, *French Painting . . . Boucicaut Master,* fig. 476. A charter of 1380 of King Richard II frames the king's standing figure in the upright of the initial *R* of his name as he extends a hand beyond the letter to grant the sealed document to a group of kneeling men on the bare page to the left of the initial. For this image, see Alexander, *Decorated Letter,* fig. 21.

23. Kris and Kurz, *Legend, Myth, and Magic,* p. 77.

24. Ibid.

25. In *Peinture médiévale à Paris,* Sterling remarks (1:245), "It is certain that the mentality of this period [the later fourteenth century] accords to the image, if not primacy over the text, at least the value of a legal proof authenticating a text, just as a seal with engraved figures authenticates a charter." One of the examples Sterling gives to support this judgment is the deliberate revision, for political motives, of the illustration of a manuscript of the *Grandes chroniques de France* (Paris, B.N.F., MS fr. 2813) to include an image of the king of England doing homage to Charles V for the duchy of Aquitaine. See also Sterling's remarks concerning the use of true-to-life portraits of individuals to reinforce the authenticating function of images in a manuscript compilation of acts of homage (1:212).

26. It is perhaps not entirely fair to say that the king's body forms the letter, for he also uses it as a stage. There is a certain spatial ambiguity in the relationship between the relatively "realistic" portrait of the king and the upright of the initial *R,* so that we can see the king's body as both forming part of the letter and standing

on and before a part of the letter. The designers of this initial may not, for ideological reasons, have wanted the king to seem to be subsumed into the letter to the same extent as the kneeling monks on the right.

27. Gutbrod, *Die Initiale,* pp. 148–55, discusses and reproduces several examples, including this one, of what he calls "held or carried" letters. In this case he argues, "The initial in the hand of the Bishop has a magical sense. With it he conquers the dragon embodying evil. Like a vice, the divided shaft of the *C* grasps the neck of the demon. The foliage emanating from the maw of the dragon, which symbolizes evil, is mastered and compressed by the contour of the letter. This manner of representation would demonstrate the magic power of the letter and of the holy word" (p. 153).

28. Lecoq, "Cadre et rebord," p. 19, suggests that, like the "portraits" of donors in prayer or devotion, artists' signatures in religious paintings may have an ex-voto function: "[T]he deposit of a *cartellino* or of an engraved signature parallels the introduction, by means of a portrait, of the donor (and sometimes of the artist himself) into the sacred space and the glorious company of the Saints. . . . [T]he presence of the donor in prayer indicates that this is not an historical scene, but a sort of mystical reunion. It is also an act of homage and piety. The painter, for his part, in executing his work as best he can, participates in the pious work. To place his name at the feet of the saintly figure is also a mark of devotion and humility. The signature thus takes on the value of a tiny *ex-voto.*" In his introduction to this special issue of *Revue de l'art* entitled *L'Art de la signature,* Chastel judged that the artist's signature on a work of religious art before the fourteenth or fifteenth centuries almost always appeared "in a devotional context" ("Signature et signe," p. 12). As Lecoq noted, late medieval artists tended to avoid infringing on the "field of activity" of the depicted saintly or sacred figures by painting their own signatures on steps, scraps of paper, and little placards on the floor or on internal "frames" (signifying their humility and marginality). In contrast, an earlier medieval scribe such as Valerianus did not hesitate to inscribe his own name in the very center of the cross to place himself at the epicenter of divine influence (my fig. 87). (Valerianus's "signature" occurs in the context of a devotional colophon in which he also requests the prayers of eventual readers for his salvation.)

29. For example, to defend themselves against the iconoclasts' charges that they were encouraging idolatry, eighth-century opponents of iconoclasm developed a theory of representation based on recognition of the difference between image and prototype. This iconophile theory of representation is treated by Sahas, *Icon and Logos,* especially pp. 77, 89–92.

30. In "Image of the Book-Owner," pp. 79–80, Sandler suggests that portraits of book owners (who, in the cases she studied, were also the scribes and designers of their texts) may serve as surrogates for them: "The portrait of the owner in

prayer may even be the surrogate for actual supplication, a kind of permanent effigy of repeated acts of devotional piety."

31. Minnis, *Medieval Theory of Authorship,* p. 5. He goes on to quote Beryl Smalley on this point: "The scheme [of the four causes] had the advantage of focusing attention on the author of the book and on the reasons which impelled him to write. The book ceased to be a mosaic of mysteries and was seen as the product of a human, although divinely inspired, intelligence instead."

32. This tendency to depict the human author of Holy Scripture using the initial letter as a stage, prop, or support for addressing the reader/viewer can already be seen, for example, in a Bible dated around 1070 made in the monastery of Mont Saint-Michel (Bordeaux, Bibliothèque Municipale, MS 1). The haloed prophet Jeremiah, holding a book and receiving the inspiration of an angel, stands on the initial *V* at its center (fol. 168v); the haloed prophet Micah stands just in front of an initial *V* shaped as a dragon, holds up a circle marked with a cross in one hand, and, wrapping his other arm around the upright dragon's tail as though leaning on it, holds up a finger in admonitory prophetic speech, or to indicate the source of his inspiration (fol. 240v). For color reproductions of these two initials, see figs. 7 and 8 in Dosdat, *L'enluminure romane au Mont Saint-Michel.*

33. This author figure from a three-volume manuscript in the Vatican Library (MS Palat. lat. 3-4-5) is reproduced with no folio number by Cahn, *Romanesque Bible Illumination,* catalog fig. 135. See Cahn's catalog figs. 129, 130, and 132 for further examples from late eleventh- and early twelfth-century Italian Bibles of Old Testament authors detached from the initial letters of their texts, either standing over them, or floating or standing in front of the backdrop of the letter.

34. This generalization can be verified for Insular manuscript illumination by leafing through the reproductions in Morgan, *Early Gothic Manuscripts, 1190–1250* and *Early Gothic Manuscripts, 1250–1285;* Sandler, *Gothic Manuscripts, 1285–1385;* and Scott, *Later Gothic Manuscripts, 1390–1490.*

35. In some late medieval and Renaissance manuscripts, the animal symbols of evangelical inspiration are brought down to earth and turned into companionable "pets" for the writers, patiently keeping them company during their authorial labors. The Spirit-as-angel who inspired Matthew is, in the Hours of Catherine of Valois (c. 1420–1437), turned into an apprentice-like helper who stands beside the evangelist, holding up his inkpot for him with an expectant look, while Matthew, his quill poised near his mouth, looks into space as if searching for the right words (and not as if mesmerized by an inner vision). For this image from London, British Library, MS Add. 65100, fol. 21v, see Scott, *Later Gothic Manuscripts,* vol. 1, fig. 287.

36. For reproductions from London, British Library, MS Harley 2904, fol. 3v; London, British Library, MS Cotton, Titus D. XXVII, fol. 65v; and New York,

Pierpont Morgan, MS 709, fol. 1v, see Temple, *Anglo-Saxon Manuscripts,* figs. 142, 246, and 289.

37. Lewis, "Apocalypse of Isabella of France," p. 250. The gesture Lewis identifies as nail biting may be a version of the meditative hand-to-mouth gesture of certain classical depictions of philosophers and authors. For further discussion of the increasing visual emphasis on John as human author in thirteenth-century Apocalypse manuscripts, see Lewis, *Reading Images,* pp. 24–25.

38. Eleen, *Illustration of the Pauline Epistles,* p. 51, and fig. 61 for a dove at Paul's ear.

39. In "Visualizing in the Vernacular," Camille has noted that vernacular Bibles more often than Latin ones exteriorize depiction in framed vignettes above the letter: "Fourteenth-century Vulgate Bibles continued to emphasize the Word by containing the images within initial letters, whereas in our vernacular Bible the image has taken over" (p. 99). This observation is equally true of the illuminated manuscripts of romances and other vernacular genres in the later Middle Ages, as compared to sacred and religious Latin texts; the latter continued to present author portraits, for example, within initial letters rather than framed above them.

40. Salter and Pearsall, "Pictorial Illustration," pp. 115–16. I have left out of this list the manuscript numbers exemplifying the different types of author portrait.

41. Early in their essay, Salter and Pearsall warn literary scholars "tempted" to overinterpret that such depictions may have no "literary significance," no value as contemporary medieval response to the particular text, because they may be merely "stock motifs": "Such scenes are often chosen because they provide opportunities for the employment of traditional iconographical models from the illustration of religious MSS: it is not that any underlying religious significance is being brought out, but that the availability of appropriate compositional models is an important consideration of the professional illustrator" (p. 104). Salter and Pearsall go on to suggest that we should not forget to consider several pragmatic reasons for the illustration of manuscripts of medieval secular literary works: complimenting or increasing the prestige of the patron or the person for whom the book was made, increasing the material value of the manuscript itself ("saleability in certain markets"), and diverting the reader (providing "a resting point for the eye, or a pleasant substitute for reading the text") (p. 106). That such desires may have motivated manuscript illumination cannot be contested, nor that illuminators of vernacular texts often drew upon and adapted religious models (although by no means always unthinkingly). Yet such explanations do not account adequately for the very phenomenon of the frontispiece or prefatory "author portrayal" (the author presenting or presiding over his text in various ways) that Salter and Pearsall so convincingly demonstrate.

42. Of fourteenth- through early sixteenth-century manuscripts made in En-

gland, Scott writes, "This frequent selection for representation of an author, narrator or main character over an event from a story or life indicates an attitude in which the author or narrator, etc., rather than the fictional or historical events of the narrative, was viewed as the authority or embodiment of truth even though the narrative events might depict Christian truth in action" ("Design, Decoration and Illustration," p. 47). Scott estimates that one in forty English codices of this period had "illustrations or other pictures" and one in twenty some "framing decorative work at one or more textual units" (p. 31). The percentages for France at the same period would be higher.

43. Windeatt provides a list of the contents of the surviving codices containing *Troilus* in the introduction to his critical edition of *Troilus and Criseyde*. A few other codices—such as Cambridge University Library MS Gg.4.27, British Library MS Harley 1239, and Bodleian Library MS Rawlinson Poet. 163—are devoted entirely to Chaucer's works, or those probably thought by the medieval compilers to have been written by Chaucer.

44. Hult, *Self-Fulfilling Prophecies*, p. 74. Elsewhere Hult remarks, "The author figure represents an anthropomorphization of the literary work, an abstraction, an allegory, which provides a biological referent for the otherwise distant collection of written signs constituting the work as a concrete entity" (p. 99). Reproductions of illuminations from different manuscripts of the *Roman de la rose*, including author portraits, are increasingly abundant and may be found, for example, in Kuhn, *Die Illustration des Rosenromans;* Tuve, *Allegorical Imagery;* Fleming, *"Roman de la Rose";* Hult, *Self-Fulfilling Prophecies;* Brownlee and Huot, *Rethinking the "Romance of the Rose";* and Huot, *The "Romance of the Rose" and Its Medieval Readers.*

45. In "Manuscrits enluminés de Guillaume de Machaut," p. 132, Avril proposed for the first time that Machaut, for whom "text and image formed an indissociable whole," gave "precise indications to the illuminators" of his codex, Paris, B.N.F., MS fr. 1584. On the basis of the illuminations, Avril dated this manuscript and another, Paris, B.N.F., MS fr. 1586, within Machaut's lifetime, the latter around 1350. Huot devotes a chapter to each of these codices in *From Song to Book* and argues, pp. 242–301, that Machaut supervised the compilation and illumination of both of them.

46. In an earlier codex of his collected works, B.N.F., MS fr. 1586, Machaut is pictured in the illuminations of his *Remède de fortune* taking dictation onto a scroll from female figures such as Hope, whose diaphanous veil floats as if in a breeze (perhaps suggestive of "inspiration"). Huot has reproduced an illumination of Loyalty dictating to Machaut in this fashion in *From Song to Book*, p. 261, fig. 22.

47. This general "prologue" is edited by Hoepffner, *Oeuvres de Guillaume de Machaut,* vol. 1, pp. 1–12. In his introduction to it, Hoepffner makes no mention

of reversing the order of the speakers (and the pictures) in his base manuscript (B.N.F., MS fr. 1584).

48. In "The Annunciation to Christine," Kolve calls attention to Christine's use in *The Book of the City of Ladies* of implicit verbal comparisons between herself and the Virgin of the Annunciation, allusions that serve to authorize her daring feminist writing. Given this rhetoric, as Kolve remarks, it is surprising that the program of three illuminations planned by Christine herself for this book did *not* make visual reference to the Annunciation in an author portrait (pp. 174–75, 186–89). See also Quilligan, *Allegory of Authority,* pp. 54–55.

49. On the self-authorizing tactics of late medieval vernacular writers—including Gautier de Coinci and Giraut Riquier in the thirteenth century, and Francesco da Barberino at the beginning of the fourteenth—who glossed, commented on, or directed the compilation and illumination of their own works, see Kendrick, "The Monument and the Margin." On John Gower and self-authorizing methods, see Pearsall, "Gower's Latin in the *Confessio Amantis,*" and Griffiths, "*Confessio Amantis*: The Poem and Its Pictures." Christine de Pizan's role in the early fifteenth century as director of the "publication" of editions of her own collected works has been treated by Laidlaw, "Christine de Pizan: A Publisher's Progress," and Hindman, *Christine de Pizan's "Epistre Othéa."*

50. The French king's hands were one of the parts of his body anointed by sacred oil at his consecration, and this gave his touch a power similar to that of a saint's relic. The king touched sufferers of certain skin diseases to cure them, for example. The pious Charles V is often pictured wearing gloves over his sanctified hands, and it seems plausible that presentation portraits in which the king receives a book into his own hand might, to a medieval viewer familiar with French royal traditions, suggest that the book had been sanctified by contact with the king's sanctified hand. On the royal unction and its curative effects, see Bloch, *Rois thaumaturges*. Depictions of Charles V in gloves or holding gloves may be found in Sherman, *Portraits of Charles V of France*.

51. Even relatively recent vernacular authors could be depicted, like Augustine, "backing" and encouraging their translators, as is the case in the presentation frontispiece of Paris, B.N.F., MS fr. 131, fol. 1r, where a magisterial Boccaccio stands behind Laurent de Premierfait's presentation to Jean de Berry of his French translation of Boccaccio's *De casibus virorum illustrium*. For a reproduction of this miniature, see Meiss, *French Painting . . . Patronage of the Duke,* plate volume, fig. 500.

52. Sherman, *Imaging Aristotle,* pp. 47, 350 n. 1: "The presence of a courtier at the extreme right of the dedication portraits of the A miniatures (Figs. 6 and 7) does not jeopardize the direct communication of Oresme and Charles V." This same scene is reproduced a second time in the manuscript, on folio 2v, as the first in a series of four scenes occupying the top half of the page and narrating steps in

the transmission of Aristotle's text at Charles V's court. In this second instance, the face of the bearded man looking out from behind the curtain seems younger. Nevertheless, he is the only bearded figure in these scenes.

53. Ibid., p. 207.

54. This frontispiece from Rome, Biblioteca Vallicelliana, MS B25 superscript 2, fol. 2r, is reproduced by Osborne in "Use of Painted Initials," fig. 7.

55. For reproductions of two double-page presentation scenes of this type (fols. 16v–17r and 18v–19r) from the Egbert Psalter produced at the monastery of Reichenau toward the end of the tenth century, the first showing the scribe Ruodpreht offering the Psalter he has written to Archbishop Egbert of Trier, the second showing Egbert offering the same codex to Saint Peter, see Mayr-Harting, *Ottonian Book Illumination,* vol. 2, figs. 36–39. The manuscript is now in Cividale del Friuli, Museo Archaeologico, MS CXXXVI.

56. This tendency to identify the codex depicted in a presentation scene with the one in which the scene is depicted is illustrated by the fact that earlier medievalists sometimes attributed manuscripts to royal or ducal collections on the basis of such presentation scenes alone, in the absence of inventory records or identifying marks in the margins such as heraldic emblems. For example, in *French Painting . . . the Patronage of the Duke,* plate volume, p. 93, Meiss points out that two manuscripts of Laurent de Premierfait's French translation of Boccaccio's *De casibus virorum illustrium* (Paris, B.N.F., MSS fr. 131 and 226) contain absolutely no evidence of Jean de Berry's ownership other than the suggestion of their presentation miniatures. The scene in MS fr. 131, fol. 1r (Meiss, fig. 500), where a magisterial Boccaccio backs and encourages Laurent's presentation of his translation to Jean de Berry, is just as fanciful as that in which we saw Saint Augustine sanction and encourage Raoul de Presles's presentation of his translation of *The City of God* to Charles V (my fig. 94). In MS fr. 226 (Meiss, fig. 503), the image of Boccaccio has been eliminated from the scene, making it seem more realistic. Yet, as Meiss rightly insists (p. 318), "neither Laurent's [verbal] dedication to Jean de Berry nor the portrait of him in the scene of presentation proves that the manuscript belonged to him." If we tend to believe otherwise, it is because the pictured presentation scene has served to authenticate the copy as the original one accepted by the ruler.

## Conclusion

1. This generalization holds true despite efforts by some early printers to imitate the designs and colors of manuscript initials by printing woodcuts and washing these with color. The technical and economic constraints of print can be seen

in this very book, whose strictly illustrative pictures have had to be drained of their original color by photographic reproduction in more economical black and white.

2. Many other Renaissance manuscripts, in addition to the ones I have arbitrarily chosen, might have been used to exemplify the changes and trends I evoke in this brief conclusion. As one of my press readers remarked, a page from Harvard's Houghton Library, MS TYP 219, would have made a striking example, for it too "'stretches' the text on a piece of hanging parchment and depicts a scene in perspective beyond the parchment; but it also includes a trompe-l'oeil fly viewed from above that seems to have landed on the book page."

3. Pächt, *Book Illumination in the Middle Ages,* p. 201. Immediately preceding this quotation, Pächt writes: "The picture with its space shifts into the border zone, and in the centre, by way of a break, the page of script appears, like a placard suspended in air, often attached to the pictorial space by ropes. Now even the script is part of an observed space: the border here is set back into the distance, and the script in the centre appears closer so that we can read it."

4. A more violent representation of the idea of "reading through"—in which the piercing of a curtain of letters allows the vision of a pictorially represented truth—can be found in a Book of Hours made for Jean Lallemant the Younger of Bourges in the first part of the sixteenth century (Baltimore, Walters Art Gallery, MS W.446, fol. 52v). In a rectangular window frame hangs an opaque curtain on which are embroidered Roman capitals, widely and neatly spaced in rows. Although the bright letters stand out against the dark background of the curtain, they do not seem to form any legible words. This lettered curtain has been torn by what would seem to be a violent impact to produce a large, jagged hole (more characteristic of the way a parchment might be pierced and torn than the way woven cloth tears). The torn edges of the cloth hanging down show that the reverse side of the curtain is striped, so that the curtain would also have the effect of "barring" the window (if seen from the reverse). Yet the barring veil of this curtain has been pierced. Through the hole in the curtain of letters, the viewer perceives, in the foreground, a hairshirt, and in a burst of light in the distant background, a very tiny kneeling figure with arms outstretched in prayer. For a reproduction of this image, and identification of the tiny figure as the penitent David, see Orth, "What Goes Around," p. 195, fig. 13.

## Appendix

Originally read in the form of a paper at the July 1994 New Chaucer Society Congress in Dublin, Ireland, an earlier version of this essay was published in French under the title "Les 'bords' des *Contes de Cantorbéry* et des manuscrits enluminés."

1. Salter, "Medieval Poetry," p. 30.

2. Randall, *Images in the Margins,* pp. 10–11.

3. Randall, "Exempla in Gothic Marginal Illumination," p. 101: "It was inevitable that the precedent established by secular, and often obscene, narratives introduced under the cloak of moralization at the end of the sermon paved the way for the representation of analogous subjects in the margins of manuscripts, regardless of whether they were designed for private or liturgical use."

4. Caviness, "Patron or Matron?"; Sandler, "Word in the Text."

5. For this theory, see *Book of Memory,* pp. 245–48, where Carruthers suggests that some of the figures in the margins, engaged in such activities as hunting, fishing, and tracking prey, are common tropes for recollection.

6. Camille, *Image on the Edge,* pp. 41–42. See Sandler, "Word in the Text," pp. 91–92, for further examples.

7. Kendrick, *Game of Love,* pp. 114–20.

8. For French and Anglo-Norman cognates, see Godefroy, *Dictionnaire de l'ancienne langue française,* and *Anglo-Norman Dictionary,* edited by Stone, Rothwell, and Reid.

9. Randall, *Images in the Margins,* pp. 8–9:

> Shortly after the middle of the thirteenth century extensive ornamentation begins to fill the margins in both religious and secular texts. . . . It is noteworthy that the region where marginal illumination was most fully developed in the decades preceding and following the turn of the fourteenth century coincides with one of the most active trading areas in northern Europe at this time. There was constant interchange, both commercial and cultural, between England and the provinces of particular interest in the present context, Artois, Hainaut, Picardy, Flanders, Brabant, Liège.

10. Roy, *Culture de l'équivoque.*

11. Laborde, *Notice des émaux,* p. 169.

12. For example, in the Luttrell Psalter (London, B. L., MS Add. 42130, fol. 160r), there is an aerial perspective of two men pulling a large boat down the border, with four rowing men on board. See Randall, *Images in the Margins,* figs. 469, 722, and others under "boat" in her index.

13. The long board of a table, set for a meal, is featured at the bottom of fol. 208r in the Luttrell Psalter (Randall, *Images in the Margins,* fig. 74); in the Rutland Psalter (London, B. L., MS 62925) a naked man and a clothed one play at a large checkered gaming board on fol. 78v (Randall, *Images in the Margins,* see figs. 102–4 for other board games).

14. An enormous, gourd-headed staff has been used to club a rabbit at the bottom of fol. 69r in the Hours of Saint Omer (London, B. L., MS Add. 36684); for a

monkey playing a bagpipe, see Randall, *Images in the Margins,* fig. 56, and others under the index entry of "man playing bagpipe."

15. For bordels in the borders, see Randall, *Images in the Margins,* figs. 392 and 393.

16. Randall, *Images in the Margins,* provides numerous examples of different types of humorous entertainment performed by jesters and jongleurs, such as, for example, the balancing of objects on the nose or other bodily parts (figs. 410–15, 418–21).

17. For example, plowing or harvesting (ibid., figs. 465, 466, 469, and 470).

18. At the bottom of one page of the *Romance of Alexander* (Oxford, Bodleian, MS Douce 62, fol. 56r), there are two kinds of tilting scenes that burlesque the knightly piercing of the dragon's maw pictured in a framed vignette in the upper register of this same page. At the bottom left, three naked men tilt together at the hole in a barrel; at the bottom right, a man exposes his buttocks as visual target in the direct line of sight of a kneeling woman. For further border images of jousts and tilts, often involving animals in place of humans and women in place of men, see Randall, *Images in the Margins,* figs. 61, 316, 318, 706–10, and 719ff.

19. Muscatine, *Chaucer and the French Tradition,* p. 171.

20. Randall, *Images in the Margins,* fig. 336. Carruthers, *Book of Memory* (p. 344 n. 60), suggests that the scenes Randall identifies and indexes as "man defecating" depict, instead, the fabliau of the squire who laid eggs.

21. In *Image on the Edge,* figs. 21 and 22, Camille reproduces the double-page spread of these two pages from the Rutland Psalter, but he misses the illuminator's jesting "point" of putting the two images on separate pages. The Rutland Psalter's joke is a burlesque of the high seriousness evidenced in the use of the double-page spread and the mechanism of page turning to present a book to a patron or ruler, as we saw in the Ottonian example of chapter 6.

# WORKS CITED

Adomnan. *Life of Saint Columba*. Edited and translated by William Reeves. 1874. Reprint. Lampeter, England: Llanerch, 1988.

Aethelwulf. *De abbatibus*. Edited and translated by A. Campbell. Oxford: Clarendon, 1967.

Alexander, J. J. G. *The Decorated Letter*. New York: Braziller, 1978.

———. "Ideological Representation of Military Combat in Anglo-Norman Art." In *Anglo-Norman Studies 15: Proceedings of the Battle Conference, 1992*, edited by Marjorie Chibnall. Woodbridge, Conn.: Boydell, 1993.

———. *Insular Manuscripts, Sixth to the Ninth Century*. London: Harvey Miller, 1978.

———. *Medieval Illuminators and Their Methods of Work*. New Haven, Conn.: Yale University Press, 1992.

———. *Norman Illumination at Mont St. Michel, 966–1100*. Oxford: Clarendon, 1970.

———. "Scribes as Artists: The Arabesque Initial in Twelfth-Century English Manuscripts." In *Medieval Scribes, Manuscripts and Libraries: Essays Presented to N. R. Ker*, edited by M. B. Parkes and A. G. Watson. London: Scolar Press, 1978.

Ambrose. *Enarrationes in psalmos*. Vol. 14 of *PL*.

———. *Expositio in psalmum 118*. Vol. 15 of *PL*.

———. *Hexaemeron*. Vol. 14 of *PL*.

Aston, Margaret. *Lollards and Reformers: Images and Literacy in Late Medieval Religion*. London: Hambledon, 1984.

Augustine. *The City of God against the Pagans.* Edited and translated by George McCracken, William C. Greene, et al. 7 vols. London: Heinemann, 1969–88.

———. *De catechizandis rudibus.* Vol. 40 of *PL.*

———. *De doctrina christiana.* Vol. 34 of *PL,* vol. 32 of *CCL.*

———. *De moribus ecclesiae catholicae.* Vol. 32 of *PL.*

———. *Enarrationes in psalmos.* Vols. 36–37 of *PL,* vols. 38–40 of *CCL.*

———. *In Johannis evangelium.* Vol. 36 of *CCL.*

———. *On Christian Doctrine.* Translated by D. W. Robertson. New York: Macmillan, 1958.

———. *Sermones ad populum: De tempore.* Vol. 38 of *PL.*

Avril, François. "Les manuscrits enluminés de Guillaume de Machaut." In *Guillaume de Machaut, poète et compositeur.* Colloquium organized by the University of Rheims, 19–22 April 1978. Paris: Klincksieck, 1982.

Avril, François, and Jean Lafaurie. *La librairie de Charles V.* Paris: Bibliothèque Nationale, 1968.

Balogh, Joseph. "Voces paginarum." *Philologus* 82 (1926): 84–109, 202–40.

Baltrušaitis, Jurgis. *Réveils et prodiges.* Paris: Flammarion, 1988.

Barthes, Roland. *L'obvie et l'obtus: Essais critiques III.* Paris: Seuil, 1982.

Basil. *In psalmos.* Vol. 29 of *PG.*

———. *Saint Basil: Exegetic Homilies.* Translated by Agnes Clare Way. Washington, D.C.: Catholic University of America Press, 1963.

Bastard, Auguste de. *Peintures et ornements des manuscrits classés dans un ordre chronologique pour servir à l'histoire des arts du dessin depuis le quatrième siècle de l'ère chrétienne jusqu'à la fin du seizième.* 11 vols. Paris: Imprimerie impériale, 1832–69.

Bearman, Frederick. "The Origins and Significance of Two Late Medieval Textile Chemise Bookbindings in the Walters Art Gallery." *Journal of the Walters Art Gallery* 54 (1996): 163–87.

Beatus of Liébana. *Adversus Elipandum.* Vol. 96 of *PL,* vol. 59 of *CCM.*

Bede. *De templo.* Vol. 91 of *PL,* vol. 119 of *CCL.*

———. *Hexameron.* Vol. 91 of *PL.*

———. *In Lucae evangelium.* Vol. 92 of *PL,* vol. 120 of *CCL.*

———. *In Marci evangelium.* Vol. 92 of *PL,* vol. 120 of *CCL.*

Beeren, Wim, and Talitha Schoon, eds. *Graffiti.* Rotterdam: Boymans van Beuningen Museum, 1983.

Belting, Hans. *Likeness and Presence: A History of the Image before the Era of Art.* Translated by Edmund Jephcott. Chicago: University of Chicago Press, 1994.

Bennett, Adelaide. "A Thirteenth-Century French Book of Hours for Marie." *Journal of the Walters Art Gallery* 54 (1996): 21–50.

Benoit, Pierre. "L'inspiration des septante d'après les pères." In *L'homme devant Dieu: Mélanges offerts au Père Henri de Lubac,* vol. 1. Paris: Aubier, 1963.

Bernard. *In epiphania domini.* Vol. 183 of *PL.*

Bethe, Erich. *Buch und Bild im Altertum.* Leipzig: Harrassowitz, 1945.

Bible, English. *The Holy Bible.* Douay-Rheims translation of the Vulgate. 1899. Reprint. Rockford, Ill.: Tan, 1971.

Bible, Vulgate. *Biblia sacra iuxta vulgatam versionem.* Edited by Robert Weber, Roger Gryson, et al. 4th ed. Stuttgart: Deutsche Bibelgesellschaft, 1994.

Bishop, Bernard. *Latin Palaeography: Antiquity and the Middle Ages.* Translated by D. Cróinín and D. Ganz. Cambridge: Cambridge University Press, 1990.

Bloch, Marc. *Les rois thaumaturges.* 1924. Reprint. Paris: Gallimard, 1983.

Bonne, Jean-Claude. "Rituel de la couleur: Fonctionnement et usage des images dans le Sacramentaire de Saint-Etienne de Limoges (B.N. lat. 94380)." In *Image et signification.* Rencontres de l'Ecole du Louvre, no. 2. Paris: La documentation française, 1983.

Bosworth, Joseph, and T. N. Toller, eds. *An Anglo-Saxon Dictionary.* 1898. Reprint. Oxford: Oxford University Press, 1972.

Bouché-Leclercq, A. *Histoire de la divination dans l'antiquité.* 4 vols. Paris: Leroux, 1879–82.

Brosses, Charles de. *Du culte des dieux fétiches.* 1760. Reprint. Paris: Fayard, 1988.

Brown, Michelle P. *The Book of Cerne: Prayer, Patronage and Power in Ninth-Century England.* London: British Library, and Toronto: University of Toronto Press, 1996.

———. "The Lindisfarne Scriptorium from the Late Seventh to the Early Ninth Century." In *Saint Cuthbert, His Cult and His Community to A.D. 1200,* edited by Gerald Bonner et al. Woodbridge, Conn.: Boydell, 1989.

Brownlee, Kevin, and Sylvia Huot, eds. *Rethinking the "Romance of the Rose": Image, Text, Reception.* Philadelphia: University of Pennsylvania Press, 1992.

Brunn, Patrick. "Symboles, signes et monogrammes." In *Sylloge inscriptionum christianarum veterum musei vaticani,* edited by Henrico Zilliacus. Vol. 2. Helsinki: Helsingfors, 1963.

Bruyne, Donatien de. *Préfaces de la Bible latine.* Namur, Belgium: Godenne, 1920.

Burchard of Worms. *Decretorum.* Vol. 140 of *PL.*

Bynum, Caroline Walker. *The Resurrection of the Body in Western Christianity, 200–1336.* New York: Columbia University Press, 1995.

Cabrol, Fernand, and Henri Leclercq, eds. *Dictionnaire d'archéologie chrétienne et de liturgie.* 15 vols. Paris: Letouzey, 1924–51.

Cahn, Walter. *Romanesque Bible Illumination.* Ithaca, N.Y.: Cornell University Press, 1982.

Calkins, Robert. "Liturgical Sequence and Decorative Crescendo in the Drogo Sacramentary." *Gesta* 25 (1986): 17–23.

Camille, Michael. *Image on the Edge: The Margins of Medieval Art.* Cambridge, Mass.: Harvard University Press, 1992.

———. *Master of Death: The Lifeless Art of Pierre Remiet, Illuminator.* New Haven, Conn.: Yale University Press, 1996.

———. "Philological Iconoclasm: Edition and Image in the *Vie de Saint Alexis.*" In *Medievalism and the Modernist Temper,* edited by R. Howard Bloch and Stephen G. Nichols. Baltimore: Johns Hopkins University Press, 1996.

———. "Visualizing in the Vernacular: A New Cycle of Early Fourteenth-Century Bible Illustrations." *Burlington Magazine* 130 (1988): 97–106.

———. "Visual Signs of the Sacred Page: Books in the *Bible moralisée.*" *Word and Image* 5 (1989): 111–30.

Carruthers, Mary J. *The Book of Memory: A Study of Memory in Medieval Culture.* Cambridge: Cambridge University Press, 1990.

Cassian. *Collationes.* Vol. 49 of *PL,* vol. 54 of *SC.*

Cassin, Elena. "Le sceau: Un fait de civilisation dans la Mésopotamie ancienne." *Annales (Economies, Sociétés, Civilisations)* 15 (1960): 742–51.

Cassiodorus. *Cassiodori senatoris institutiones.* Edited by R. A. B. Mynors. Oxford: Clarendon, 1937.

———. *De institutione divinarum litterarum.* Vol. 70 of *PL.*

———. *An Introduction to Divine and Human Readings by Cassiodorus Senator.* Translated by L. W. Jones. New York: Columbia University Press, 1946.

Caviness, Madeline. "Anchoress, Abbess, and Queen: Donors and Patrons or Intercessors and Matrons?" In *The Cultural Patronage of Medieval Women,* edited by June Hall McCash. Athens: University of Georgia Press, 1996.

———. "Patron or Matron? A Capetian Bride and a Vade Mecum for Her Marriage Bed." *Speculum* 68 (1993): 333–62.

Chadwick, William O. *Western Asceticism.* London: SCM Press, 1958.

Chastel, André. "Signature et signe." *Revue de l'art* 26 (1974): 8–14.

Chaucer, Geoffrey. *The Canterbury Tales* and *Treatise on the Astrolabe.* In *The Riverside Chaucer,* 3d ed., edited by Larry D. Benson. Boston: Houghton Mifflin, 1987.

Chazelle, Celia M. "Matter, Spirit, and Image in the *Libri Carolini.*" *Recherches Augustiniennes* 21 (1986): 163–84.

———. "Pictures, Books, and the Illiterate: Pope Gregory I's Letters to Serenus of Marseilles." *Word and Image* 6 (1990): 138–53.

Chenu, M.-D. "Auctor, actor, autor." *Bulletin du Cange* 3 (1927): 81–86.

Clanchy, Michael T. *From Memory to Written Record: England 1066–1307.* 2d ed. Oxford: Blackwell, 1993.

Clement of Alexandria. *Paedagogum.* Vol. 8 of *PG,* vol. 158 of *SC.*

———. *Stromates.* Vol. 8 of *PG.*

Clerc, Charly. *Les théories relatives au culte des images chez les auteurs grecs du deu-xième siècle après Jhésu-Christ.* Paris: Fontemoing, 1915.

Cockayne, Oswis. *Leechdoms, Wortcunning, and Starcraft of Early England.* 3 vols. London: Longman, 1864–66.

*Codex purpureus rossanensis.* 2 vols. Facsimile and commentary, edited by Guglielmo Cavallo, William C. Loerke, et al. Rome, Salerno, and Graz: Akademische Druck, 1987.

Comparetti, Domenico. *Vergil in the Middle Ages.* Translated by E. F. M. Benecke. 1908. Reprint. Hamden, Conn.: Archon, 1966.

Coomaraswamy, Ananda K. *Christian and Oriental Philosophy of Art.* New York: Dover, 1956.

Courcelle, Pierre. "Les exégèses chrétiennes de la quatrième églogue." *Revue des études anciennes* 59 (1957): 294–319.

Day, Cyrus L. *Quipus and Witches' Knots: The Role of the Knot in Primitive and Ancient Cultures.* Lawrence: University of Kansas Press, 1967.

Derrida, Jacques. *L'écriture et la différence.* Paris: Seuil, 1967.

———. *Of Grammatology.* Translated by Gayatri Chakravorty Spivak. Baltimore: Johns Hopkins University Press, 1974.

Dioscurides. *Codex Vindobonensis Med. Gr. 1 der österreichischen Nationalbibliothek.* Facsimile edited by Hans Gerstinger. Graz, Austria: Akademische Druck, 1970.

Diringer, David. *Writing.* London: Thames and Hudson, 1962.

Dodwell, C. R. *Anglo-Saxon Art: A New Perspective.* Ithaca, N.Y.: Cornell University Press, 1982.

———. *The Canterbury School of Illumination, 1066–1200.* Cambridge: Cambridge University Press, 1954.

Dölger, Franz. *IXΘΥΣ: Das Fischsymbol in frühchristlicher Zeit.* Rome: Spithöver, 1910.

Dosdat, Monique. *L'enluminure romane au Mont Saint-Michel, dixième au douzième siècles.* Rennes, France: Ouest-France, 1991.

Drewer, Lois. "Fisherman and Fish Pond: From the Sea of Sin to the Living Waters." *Art Bulletin* 63 (1981): 533–47.

Drogin, Marc. *Biblioclasm: The Mythical Origins, Magical Powers, and Perishability of the Written Word.* Lantham, Md.: Rowman and Littlefield, 1989.

Duby, Georges. *Le moyen âge: Adolescence de la chrétienté occidentale, 980–1140.* Geneva: Skira, 1984.

Duffy, Eamon. *The Stripping of the Altars: Traditional Religion in England, 1400–1580.* New Haven, Conn.: Yale University Press, 1992.

Duggan, Lawrence. "Was Art Really the 'Book of the Illiterate'?" *Word and Image* 5 (1989): 227–51.

Dumézil, Georges. "La tradition druidique et l'écriture: Le vivant et le mort." In *Georges Dumézil,* edited by Jacques Bonnet. Pour un temps, no. 3. Paris: Centre Georges Pompidou, 1981.

Durandus of Mende. *Guillelmi Duranti: Rationale divinorum officiorum, I–IV.* Vol. 140 of *CCM.*

Durrow, Book of. *Evangeliorum quattuor codex Durmachensis.* Facsimile edited by A. A. Luce, P. Meyer, G. O. Simmons, and L. Bieler. 2 vols. Olten, Switzerland: Urs Graf, 1960.

Dutton, Paul Edward, and Herbert Kessler. *The Poetry and Paintings of the First Bible of Charles the Bald.* Ann Arbor: University of Michigan Press, 1997.

Dynes, Wayne. "Imago Leonis." *Gesta* 20 (1981): 35–41.

Eadmer. *Historia novorum in anglia.* Edited by Martin Rule. London: Longman, 1884.

Eleen, Luba. *The Illustration of the Pauline Epistles in French and English Bibles of the Twelfth and Thirteenth Centuries.* Oxford: Clarendon, 1982.

Eliade, Mircea. "Le 'dieu lieur' et le symbolisme des noeuds." In *Images et symboles: Essais sur le symbolisme magico-religieux.* Paris: Gallimard, 1952.

Ermini, Filippo. *Il centone di Proba e la poesia centonaria latina.* Rome: Loescher, 1909.

Farr, Carol Ann. *The Book of Kells: Its Function and Audience.* London: British Library, and Toronto: University of Toronto Press, 1997.

Finlayson, C. P. *Celtic Psalter, Edinburgh University Library MS. 56.* Amsterdam: North Holland, 1962.

Fleming, John. *The "Roman de la Rose": A Study in Allegory and Iconography.* Princeton, N.J.: Princeton University Press, 1969.

Foucault, Michel. *L'ordre du discours.* Paris: Gallimard, 1971.

———. "What Is an Author?" In *Textual Strategies: Perspectives in Post-Structuralist Criticism,* edited by Josué V. Harari. Ithaca, N.Y.: Cornell University Press, 1979.

Fox, Robin Lane. "Literacy and Power in Early Christianity." In *Literacy and Power in the Ancient World,* edited by Alan Bowman and Greg Woolf. Cambridge: Cambridge University Press, 1994.

Fraenkel, Béatrice. *La signature: Genèse d'un signe.* Paris: Gallimard, 1992.

Freedberg, David. *The Power of Images: Studies in the History and Theory of Response.* Chicago: University of Chicago Press, 1989.

Friend, A. M., Jr. "The Portraits of the Evangelists in Greek and Latin Manuscripts: Part 1." *Art Studies* 5 (1927): 115–47.

————. "The Portraits of the Evangelists in Greek and Latin Manuscripts: Part 2." *Art Studies* 7 (1929): 3–29.

Gandilhon, René. "La dactyloscopie et les sceaux." *Mémoires de la société historique, littéraire et scientifique du Cher,* 4th series, 39 (1932): 98–102.

Ganz, David. "'Mind in Character': Ancient and Medieval Ideas about the Status of the Autograph as an Expression of Personality." In *Of the Making of Books: Medieval Manuscripts, Their Scribes and Readers: Essays Presented to M. B. Parkes,* edited by P. R. Robinson and Rivkali Zim. Aldershot, England: Scolar, 1997.

Garnier, François. *Le langage de l'image au moyen âge.* Paris: Léopard d'or, 1982.

————. "La lecture de l'image médiévale." In *Image et signification.* Rencontres de l'Ecole du Louvre, no. 2. Paris: La documentation française, 1983.

Geary, Patrick. *Furta Sacra: Thefts of Relics in the Central Middle Ages.* Princeton, N.J.: Princeton University Press, 1978.

Gerald of Wales. *Topographia hibernica.* Vol. 5 of *Opera,* edited and translated by J. F. Dimock. London: Longman, 1867.

Ginzburg, Carlo. *Myths, Emblems, Clues.* Translated by John Tedeschi and Anne Tedeschi. London: Hutchinson, 1990.

Giry, Arthur. *Manuel de diplomatique.* Paris: Hachette, 1894.

*Glossa ordinaria.* Vol. 113 of *PL.*

Godefroy, Frédéric. *Dictionnaire de l'ancienne langue française et de tous ses dialectes du neuvième au quinzième siècle* and *Complément.* 10 vols. 1881–1902. Reprint. Geneva: Slatkine, 1982.

Gollancz, Israel. Introduction to *Pearl, Cleanness, Patience, and Sir Gawain and the Green Knight, Reproduced in Facsimile from the Unique MS Cotton Nero A.x in the British Museum.* Early English Text Society, no. 162. London: Oxford University Press, 1923.

————, ed. *Sir Gawain and the Green Knight.* Early English Text Society, no. 210. London: Oxford University Press, 1940.

Gombrich, E. H. *The Sense of Order: A Study in the Psychology of Decorative Art.* Ithaca, N.Y.: Cornell University Press, 1979.

Goodman, Martin. "Sacred Scripture and 'Defiling the Hands.'" *Journal of Theological Studies* 41 (1990): 99–107.

————. "Texts, Scribes and Power in Roman Judaea." In *Literacy and Power in the Ancient World,* edited by Alan Bowman and Greg Woolf. Cambridge: Cambridge University Press, 1994.

Gouillard, Jean. "Le synodikon de l'orthodoxie." In *Travaux et mémoires II.* Centre de recherche d'histoire et civilisation byzantines. Paris: E. de Boccard, 1967.

Grabar, André. *Ampoules de Terre Sainte (Monza, Bobbio).* Paris: Klincksieck, 1958.

———. *L'iconoclasme byzantin: Le dossier archéologique.* Paris: Flammarion, 1984.

———. *Le premier art chrétien (200–395).* Paris: Gallimard, 1966.

Grabar, André, and Carl Nordenfalk. *Romanesque Painting from the Eleventh to the Thirteenth Century.* New York: Skira, 1958.

Grabar, Oleg. *The Mediation of Ornament.* Princeton, N.J.: Princeton University Press, 1992.

Gregory I, Pope (Gregory the Great). *Epistolae.* Vol. 140 of *CCL.*

———. *Homiliae in Hiezechihelem prophetam.* Vol. 76 of *PL,* vol. 142 of *CCL.*

———. *In librum I regum.* Vol. 79 of *PL,* vol. 144 of *CCL.*

———. *Moralia in Job.* Vol. 75 of *PL,* vol. 143 of *CCL.*

———. *Quadraginta homiliarum in evangelia.* Vol. 76 of *PL.*

Gregory of Tours. *Historia Francorum.* Edited by Wilhelm Arndt and Bruno Krush. Hannover: Hahnsche, 1884.

Gribomont, Jean. "Les plus anciennes traductions." In *Le monde antique et la Bible,* edited by Jacques Fontaine and Charles Pietri. Paris: Beauchesne, 1985.

Griffiths, Jeremy. "*Confessio Amantis*: The Poem and Its Pictures." In *Gower's "Confessio Amantis": Responses and Reassessments,* edited by A. J. Minnis. Woodbridge, Conn.: Brewer, 1983.

Grundmann, H. "Die Frauen und die Literatur im Mittelalter." *Archiv für Kulturgeschichte* 26 (1936): 129–61.

Gutbrod, Jürgen. *Die Initiale in Handschriften des achten bis dreizehnten Jahrhunderts.* Stuttgart: Kohlhammer, 1965.

Hamburger, Jeffrey F. *The Rothschild Canticles: Art and Mysticism in Flanders and the Rhineland circa 1300.* New Haven, Conn.: Yale University Press, 1990.

Haseloff, Günther. *Die Psalterillustration in dreizehnten Jahrhundert: Studien zur Geschichte der Buchmalerei in England, Frankreich und den Niederlanden.* Kiel, Germany: n.p., 1939.

Havelock, Eric. *Preface to Plato.* Cambridge, Mass.: Harvard University Press, 1963.

Heffernan, Thomas J. *Sacred Biography: Saints and Their Biographers in the Middle Ages.* New York: Oxford University Press, 1988.

Helsinger, Howard. "Images on the *Beatus* Page of Some Medieval Psalters." *Art Bulletin* 53 (1971): 161–76.

Henderson, George. "Cassiodorus and Eadfrith Once Again." In *The Age of Migrating Ideas: Early Medieval Art in Northern Britain and Ireland,* edited by R. Michael Spearman and John Higgitt. Edinburgh: National Museums of Scotland, 1993.

———. *From Durrow to Kells.* London: Thames and Hudson, 1987.

Henry, Françoise. *The Book of Kells: Reproductions from the Manuscript in Trinity College Dublin with a Study of the Manuscript.* New York: Knopf, 1974.

———. *Irish Art in the Early Christian Period to 800 A.D.* Ithaca, N.Y.: Cornell University Press, 1965.

Higgitt, John. "The Display Script of the Book of Kells and the Tradition of Insular Decorative Capitals." In *The Book of Kells: Proceedings of a Conference at Trinity College, Dublin, 6–9 September 1992,* edited by Felicity O'Mahony. Aldershot, England: Scolar Press, 1994.

Hindman, Sandra L. *Christine de Pizan's "Epistre Othéa": Painting and Politics at the Court of Charles VI.* Toronto: University of Toronto Press, 1986.

Hoepffner, Ernest, ed. *Oeuvres de Guillaume de Machaut.* 3 vols. Paris: Firmin Didot, 1908–21.

Hornung, Erik. "Hieroglyphs: Signs and Art." In *World Art: Themes of Unity in Diversity,* edited by Irving Lavin, vol. 2. University Park: Penn State University Press, 1989.

Hugh of Saint Victor. *De arca Noe mystica.* Vol. 176 of *PL.*

———. *Didascalicon.* Translated by Jerome Taylor. New York: Columbia University Press, 1961.

Hult, David. *Self-Fulfilling Prophecies: Readership and Authority in the First "Roman de la Rose."* Cambridge: Cambridge University Press, 1986.

Huon le Roi de Cambrai. *Li abéces par ekivoche et li signification des lettres.* In *Oeuvres,* edited by Artur Langfors, vol. 1. Paris: Champion, 1913.

Huot, Sylvia. *From Song to Book: The Poetics of Writing in Old French Lyric and Lyrical Narrative Poetry.* Ithaca, N.Y.: Cornell University Press, 1987.

———. *The "Romance of the Rose" and Its Medieval Readers.* Cambridge: Cambridge University Press, 1993.

Hust, Pierre d'. *Les signatures célèbres: Miroirs de la personnalité.* Paris: Hermé, 1991.

Irenaeus. *Adversus haereses.* Vol. 7 of *PG,* vol. 211 of *SC.*

Isidore of Seville. *De ecclesiasticis officiis.* Vol. 83 of *PL,* vol. 113 of *CCL.*

Jerome. "Ad Fabiolam." *Epistolae.* Vol. 22 of *PL.*

———. "Ad Laetam." In *Selected Letters of St. Jerome,* translated by F. A. Wright. London: Heinemann, 1954.

———. "Ad Laetam, de institutione filiae." *Epistolae.* Vol. 22 of *PL.*

———. *Breviarum in psalmos.* Vol. 26 of *PL.*

———. *Commentaria in Ezechielem.* Vol. 25 of *PL,* vol. 75 of *CCL.*

———. *Tractatus in psalmos.* Vol. 26 of *PL,* vol. 78 of *CCL.*

John Chrysostom. *Homilies on the Gospel of St. John and the Epistle to the Hebrews.* Translated by Frederic Gardiner. New York: Christian Literature Co., 1890.

————. *In epistolam ad Hebraeos.* Vol. 63 of *PG.*

John of Damascus. *Orationes pro sacris imaginibus.* Vol. 94 of *PG.*

John the Scot. *Commentarius in evangelium Iohannis.* Vol. 122 of *PL,* vol. 180 of *SC.*

————. *De divisione naturae.* Vol. 122 of *PL.*

Jonas of Orleans. *De institutione laicali.* Vol. 106 of *PL.*

Jordan, Robert. *Chaucer and the Shape of Creation.* Cambridge, Mass.: Harvard University Press, 1967.

Jousse, Marcel. *L'anthropologie du geste.* Paris: Gallimard, 1975.

————. *La manducation de la parole.* Paris: Gallimard, 1975.

Karkov, Catherine. "The Chalice and Cross in Insular Art." In *The Age of Migrating Ideas: Early Medieval Art in Northern Britain and Ireland,* edited by R. Michael Spearman and John Higgit. Edinburgh: National Museums of Scotland, 1993.

Kauffmann, C. M. *Romanesque Manuscripts, 1066–1190.* London: Harvey Miller, 1975.

Kells, Book of. *Evangeliorum quattuor codex cenannensis.* Facsimile edited by E. H. Alton and Peter Meyer. 3 vols. Berne, Switzerland: Urs Graf, 1950.

Kelly, Eamonn P. "The Lough Kinale Book Shrine: The Implication for the Manuscripts." In *The Book of Kells: Proceedings of a Conference at Trinity College, Dublin, 6–9 September 1992,* edited by Felicity O'Mahony. Aldershot, England: Scolar Press, 1994.

Kendrick, Laura. "Les 'bords' des *Contes de Cantorbéry* et des manuscrits enluminés." *Bulletin des anglicistes médiévistes* 45 (1994): 926–43.

————. "1123? A Richly Illustrated Latin Psalter Prefaced by a Vernacular *Chanson de Saint Alexis* Is Being Executed at the Monastery of Saint Albans, England, for Christina of Markyate." In *A New History of French Literature,* edited by Denis Hollier. Cambridge, Mass.: Harvard University Press, 1989.

————. *The Game of Love: Troubadour Wordplay.* Berkeley: University of California Press, 1988.

————. "The Monument and the Margin." *South Atlantic Quarterly* 91 (1992): 835–64.

Kessler, Herbert L. "Diction in the 'Bibles of the Illiterate.'" In *World Art: Themes of Unity in Diversity,* edited by Irving Lavin, vol. 2. University Park: Penn State University Press, 1986.

————. *The Illustrated Bibles from Tours.* Princeton, N.J.: Princeton University Press, 1977.

————. "Interlace and Icons: Form and Function in Early Insular Art." In *The Age of Migrating Ideas: Early Medieval Art in Northern Britain and Ireland,* edited by R. Michael Spearman and John Higgitt. Edinburgh: National Museums of Scotland, 1993.

————. "Medieval Art as Argument." In *Iconography at the Crossroads: Papers from the Colloquium Sponsored by the Index of Christian Art, Princeton University, 23–24 March 1990,* edited by Brendan Cassidy. Princeton, N.J.: Department of Art and Archaeology, Princeton University, 1993.

————. "On the State of Medieval Art History." *Art Bulletin* 70 (1988): 166–87.

————. "Pictorial Narrative and Church Mission in Sixth-Century Gaul." In *Pictorial Narrative in Antiquity and the Middle Ages,* edited by Herbert Kessler and Marianna Shreve Simpson. Washington, D.C.: National Gallery of Art, 1985.

Kitzinger, Ernst. "The Cult of Images in the Age before Iconoclasm." In *The Art of Byzantium and the Medieval West: Selected Studies,* edited by W. Eugene Kleinbauer. Bloomington: Indiana University Press, 1976.

Kolve, V. A. "The Annunciation to Christine: Authorial Empowerment in *The Book of the City of Ladies.*" In *Iconography at the Crossroads: Papers from the Colloquium Sponsored by the Index of Christian Art, Princeton University, 23–24 March 1990,* edited by Brendan Cassidy. Princeton, N.J.: Department of Art and Archaeology, Princeton University, 1993.

————. *Chaucer and the Imagery of Narrative.* Stanford, Calif.: Stanford University Press, 1984.

Kris, Ernst, and Otto Kurz. *Legend, Myth, and Magic in the Image of the Artist.* New Haven, Conn.: Yale University Press, 1979.

Kristeva, Julia. *Le langage cet inconnu.* Paris: Seuil, 1981.

Kuhn, Alfred. *Die Illustration des Rosenromans.* Freiburg: Wagners, 1911.

Kurath, Hans, and Sherman Kuhn, eds. *The Middle English Dictionary.* Ann Arbor: University of Michigan Press, 1952–.

Laborde, Léon de. *Notice des émaux exposés dans les galeries du Musée du Louvre.* Paris: Vinchon, 1853.

Lafont, Robert, ed. *Anthropologie de l'écriture.* Paris: Centre Georges Pompidou, 1984.

Laidlaw, James C. "Christine de Pizan: A Publisher's Progress." *Modern Language Review* 82 (1987): 35–75.

Lanham, Richard. *The Electronic Word: Democracy, Technology, and the Arts.* Chicago: University of Chicago Press, 1993.

Lecoq, Anne-Marie. "Cadre et rebord." *Revue de l'art* 26 (1974): 15–20.

Lerer, Seth. *Literacy and Power in Anglo-Saxon Literature.* Lincoln: University of Nebraska Press, 1991.

Lerner, Robert E. "Ecstatic Dissent." *Speculum* 67 (1992): 33–57.

Leroquais, Victor. *Les livres d'heures manuscrits de la Bibliothèque nationale.* 2 vols. and plate album. Mâcon, France: Protat, 1927.

Lewis, Suzanne. "The Apocalypse of Isabella of France: Paris, Bibl. Nat. MS Fr. 13096." *Art Bulletin* 72 (1990): 224–60.

———. "The Enigma of Fr. 403 and the Compilation of a Thirteenth-Century English Illustrated Apocalypse." *Gesta* 29 (1990): 31–43.

———. *Reading Images: Narrative Discourse and Reception in the Thirteenth-Century Illuminated Apocalypse.* Cambridge: Cambridge University Press, 1995.

———. "Sacred Calligraphy: The Chi Rho Page in the Book of Kells." *Traditio* 36 (1980): 139–59.

*Libri carolini.* Vol. 98 of *PL.*

Lindisfarne, Gospels of. *Evangeliorum quattuor codex Lindisfarnensis.* Facsimile edited by T. D. Kendrick, T. J. Brown, and R. L. S. Bruce-Mitford. 2 vols. Olten, Switzerland: Urs Graf, 1960.

*Lindisfarne Gospels, The.* Introduced by E. G. Millar. London: British Museum, 1923.

*Lives of Saints from the Book of Lismore.* Edited and translated by Whitley Stokes. Oxford: Clarendon, 1890.

Loos, Adolf. "Ornament and Crime." In *The Architecture of Adolf Loos,* edited and translated by Yehuda Safran and Wilfried Wang. London: Arts Council of Great Britain, 1985.

Lowe, E. A., ed. *Codices latini antiquiores.* 11 vols. and supplement. Oxford: Clarendon, 1934–72.

Lubac, Henri de. *Exégèse médiévale: Les quatre sens de l'Ecriture.* 2 vols. Paris: Aubier, 1959–64.

———. *Histoire et esprit: L'intelligence de l'Ecriture d'après Origène.* Paris: Aubier, 1950.

Manegold of Lautenbach. *In librum psalmorum.* Vol. 93 of *PL.*

Manguel, Alberto. *A History of Reading.* London: Harper Collins, 1996.

Marrou, Henri-Irénée. *Histoire de l'éducation dans l'Antiquité.* 2 vols. Paris: Seuil, 1948.

Maximus the Confessor. *Capita theologiae et oeconomiae.* Vol. 90 of *PG.*

Mayr-Harting, Henry. *Ottonian Book Illumination: An Historical Study.* 2 vols. London: Harvey Miller, 1991.

McCoy, Katherine. "Graphic Design: Sources of Meaning in Word and Image." *Word and Image* 4 (1988): 116–30.

McCulloch, Florence. *Medieval Latin and French Bestiaries.* Chapel Hill: University of North Carolina Press, 1962.

———. "Le Tigre au miroir: La vie d'une image de Pline à Pierre Gringore." *Revue des sciences humaines* 33 (1968): 149–60.

McGurk, Patrick. "The Oldest Manuscripts of the Latin Bible." In *The Early Medieval Bible: Its Production, Decoration and Use,* edited by Richard Gameson. Cambridge: Cambridge University Press, 1994.

Meiss, Millard. *French Painting in the Time of Jean de Berry: The Boucicaut Master.* London: Phaidon, 1968.

———. *French Painting in the Time of Jean de Berry: The Late Fourteenth Century and the Patronage of the Duke.* Plate volume. London: Phaidon, 1967.

Metzger, Bruce. *The Early Versions of the New Testament.* Oxford: Oxford University Press, 1977.

Meyer, Peter. "Notes on the Art and Ornament of the Book of Kells." In *Evangeliorum quattuor codex cenannensis,* facsimile edition by E. H. Alton and Peter Meyer, vol. 3. Berne, Switzerland: Urs Graf, 1950.

Meyvaert, Paul. "Bede and the Church Paintings at Wearmouth-Jarrow." *Anglo-Saxon England* 8 (1979): 63–77.

*Middle English Dictionary.* See Kurath.

Minnis, A. J. *Medieval Theory of Authorship: Scholastic Literary Attitudes in the Later Middle Ages.* London: Scolar Press, 1984.

Morgan, Nigel. *Early Gothic Manuscripts, 1190–1250.* London: Harvey Miller, 1982.

———. *Early Gothic Manuscripts, 1250–1285.* London: Harvey Miller, 1988.

Morin, Germain. *Etudes, textes, découvertes.* Paris: Picard, 1913.

Muscatine, Charles. *Chaucer and the French Tradition.* Berkeley: University of California Press, 1957.

Mütherich, Florentine, and Joachim Gaehde. *Carolingian Painting.* New York: Braziller, 1976.

Nees, Lawrence. "A Fifth-Century Book Cover and the Origin of the Four Evangelist Symbols Page in the Book of Durrow." *Gesta* 17 (1978): 3–8.

———. "Ultan the Scribe." In *The Age of Migrating Ideas: Early Medieval Art in Northern Britain and Ireland,* edited by R. Michael Spearman and John Higgit. Edinburgh: National Museums of Scotland, 1993.

Nersessian, V. *Armenian Illuminated Gospel Books.* London: British Library, 1987.

Neuman de Vegvar, Carol. *The Northumbrian Renaissance: A Study in the Transmission of Style.* Selinsgrove, Pa.: Susquehanna University Press, 1987.

Nieuwdorp, Hans, ed. *Musée Mayer van den Bergh, Anvers.* Antwerp: Musea Nostra, n.d.

Nordenfalk, Carl. "Before the Book of Durrow." *Acta Archaeologica* 18 (1947): 141–74.

———. *Celtic and Anglo-Saxon Painting: Book Illumination in the British Isles, 600–800.* New York: Braziller, 1977.

———. *Die spätantiken Kanontafeln.* Göteborg, Sweden: O. Isacsons, 1938.

———. *Die spätantiken Zierbuchstaben.* Stockholm: n.p., 1970.

————, ed. *Vergilius Augusteus.* Facsimile edition. Graz, Austria: Akademische Druck, 1976.

O'Carragáin, Eamonn. "*Traditio evangeliorum* and *sustentatio*: The Relevance of Liturgical Ceremonies to the Book of Kells." In *The Book of Kells: Proceedings of a Conference at Trinity College, Dublin, 6–9 September 1992,* edited by Felicity O'Mahony. Aldershot, England: Scolar Press, 1994.

Openshaw, Kathleen M. "The Battle between Christ and Satan in the Tiberius Psalter." *Journal of the Warburg and Courtauld Institutes* 52 (1989): 14–33.

————. "Weapons in the Daily Battle: Images of the Conquest of Evil in the Early Medieval Psalter." *Art Bulletin* 75 (1993): 17–38.

Origen. *In canticum canticorum.* Vol. 13 of *PG,* vol. 376 of *SC.*

————. *Commentaria in evangelium secundum Joannem.* Vol. 14 of *PG.*

————. *Commentaria in evangelium secundum Matthaeum.* Vol. 13 of *PG.*

————. *In Leviticum.* Vol. 12 of *PG,* vol. 286 of *SC.*

————. *Selecta in psalmos.* Vol. 12 of *PG.*

Orth, Myra D. "What Goes Around: Borders and Frames in French Manuscripts." *Journal of the Walters Art Gallery* 54 (1996): 189–201.

Osborne, John. "The Use of Painted Initials by Greek and Latin Scriptoria in Carolingian Rome." *Gesta* 29 (1990): 76–85.

Oursel, Charles. *Miniatures cisterciennes, 1109–1134.* Mâcon, France: Protat, 1960.

Pächt, Otto. *Book Illumination in the Middle Ages.* Translated by Kay Davenport. London: Harvey Miller, 1986.

Pächt, Otto, C. R. Dodwell, and Francis Wormald. *The St. Albans Psalter.* London: Warburg Institute, 1960.

Paris, Gaston, and Léopold Pannier. *La vie de Saint Alexis, poème du onzième siècle et renouvellements des douzième, treizième, et quatorzième siècles.* Paris: Franck, 1872.

Parkes, Malcolm. *Pause and Effect: An Introduction to the History of Punctuation in the West.* Berkeley: University of California Press, 1993.

Paulinus of Nola. *Libellus sacrosyllabus contra Elipandum.* Vol. 99 of *PL.*

Pearsall, Derek. "Gower's Latin in the *Confessio Amantis.*" In *Latin and Vernacular: Studies in Late-Medieval Texts and Manuscripts,* edited by A. J. Minnis. Woodbridge, Conn.: Brewer, 1989.

Peter Damien. *Antilogus contra Judaeos.* Vol. 145 of *PL.*

Petitmengin, Pierre. "Les plus anciens manuscrits de la Bible latine." In *Le monde antique et la Bible,* edited by Jacques Fontaine and Charles Pietri. Paris: Beauchesne, 1985.

Philip of Harveng. *Epistolae.* Vol. 203 of *PL.*

Plato. *The Collected Dialogues of Plato.* Edited by Edith Hamilton and H. Cairns, translated by R. Hackforth. New York: Pantheon, 1961.

Porfyrius. *Publilii Optatiani Porfyrii: Carmina.* Edited by Johannes Polara. 2 vols. Turin: G. B. Paravia, 1973.

Poulin, Joseph-Claude. "Entre magie et religion: Recherches sur les utilisations marginales de l'écrit dans la culture populaire du haut moyen âge." In *La culture populaire au moyen âge,* edited by Pierre Boglioni. Montreal: Univers, 1979.

Pulver, Max. *Le symbolisme de l'écriture.* Translated by Marguerite Schmid and Maurice Delmain. Paris: Stock, 1982.

Quilligan, Maureen. *The Allegory of Authority: Christine de Pizan's "Cité des Dames."* Ithaca, N.Y.: Cornell University Press, 1991.

Quintilian. *The Institutio oratoria.* Edited and translated by H. E. Butler. 4 vols. London: Heinemann, 1979–86.

Randall, Lilian. "Exempla in Gothic Marginal Illumination." *Art Bulletin* 39 (1957): 97–107.

———. *Images in the Margins of Gothic Manuscripts.* Berkeley: University of California Press, 1966.

Rhabanus Maurus. *Allegoriae in sacram scripturam.* Vol. 112 of *PL.*

———. *Hrabanus Maurus, "De laudibus sancta crucis."* Facsimile edited by Hans-Georg Müller. Düsseldorf: Henn, 1973.

———. *De laudibus sanctae crucis.* Vol. 107 of *PL.*

Richard of Saint Victor. *Expositio in cantica canticorum.* Vol. 196 of *PL.*

Riché, Pierre. "Le rôle de la mémoire dans l'enseignement médiéval." In *Jeux de mémoire: Aspects de la mnémotechnie médiévale,* edited by Bruno Roy and Paul Zumthor. Paris: Vrin, 1985.

Riché, Pierre, and Guy Lobrichon. *Le moyen âge et la Bible.* Paris: Beauchesne, 1984.

Rickert, Margaret. Untitled chapter on illuminated manuscripts in *The Text of the Canterbury Tales,* edited by John M. Manly and Edith Rickert, vol. 1. Chicago: University of Chicago Press, 1940.

Riegl, Alois. *Altorientalische Teppiche.* Leipzig: Wiegel, 1891.

Robertson, D. W. *A Preface to Chaucer.* Princeton, N.J.: Princeton University Press, 1962.

Robinson, Pamela R. "A Twelfth-Century *Scriptrix* from Nunnaminster." In *Of the Making of Books: Medieval Manuscripts, Their Scribes and Readers: Essays Presented to M. B. Parkes,* edited by P. R. Robinson and Rivkali Zim. Aldershot, England: Scolar, 1997.

Rossano Gospels. See *Codex purpureus rossanensis.*

Rossi, G. B. de. *Inscriptiones christianae urbis romae.* 2 vols. and plate album. Rome: Cuggiani, 1861.

———. *La Roma sotterranea cristiana.* 3 vols. Rome: Cromolitografia pontifica, 1864–77.

Roy, Bruno. *Une culture de l'équivoque.* Montreal: Presses Universitaires de Montréal, 1992.

Rudolph of Saint Trond. *Vita sancti Lietbierti.* Vol. 146 of *PL.*

Rudolph, Conrad. "Bernard of Clairvaux's *Apologia* as a Description of Cluny, and the Controversy over Monastic Art." *Gesta* 27 (1988): 125–32.

Rupert of Deutz. *De sancta Trinitate: In exodum.* Vol. 167 of *PL,* vol. 22 of *CCM.*

———. *De Trinitate: In Ezechielem.* Vol. 167 of *PL,* vol. 23 of *CCM.*

———. *Super Mattheum.* Vol. 168 of *PL,* vol. 29 of *CCM.*

Ryan, Michael. "The Book of Kells and Metalwork." In *The Book of Kells: Proceedings of a Conference at Trinity College, Dublin, 6–9 September 1992,* edited by Felicity O'Mahony. Aldershot, England: Scolar Press, 1994.

Saenger, Paul. "Silent Reading." *Viator* 13 (1982): 367–414.

Sahas, Daniel J. *Icon and Logos: Sources in Eighth-Century Iconoclasm.* Toronto: University of Toronto Press, 1986.

Salmon, Pierre. *Les 'Tituli psalmorum' des manuscrits latins.* Paris: Cerf, 1959.

Salter, Elizabeth. "Medieval Poetry and the Visual Arts." *Essays and Studies* 22 (1969): 16–32.

Salter, Elizabeth, and Derek Pearsall. "Pictorial Illustration of Late Medieval Poetic Texts: The Role of the Frontispiece or Prefatory Picture." In *Medieval Iconography and Narrative: A Symposium,* edited by Flemming G. Andersen et al. Odense, Denmark: Odense University Press, 1980.

Sandler, Lucy Freeman. *Gothic Manuscripts, 1285–1385,* 2 vols. London: Harvey Miller, 1986.

———. "The Image of the Book-Owner in the Fourteenth Century: Three Cases of Self-Definition." In *England in the Fourteenth Century,* edited by Nicholas Rogers. Stamford, Conn.: Paul Watkins, 1993.

———. "Reflections on the Construction of Hybrids in English Gothic Marginal Illustration." In *Art, the Ape of Nature: Studies in Honor of H. W. Janson,* edited by Moshe Barash and L. F. Sandler. New York: Abrams, 1981.

———. "The Word in the Text and the Image in the Margin: The Case of the Luttrell Psalter." *Journal of the Walters Art Gallery* 54 (1996): 87–99.

Schmitt, Jean-Claude. *La raison des gestes dans l'occident médiéval.* Paris: Gallimard, 1990.

Scott, Kathleen. "Design, Decoration and Illustration." In *Book Production and Publishing in Britain, 1375–1475,* edited by Jeremy Griffiths and Derek Pearsall. Cambridge: Cambridge University Press, 1989.

———. *Later Gothic Manuscripts, 1390–1490.* 2 vols. London: Harvey Miller, 1996.

Sears, Elizabeth. "Word and Image in Carolingian *Carmina Figurata.*" In *World*

*Art: Themes of Unity in Diversity,* edited by Irving Lavin, vol. 2. University Park: Penn State University Press, 1989.

Sherman, Claire Richter. *Imaging Aristotle: Verbal and Visual Representation in Fourteenth-Century France.* Berkeley: University of California Press, 1995.

———. *The Portraits of Charles V of France (1338–1380).* New York: New York University Press, 1969.

Simeon of Durham. *Historia ecclesiae dunhelmensis.* Vol. 1 of *Symeonis monachi opera omnia,* edited by Thomas Arnold. London: Longman, 1882.

Sims-Williams, Patrick. *Religion and Literature in Western England, 600–800.* Cambridge: Cambridge University Press, 1990.

Smalley, Beryl. *The Study of the Bible in the Middle Ages.* Oxford: Oxford University Press, 1952.

Smith, Lesley. "*Scriba Femina*: Medieval Depictions of Women Writing." In *Women and the Book: Assessing the Visual Evidence,* edited by Lesley Smith and Jane H. M. Taylor. London: British Library, 1997.

Smith, Sarah Stanbury. "'Game in Myn Hood': The Traditions of a Comic Proverb." *Studies in Iconography* 9 (1983): 1–12.

Speer, Mary. "Editing Old French Texts in the Eighties: Theory and Practice." *Romance Philology* 45 (1991): 7–44.

Steiner, Wendy. "Postmodernism and the Ornament." *Word and Image* 4 (1988): 60–66.

Sterling, Charles. *La peinture médiévale à Paris, 1300–1500.* 2 vols. Paris: Wildenstein Foundation, 1987–90.

Stone, Louise W., William Rothwell, and T. B. W. Reid, eds. *The Anglo-Norman Dictionary.* 7 vols. London: Modern Humanities Research Association, 1977–92.

Storms, G. *Anglo-Saxon Magic.* The Hague: Nijhoff, 1948.

Strzygowski, Josef. *Der Dom zu Aachen und seine Entstellung.* Leipzig: Hinrichs, 1904.

Suntrup, Rudolf. "*Te Igitur*-Initialen und Kanonbilder in mittelalterlichen Sakramentarhandschriften." In *Text und Bild: Aspekte des Zusammenwirkens zweier Künste in Mittelalter und früher Neuzeit,* edited by Christel Meier and Uwe Ruberg. Wiesbaden: Reichert, 1980.

Svenbro, Jesper. "La Grèce archaïque et classique: L'invention de la lecture silencieuse." In *Histoire de la lecture dans le monde occidental,* edited by Guglielmo Cavallo and Roger Chartier. Paris: Seuil, 1997.

Temple, Elzbieta. *Anglo-Saxon Manuscripts, 900–1066.* London: Harvey Miller, 1976.

Tertullian. *De baptismo.* Vol. 1 of *PL,* vol. 1 of *CCL.*

Tory, Geoffroy. *Champ fleury.* Translated by George B. Ives. New York: Dover, 1967.

Toubert, Hélène. "Formes et fonctions de l'enluminure." In *Le livre conquérant: Du moyen âge au milieu du dix-septième siècle.* Vol. 1 of *Histoire de l'édition française,* edited by Henri-Jean Martin and Roger Chartier. Paris: Promodis, 1982.

———. "La lettre ornée." In *Mise en page et mise en texte du livre manuscrit,* edited by Henri-Jean Martin and Jean Vezin. Paris: Promodis, 1990.

Tuve, Rosemund. *Allegorical Imagery: Some Medieval Books and Their Posterity.* Princeton, N.J.: Princeton University Press, 1966.

Underwood, Paul. "The Fountain of Life in MSS. of the Gospels." *Dumbarton Oaks Papers* 5 (1950): 41–138.

Van Moé, Emile. *La lettre ornée dans les manuscrits du septième au douzième siècle.* Paris: Du Chêne, 1949.

*Vergilius Augusteus.* See Nordenfalk.

*Vergilius Romanus.* Facsimile edition. Milan: Jaca, 1985. Commentary volume by Italo Lana. Milan: Jaca, 1986.

*Vergilius Vaticanus.* Facsimile edition. Graz, Austria: Akademische Druck, 1980. Commentary volume by David H. Wright. Graz: Akademische Druck, 1984.

Vernant, Jean-Pierre. "De la présentification de l'invisible à l'imitation de l'apparence." In *Image et signification.* Rencontres de l'Ecole du Louvre, no. 2. Paris: La documentation française, 1983.

Waldensis, Thomas. *Doctrinale antiquitatum fidei catholicae ecclesiae.* 3 vols. 1759. Reprint. Farnborough, England: Gregg Press, 1967.

Weitzmann, Kurt. *Ancient Book Illumination.* Cambridge, Mass.: Harvard University Press, 1959.

———. *Illustrations in Roll and Codex: A Study of the Origin and Method of Text Illustration.* Princeton, N.J.: Princeton University Press, 1947.

———. "Loca Sancta and the Representational Arts of Palestine." *Dumbarton Oaks Papers* 28 (1974): 31–55.

———. *Manuscrits gréco-romains et paléochrétiens.* Translated by M. Courtois. Paris: Chêne, 1977.

Werner, Martin. "The Cross-Carpet Page in the Book of Durrow: The Cult of the True Cross, Adomnan, and Iona." *Art Bulletin* 72 (1990): 174–223.

Wilpert, Giuseppe. "La croce sui monumenti della catacombe." *Nuova bulletino di archeologia cristiana* 8 (1902): 5–14.

———. "Drei altchristliche Epitaphfragmente aus den römischen Katakomben." *Römische Quartalschrift für christliche Altertumskunde und für Kirchengeschichte* 6 (1892): 366–78.

Windeatt, B. A., ed. *Geoffrey Chaucer: Troilus and Criseyde.* London: Longman, 1984.

Wingo, E. O. *Latin Punctuation in the Classical Age.* The Hague: Mouton, 1972.

Wirth, Jean. *L'image médiévale: Naissance et développements (sixième au quinzième siècle).* Paris: Klincksieck, 1989.

Wormald, Francis. *The Miniatures in the Gospels of Saint Augustine: Corpus Christi College MS 286.* Cambridge: Cambridge University Press, 1954.

———. "The Sherborne 'Chartulary.'" In *Fritz Saxl Memorial Essays,* edited by D. J. Gordon. London: Nelson, 1957.

Yates, Francis. *The Art of Memory.* London: Routledge, 1966.

Youngs, Susan, ed. *"The Work of Angels": Masterpieces of Celtic Metalwork, Sixth to Ninth Centuries A.D.* London: British Museum, 1989.

Zimmerman, E. Heinrich. *Vorkarolingische Miniaturen.* Text volume. Berlin: Deutsch Vereins für Kunstwissenschaft, 1916.

# INDEX

*References to illustrations, by figure number, are at the end of the entries.*

# INDEX OF MANUSCRIPTS

*References to illustrations, by figure number, are at the end of the entries.*